REMEMBERING
OUR GRANDFATHERS' EXILE

REMEMBERING OUR GRANDFATHERS' EXILE

US Imprisonment of Hawai'i's
Japanese in World War II

Gail Y. Okawa

University of Hawai'i Press
Honolulu

25 24 23 22 21 20   6 5 4 3 2 1

Library of Congress Cataloging-in-Publication Data

Names: Okawa, Gail Y., author.
Title: Remembering our grandfathers' exile : US imprisonment of Hawai'i's
  Japanese in World War II / Gail Y. Okawa.
Description: Honolulu : University of Hawai'i Press, [2020] | Includes
  bibliographical references and index.
Identifiers: LCCN 2019044475 | ISBN 9780824881191 (paperback) | ISBN
  9780824881207 (hardcover) | ISBN 9780824883195 (adobe pdf) | ISBN
  9780824883201 (epub) | ISBN 9780824883218 (kindle edition)
Subjects: LCSH: Japanese Americans—Hawaii—Evacuation and relocation,
  1942–1945. | World War, 1939–1945—Evacuation of civilians—Hawaii.
Classification: LCC D769.8.A6 O34 2020 | DDC 940.53/177309239560969—dc23
LC record available at https://lccn.loc.gov/2019044475

Cover art: Painting of Santa Fe Internment Camp. Artist unknown, possibly a camp art teacher;
color rendered by Rev. Gyokuei Matsuura, SFIC. Courtesy Matsuura Family Collection.

To my grandfather, Reverend Tamasaku Watanabe,
and all Hawaiʻi Issei exiled on the U.S. mainland during World War II,
and to my mother, Sumi Watanabe Okawa,
without whose enduring faith
this project might not have been completed

Contents

Illustrations

Figures

Maps: Hawai'i Internees' Exile

Acknowledgments

Remembering Our Grandfathers' Exile is a composite chronicling of the Hawai'i Issei experience in mainland internment during World War II, told through the eyes of a granddaughter and researcher born during that war. As this is a composite telling of the lives of our fathers and grandfathers in exile, it is also the combined effort of scores of people, some of whom have regrettably passed away over the course of this study and writing, including my mother, Sumi, who was my constant supporter.

My deepest gratitude goes to those who shared their memories, photographs, letters, and other documents and artifacts with me, especially several Issei survivors: the late Kazumi Matsumoto, the late Reverend Gyokuei Matsuura and his family, the late Reverend Kenjyo Ohara, and the late Reverend Shingetsu Akahoshi and his family, as well as the families (Nisei/Sansei children or relatives) of the following Issei internees (listed alphabetically): Ichiji Adachi, Ryosei Aka, Seisaku Aoyagi, Seiichi Fujii, Reverend Kodo Fujitani, Itsuo Hamada, Naojiro Hirano, Masaichi Hirashima, Koichi Iida, Reverend Kinai Ikuma, Hisato Isemoto, Kyujiro Ishida, Ryozo Izutsu, Reverend Ryuten Kashiwa, Isoo Kato, Kango Kawasaki, Muneo Kimura, Ichiji Kinoshita, Aisuke Kuniyuki, Katsuichi Miho, Reverend Kinzaemon Odachi, Reverend Chikou Odate, Futoshi Ohama, Dr. Seiichi Ohata, Matsujiro Otani, Shigeo Shigenaga, Masaichiro Shinoda, Hiroshi Tahara, Shigeji Terada, Jinshichi Tokairin, Reverend Tamasaku Watanabe, Ryosen Yonahara, and Shinjiro Yoshimasu.

In gathering information for chapter 7, "Compounded Ironies I," I was also greatly aided by Andrew Ono and family members of Arthur Akira Morihara, Yukitaka Mizutari, Toshio Murakami, Hiroshi Nagami, and Saburo Maehara, and, in the cases of Murakami, Maehara, and Kihachiro Hotta, by the tenacious research of David Fukuda of the Maui Nisei Veterans Memorial Center.

This long and expanding research project might have been impossible—certainly would have encountered many more obstacles—had it not been for the generous guidance of my advisors on the mainland: Franklin Odo, the late Aiko Herzig-Yoshinaga and the late Jack Herzig, Colonel Joe Ando, and Tetsuden

Kashima, who are mentioned in chapter 1. Gary Salvner, past chair of English, Youngstown State University, and Richard Melzer, professor of history, University of New Mexico, have provided continual encouragement and advice. Further, the support—and patience—of my advisors in Honolulu has been immeasurable: Craig Howes, Stanley Schab, and John Zuern, Center for Biographical Research, University of Hawaiʻi at Mānoa, who gave me an academic home over the years; and Reverend Yoshiaki Fujitani, retired bishop, Honpa Hongwanji, who introduced me to many in Hawaiʻi's Japanese community. I also thank Tom Coffman for his writing advice and the late Patsy Sumie Saiki, whom I met in the earliest days of my project, for her pathfinding work—the springboard for subsequent research on the Hawaiʻi Issei internment on the mainland.

I am also very grateful to those who translated written or spoken Japanese texts specifically for this project, including Reiko Odate Matsumoto, Haruko Kawasaki, the late Kihei Hirai, and particularly Rev. Fujitani and Tatsumi Hayashi. Their efforts have enriched our understanding of Issei writings, experiences, and sensibilities.

The research for this project undoubtedly has been a communal and social process, involving old and new friends and colleagues whose help and encouragement I have greatly appreciated: in Ohio, Hugh McCracken, Virginia Monseau, and, more recently, Jay Gordon, Tom Copeland, and Jeffrey Buchanan; in New Mexico, Carolyn Vogel, Koichi Okada, Estevan Rael-Gálvez, Sue Rundstrom, Lisa Pacheco, Janice Baker, and Kermit Hill; and in Hawaiʻi, Naomi Kawamura, Charlotte Nagoshi, Yoshie and the late James Tanabe, Susan Tokairin, Mariko Miho, Stanley Toyama, the late Patricia Koshi, and the late Kay Yokoyama. Many thanks also to the Resource Center, Japanese Cultural Center of Hawaiʻi.

Writing, in contrast, is a solitary affair, and I would have had difficulty sustaining this work without the continual interest and moral support of Beverly Keever, a writer and longtime friend, who provided gentle nudges, and of Victor Villanueva especially, likewise a writer, editor, and longtime friend, who suffered through innumerable drafts of chapters and then the entire manuscript, providing much needed feedback on the writing. Many thanks also to University of Hawaiʻi Press's editorial and publishing staff for their fine work.

Financial support was provided by sabbatical and research grants from Youngstown State University and the resources of the Smithsonian Asian and Pacific American Program and the University of Hawaiʻi at Mānoa Center for Biographical Research.

Finally, my family has been a continual source of faith and encouragement over many years, from my work in Washington, DC, to Hawaiʻi, to New Mexico, and repeated returns. At the outset, my mother shared in the excitement of everything that I uncovered and everyone whom I met to fill in the gaps of this unfolding story.

Abbreviations

Because of the frequent use of military, government, and archival abbreviations, the following list is provided to aid the general reader, although abbreviations are generally defined in the chapters when they first appear.

AECU   Alien Enemy Control Unit, DOJ
AJA   American of Japanese Ancestry
CI   civilian internee
CWRIC   Commission on Wartime Relocation and Internment of Civilians
DOJ   U.S. Department of Justice
HJ   Hawaii Japanese (government label)
HTG   Hawaii Territorial Guard
INS   U.S. Immigration and Naturalization Service
JACL   Japanese American Citizens League
JAGD   Judge Advocate General Department, OMG
KP   kitchen patrol
MIS   Military Intelligence Service
MISLS   Military Intelligence Service Language School
NAB   National Archives Building, Washington, DC
NACP   National Archives at College Park, MD
NARA   National Archives and Records Administration
OIS   Office of Internal Security, OMG
OMG   Office of the Military Governor
OPMG   Office of the Provost Marshal General
RCT   regimental combat team
RG   record group
ROTC   Reserve Officers' Training Corps
SFIC/SFDS Santa Fe Internment Camp / Santa Fe Detention Station

TH   Territory of Hawaii
VVV   Varsity Victory Volunteers
WRA   War Relocation Authority

Names and Terminology

Japanese names are included in this text with family names following first names, for example, "Tamasaku Watanabe," rather than the traditional Japanese practice of family names preceding first names.

American Japanese	As the term *Japanese American* is associated with persons born in the United States, I use *American Japanese* to refer to all Americans of Japanese ancestry in the United States, including immigrants.
Issei	Persons of the immigrant generation, born in Japan.
Nikkei	Persons of Japanese ancestry/descent.
Japanese American	Persons of Japanese ancestry, born in the United States.
Nisei	Persons of the second generation, born in the United States.
Sansei	Persons of the third generation, born in the United States.
Hawai'i	The contemporary spelling, using the *'okina* diacritical mark, refers to the Hawaiian Islands.
Territory of Hawaii	Abbreviated *TH,* this term refers to the Hawaiian Islands under U.S. annexation following the U.S. overthrow of the Hawaiian monarchy in July 1898 and prior to the islands' being granted U.S. statehood in August 1959. No *'okina* is used.
internment	This is the official term referring specifically to the imprisonment of alien enemies by the U.S. Department of Justice in collaboration with the War Department during World War II (see Kashima 2003).

consular agent/subconsular agent   The term *consular agent(s)* appears in U.S. government wartime documents to refer to a group associated with the Japanese consulate and targeted for internment; however, the Commission on Wartime Relocation and Internment of Civilians (CWRIC) translates the Japanese term applied to such persons, *toritsuginin,* as *subconsular agent* (1997, 278), to identify the unpaid agents of the Japanese consulate who assisted the less literate Japanese with legal and government paperwork. I follow the CWRIC's practice.

Other romanized Japanese terms are generally defined in the text, parenthetically or otherwise.

Introduction
Unbundling

Unbundling

"My dear Sumi," he wrote on pale blue paper
stamped "Detained Alien Enemy Mail EXAMINED."
Thirty-five letters, formally signed,
"from your father, Tamasaku Watanabe"
from Lordsburg and Santa Fe, New Mexico,
bundled and tied with a deep red cord.
My mother's letters to him
at Lordsburg Alien Internment Camp and
Santa Fe Detention Station,
kept long past his death,
bundled and tied with care,
stored in old cardboard boxes.
Each page captures time and feeling,
constructs memory for descendants
who care to read them,
memory so fragile that it can be lost
in an oversight,
in a word.[1]

I was born during a World War II blackout, I've been told. My mother was carried to Queen's Hospital in an ambulance, probably one of the only vehicles
allowed on the road under martial law in Honolulu even a year after Pearl Harbor was attacked in December 1941. On the slopes of Punchbowl, a volcanic cra-
ter near our house, now the verdant resting place of many of America's military
dead, my mother remembered army tents scattered about. Other soldiers were
stationed at Roosevelt High School, across the street from our home. Blackout
rules were so strict and paranoia ran so high that MPs came to the house one
dark early morning to check on a tiny clock light that my father turned on
momentarily to see what time it was. But as a child, I was shielded completely

from the war with the exception of duck-and-cover exercises in preschool and the wailing ambulance sirens that terrified me for years.

I didn't know that my maternal grandfather, Tamasaku Watanabe, was absent and don't remember exactly when he appeared in my life, a tall, quiet, almost austere man, a Christian minister who was a physical presence just once or twice a year when he came to visit us in Honolulu from the island of Maui. My warmest memory of him comes from sometime in my preadolescence: When he was on one of his visits, I came down with a cold and had to stay at home from school one day. I made my favorite egg salad and Spam sandwiches for our lunch. A man of few words, he expressed his enjoyment and approval of the simple meal by smiling impishly and remarking in English that I should open a sandwich shop. I've never forgotten the compliment!

When I was in high school in Honolulu, I first learned from "Auntie" Mamie, a family friend who lived on our block, that this grandfather had been imprisoned in an American concentration camp on the mainland during World War II. I had just learned about the imprisonment of American Japanese in my American history class as something that happened on the West Coast, and perhaps we were talking about it when she mentioned this. I was stunned. Auntie Mamie was a Nisei (American-born Japanese) public health nurse and a pretty authoritative figure in my life, so I rushed home to question my parents and remember them confirming the news. "He came back a changed man," they both agreed. My family had never discussed my grandfather's internment and neither had he. It seemed to be a closed subject at that point and I don't remember pursuing it.

Decades later, in the early 1990s, my mother shared some letters that her father had written to her from Lordsburg and Santa Fe, New Mexico, mostly on light blue government aerograms printed with English, German, Italian, and Japanese imperatives, "DO NOT WRITE HERE! NICHT HIER SCHREIBEN! NON SCRIVETE QUI! KAKU NAKARE," and stamped with "Detained Alien Enemy Mail EXAMINED by [censor's initials] U.S.I.&N.S." In some cases, "Prisoner of War Mail" had been crossed out and "Internee Mail" written in its place, an appalling and revealing confusion of terms and people, a conflation that would have future repercussions. In all, there were eight letters from the Lordsburg Internment Camp (IC) and twenty-seven from the Santa Fe Detention Station (later called the Santa Fe Alien Internment Camp, according to return addresses).

Then there was the photograph. Perhaps in the late 1990s, the old trunks and cardboard boxes holding my grandfather's possessions were in danger of being disturbed. They had been stored in my uncle's basement for thirty years after my grandfather died, and my uncle had since passed away, while my aunt was growing infirm. My mother and I rescued some of the documents and artifacts during a cursory sifting.

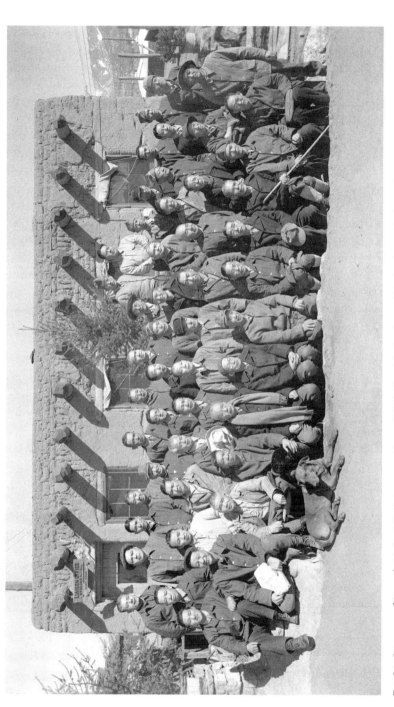

FIG. I.1. Internees of Barrack 64, Santa Fe Internment Camp (SFIC), New Mexico, June 1943–April 1945. *Left to right: row 1:* Ryozo Izutsu (6), Shinjiro Yoshimasu (8); *row 2:* Genichi Nagami (6); *row 3:* Teiichiro Maehara (6), Tamasaku Watanabe (*10*) (Tamasaku Watanabe Collection).

A sepia photograph of a group of men in front of an adobe building was among them, the only photo among the belongings that my grandfather had salvaged from his mainland internment. My mother picked her father out in the crowd. Who was this man standing so erect at the end of row three, I wondered. Was he squinting—or frowning? And where was this taken? Who were the others? My grandfather had identified some of the men on the back of the picture in Japanese, but I couldn't easily read their names. There was no mention of a date or location. Who owned the dog in the front row? I still remember the mystery of it—the excitement of initial unknowns and unknowing. The sign on the building— "Liaison Office"—was a clue, and the vigas, beams jutting out from the adobe building, reminded me of traditional New Mexican architecture I had seen, so I could guess that this picture might have been taken in Santa Fe, especially considering my mother's collection of wartime letters with a Santa Fe return address.

Initially, I thought these artifacts would provide some impartial researcher with rich material, hesitating to investigate further myself because of the academic convention of avoiding personal subjects. Yet later, as I opened box after cardboard box and found documents carefully bundled and labeled among my grandfather's papers, I began to feel that he had left them for us—for me—to understand what happened to him during those war years.

Gaps

Reverend Tamasaku Watanabe was a meticulous record keeper; he had pocket-size notebooks and diaries in his files dating from 1922 through 1967, the year before he died. Of course, I looked eagerly for any writings dated 1941, yet his notes after 7 December 1941, the date Pearl Harbor was attacked, through the war years to 1944 are mysteriously absent. And although he kept many of his important papers in English and Japanese from that period, there is no overarching narrative, so piecing them together has left gaping holes and raised further questions. Why was he arrested? What was he charged with? Where was he imprisoned? By whom? What kind of life did he lead in those facilities that Franklin D. Roosevelt referred to as "concentration camps" back in 1936?[2] Who were his friends and associates? What kinds of dilemmas did he face and how did he face them? How did he feel about it all—this pensive man who enjoyed my Spam sandwiches?

Now I know that my grandfather was one of hundreds of Issei (Japanese of the immigrant generation) in Hawai'i whose fate is still relatively unknown to the general American public. The story played out on 7 December 1941 and immediately afterward in secrecy: Agents of the Federal Bureau of Investigation (FBI), under the U.S. Department of Justice (DOJ), and military police, under the

FIG. I.2. Rev. Watanabe, detail from
internee group photo, SFIC (courtesy Kato
Family Collection).

U.S. Department of War, in some cases aided by local police, seized more than
seven thousand Japanese resident aliens from the continental United States and
the Territories of Hawaii and Alaska (Kashima 2003, 125). Those arrested in
Hawaiʻi were, like my grandfather, predominantly male immigrants,[3] heads of
households, and highly literate community leaders detained, in many cases, for
reasons no more substantial than that they were Japanese. Although most were
longtime residents of the United States like their mainland counterparts, as Japanese immigrants they were designated as "aliens ineligible for citizenship," based
on racially biased naturalization laws dating to 1790. As dictated by the Alien
Enemies Act of 1918, their immigration status would immediately change from
aliens to "alien enemies" when hostilities broke out between the United States
and their country of origin, in this case upon the declaration of war between the
United States and Japan on 8 December 1941.

In this sweep, authorities used prepared lists, evidence that plans for the Issei
imprisonment were premeditated and covert, based on long and complex surveillance operations—not simply a reaction to the Pearl Harbor bombing, as
I had so naively thought. These lists further suggest that the attack's being a

surprise may be a myth. Paul Clark relates evidence revealing that some prison camps were being prepared as early as January 1941 at Fort Stanton in New Mexico, followed by Fort Missoula in Montana and Fort Lincoln in North Dakota (1980, 8).[4] Hundreds of Issei who were detained in the islands were sent to such mainland prison camps run by the U.S. Army and the Immigration and Naturalization Service (INS), under the DOJ.

Roger Daniels, a historian who has written extensively on U.S. immigration and internment, noted in 1997, "The INS camps have been little written about and are thus largely unknown" (xii). More than ten years later, in 2008, Tetsuden Kashima, who had published a comprehensive study of the World War II incarceration of American Japanese in 2003, was still writing that "relatively few people are aware of this internment episode," referring to the Issei imprisonment in his introduction to a translation of Yasutaro Soga's internment memoir (1). Asian American studies pioneer Yuji Ichioka in 2000 called it a "conspicuous slighting of the Issei" (2006, 293).[5]

Even in the American Japanese community in the islands, I have learned, knowledge about these camps during the immediate postwar period was limited by the relative silence of the Issei who were forced to occupy them and their children's and subsequent generations' limited literacy in Japanese.[6] This was due in part to a natural acculturation in an English-dominant society, and in part to the prohibitions and stigma of maintaining the Japanese language before and during wartime, evidenced by prewar legislation, the imprisonment of Japanese language teachers, and the closing of Japanese language schools—all of which further limited access to postwar Issei writing.[7]

The more well-known story, of course, concerns the War Relocation Authority (WRA) camps, established by President Roosevelt's Executive Order (EO) 9102, following his infamous EO 9066 on 19 February 1942, establishing the Western Defense Command. The federal government removed as many as 110,000 people—"aliens and non-aliens,"[8] men, women, and children of Japanese ancestry—from their homes in Washington, Oregon, and California, incarcerating them in ten prison camps, including Manzanar and Tule Lake in inland California, Gila River in Arizona, and Jerome in Arkansas.

For Japanese resident aliens / alien enemies, the Justice and War Departments, which had entered into a collaborative agreement originally on 18 July 1941, later amended in June 1943,[9] used twenty-four prison camps, including the Kilauea Military Camp, Sand Island Internment Camp, and seven other prisons in the Territory of Hawaii; Camp McCoy, Wisconsin; Fort Sam Houston, Texas; Camp Forrest, Tennessee; Camp Livingston, Louisiana; Fort Missoula, Montana (INS/DOJ run); and Lordsburg Internment Camp, New Mexico.[10] Many of the

Hawaiʻi internees sent to the mainland passed through or had lengthy imprisonments at the Santa Fe Internment Camp, New Mexico (INS/DOJ run), over the course of the war. As Kashima points out, "This agreement, made months before the United States' entry into the ongoing war, shows that the later actions of these two federal departments were not taken in haste or fueled by wartime panic. An internment plan had been considered, discussed, and prepared" (2003, 27).

More than a Mug Shot

Remembering Our Grandfathers' Exile is written as a kind of primer not for those specialists who already know this Hawaiʻi Issei internment history but for those who don't or for those, like me, who want to research personal encounters with such major historical events. This project morphed as my awareness developed from attention to a family injury and loss to a broader, community history. In other words, the book provides a narrative starting point—a personal context for a discovery of family and archival materials—and expands to include multiple stories, perspectives, and voices of internees and/or their family members, as well as government and military officials. Perhaps Ichioka put it best: "I believe in the old-time practice of doing narrative history, of telling a story in ordinary language based on substantive research in primary sources" (2006, 296). By foregrounding and highlighting original sources, I wish to create a multivocal, multigenerational, and multigenre narrative.

My grandfather, after all, was one of hundreds from Hawaiʻi. From various hometowns and villages in Japan, the Issei had immigrated to various locations in the Hawaiian Islands and had established various productive lives. Though unique individuals, they were stereotyped and treated generically as "Japs" by their adopted country, objectified as "alien enemies," and conflated with the enemy as supposed threats to national security. To counter this portrayal—to illustrate their different circumstances, to employ their different voices, to show how unsingular the wartime imprisonment of Hawaiʻi's Japanese immigrants actually was—I have included in this narrative what I know of my grandfather's story, interwoven with experiences, writings, documents, and artifacts of scores of other internees and internee families collected during this study and in unpublished and published texts.

Although I sought to broaden my focus from one story to many stories in the course of my research, I also narrowed the subject from the Issei DOJ/army imprisonment as a whole to the internment of Hawaiʻi Issei males exiled to the mainland in particular.[11] Following the trajectory of my grandfather and others who remained attached to Hawaiʻi and together in Santa Fe, I mention the dilemma of repatriation to Japan or reunification with family members in WRA and other camps but do not focus on the stories of those who chose these paths. These pages thus provide a chronicle of a shared, collective experience, a composite overview of what happened to hundreds of Issei men forced to have a common experience as prisoners of the U.S. government in mainland concentration camps. The chronological storyline includes prewar circumstances, suspicion and arrest, initial detention, mainland exile and internment, and return to Hawai'i. Rather than a traditional academic history and historical analysis or an exhaustive or conclusive study, this book is intended to open windows into a more complex understanding—from divergent perspectives, both personal and official—of the less-known Justice/War Department internment story and its impact on those in and of Hawai'i.

Following a description of the expanding research project in chapter 1, "Discovering: A Personal and Community Recovery Project," chapters 2 and 3, "The Fate of the 'Wingless Birds' I and II," relate the immigration stories of my grandfather and others and their plight after the outbreak of the Pacific War. Chapters 4, 5, and 6, "In Exile I, II, and III," trace their removal and exile from the Territory of Hawaii to Angel Island and inland U.S. Army and INS/DOJ camps. From my vantage point in multicultural literacy and literary studies, I highlight the Issei literacy and cultural practices as ironic and deliberate acts of survival and resistance to oppressive conditions—the loss of freedom, the mistreatment, the indignity, and the mind-numbing monotony of imprisonment. Inspired by notations made by my grandfather, together with other family and government documents, chapters 7 and 8, "Compounded Ironies I and II," tell troubling stories of a distinctive subgroup of Hawai'i internees who had sons serving—and dying— in the U.S. military in Europe and the Pacific, and how the sons' service, as well as the literacy and advocacy of the internees and their families, affected the fathers' fates. Chapter 9, "Return from Exile and Rebundling," depicts the return of the Issei from their mainland imprisonment and raises questions and warnings for readers, while the epilogue offers the unique perspectives of a number of Santa Feans who have memories of the internees and the internment camp in their midst and can bear witness to the existence of the prisoners and prison camp now erased from the physical landscape.

Resources

This study follows in the tradition of Patsy Saiki's *Gambare!* (1982), the first English narrative overview of the specific Hawai'i internee experience based on research, including interviews with numerous Issei survivors and others and published memoirs in Japanese, with somewhat limited documentation. It differs in its extensive citation of revealing family and government archival documents, creating an overarching framework that leaves room for additional documents and others' stories. I have included original unpublished Japanese language sources, translated into English for this volume, and I encourage further study of numerous unpublished writings in Japanese, some collected and some yet to be discovered.

While this composite narrative also differs from the published firsthand accounts of such Hawai'i Issei writers as Yasutaro (Keiho) Soga, Otokichi (Muin) Ozaki, George Yoshio Hoshida, and Kumaji (Suikei) Furuya, which capture the singular individualized recollections of each writer, I have drawn observations from these narratives to complement the writings of others.[12] Poems written by Soga, Ozaki, and others while interned were selected from camp magazines and collections and Japanese vernacular newspapers in Hawai'i,[13] translated by Jiro Nakano and Kay Nakano, and published in *Poets behind Barbed Wire*. Primarily tanka, a Japanese indigenous poetic form of five lines, employing etched, often poignant imagery, these poems capture the Issei experience so succinctly that I include some of them in this narrative, with permission.

Besides translated Japanese texts, George Y. Hoshida, a salesman and self-made artist, composed his unpublished memoir, "Life of a Japanese Immigrant Boy in Hawaii and America," in the 1970s, based on his wartime diary; the memoir, written in English in his later years, is accompanied by extensive sketches that provide a rare illustrated narrative of internment life, among other topics. His insights and struggles, some of which I include in this volume in their original unedited form, are invaluable to this account.[14]

The most pertinent scholarly reference treating the prewar and wartime conditions and climate in the Territory of Hawaii, and thus the political and social context for the Hawai'i Issei incarceration, is Gary Okihiro's *Cane Fires: The Anti-Japanese Movement in Hawaii, 1865–1945* (1991), which is cited more extensively in chapter 2. Tetsuden Kashima's *Judgment without Trial: Japanese American Imprisonment during World War II* (2003), also referenced in chapter 2, provides us with a comprehensive overview of the wartime incarceration—both the DOJ/War Department internment and the WRA concentration camps, a complex organization of personnel and resources, while the report of the Commission on Wartime Relocation and Internment of Civilians (CWRIC), *Personal Justice Denied* (1997), outlines in scrupulous detail the people and the social, political, and legal events involved in the imprisonment process. All of these materials notwithstanding, Americans in general know little about the Issei internment, as Daniels and Kashima have bemoaned, in contrast to the more widely known, experienced, and legally contested incarceration of U.S.-born citizens and their Japanese immigrant parents on the West Coast, overseen by the WRA.

Present Memory

My intention, again, is to create less a historical artifact, more a multifaceted narrative in and for our memory in the present by integrating numerous original voices and stories of the past—the Issei and others of that period—filtered through a descendant's twenty-first-century lens. This project began in 2001 and 2002, when the political circumstances of 9/11 put the World War II internment events into particularly sharp and critical focus. Other "minority" groups have since been singled out and targeted amid a climate of hysteria. Three months after the 9/11 attack, Arab American poet Naomi Shihab Nye distilled her immediate response to that event:

> September 11, 2001, was not the first hideous day ever in the world, but it was the worst one many Americans had ever lived. . . . For people who love the Middle East and have ongoing devotion to cross-cultural understanding, the day felt sickeningly tragic in more ways than one. A huge shadow had been cast across the lives of so many innocent people and an ancient culture's pride. . . . The losses cannot be measured. They will reverberate in so many lives throughout the coming years. (2002, xv–xvii)

How the losses have reverberated and with whom, she could not have known then. As the U.S. political and social landscape has developed in the post-9/11 world, tensions and violent incidents, both domestic and abroad, have incited fear and suspicion and, with this hysteria, blatant racism and intolerance, not unlike the conditions prevailing in the United States decades before and after the outbreak of the Pacific War.

In July 1980, after a controversial decade-long process, President Jimmy Carter signed a bipartisan bill creating the Commission on Wartime Relocation and Internment of Civilians (Kashima 1997, xvii). Based on the commission's findings, the Civil Liberties Act, signed by President Ronald Reagan on 10 August 1988, set forth carefully worded language:

> The Congress recognizes that . . . a grave injustice was done to both citizens and permanent residents of Japanese ancestry by the evacuation, relocation, and internment of civilians during World War II. . . . These actions were carried out without adequate security reasons and without

any acts of espionage or sabotage . . . and were motivated largely by *racial prejudice, wartime hysteria, and a failure of political leadership*. . . . For these fundamental violations of the basic civil liberties and constitutional rights of these individuals of Japanese ancestry, the Congress apologizes on behalf of the Nation. (emphasis mine)

Whether this society can learn from the past injustice—committing so grave a wrong against its residents and citizens—and avoid the repetition of history remains to be seen. In early 2014, the late Supreme Court justice Antonin Scalia, visiting Hawai'i and speaking to University of Hawai'i Law School and other island students, commented on the World War II internment: "It was wrong, but I would not be surprised to see it happen again, in time of war. It's no justification but it is the reality" (quoted in McAvoy 2014, n.p.), a disheartening assertion, given Congress's admission of wrongdoing and national apology.

Statements such as these provide all the more reason for vigilance by citizens who value their citizenship and civil liberties, a lesson we all can learn from the fate of American citizens and immigrants of Japanese ancestry, who were denied U.S. citizenship by virtue of their race. And they provide all the more reason to use narrative—to show the common humanity of individual lives through their stories. It is, after all, an ethnic immigrant story wherein industrious men and women were forced to succumb to imprisonment en masse on the basis of their race because of the weakness of principle and will among the powerful. "It was wrong, but . . . ," said Scalia; it was a "failure of political leadership," states the Civil Liberties Act of 1988. It is essential that this story remain in the cultural memory not only of Japanese Americans but of all Americans, especially as political forces in the post-9/11 world return it to the national conversation to justify the mistreatment of others.

CHAPTER 1

Discovering

A Personal and Community Recovery Project

Over the course of the Pacific War, more than forty-five hundred men of Japanese ancestry were imprisoned in Santa Fe, New Mexico, most of them immigrants, among them my grandfather Rev. Watanabe. In one of life's ironies, I had been drawn to Santa Fe numerous times before knowing this—to the Pueblo cultures, the adobe buildings, the museums of native cultures and international folk art, the stark surrounding landscape of juniper trees and tumbleweeds, the Sangre de Cristo Mountains. Only on my visits in 1999 and 2000 did I have a vague awareness of my grandfather's presence there decades earlier. At those times, no one I spoke to could tell me where the internment camp had been located; it was as though it had never existed.

Then, in fall 2001, I learned that a group called the Committee for the World War II Santa Fe Internment Camp Historical Marker was attempting to raise funds to establish a memorial marker at the Santa Fe Internment Camp (SFIC) site, and I eagerly contacted Colonel Joe Ando, U.S. Air Force (Retired), the son of an internee and a cochairman of the committee. Finding this effort in progress, having the reality of the internment camp confirmed, and learning that there were others who sought to preserve this nearly forgotten part of history, I was inspired to develop a research project, "The Politics of Language and Identity: The Case of Japanese Immigrants in U.S. Justice Department Internment Camps during World War II." A rather ambitious and, I now know, naive proposal due to its broad scope, it set the theoretical stage for me to examine the general DOJ/War Department internment experience from the perspective of language, literacy, and identity among the Issei prisoners.

In the midst of this process, on the morning of 11 September 2001, I was driving to teach my literature and linguistics classes at Youngstown State University in Ohio and heard words on National Public Radio that reminded me of Orson Welles's *War of the Worlds*, chilling descriptions of massive destruction and chaos as they were occurring in New York City. As the unfolding events revealed that this was no fabrication, I met with my students and found myself seeking their responses to the news, asking what the possible alternatives might be to the "racial prejudice [and] wartime hysteria" that had precipitated the imprisonment of Japanese immigrants and their American-born children after the attack on Pearl Harbor,[1] responses that could be unleashed against other groups as a result of 9/11. Suddenly this was no longer an academic question about a past occurrence; the parallels and immediate relevance of my research to contemporary events grew undeniably and increasingly clear.

The Road to Santa Fe

Although the project itself was clearly outlined, the road to Santa Fe, literally and figuratively, was indirect. I learned the roles of disappointment, success, spontaneity, and serendipity in research and the importance of being open to any encounter. Granted a research leave by my university in winter 2002, I focused first on learning what I could about Rev. Watanabe's story and traveled to the island of Hawaiʻi (the Big Island) to find the Olaʻa Japanese Christian Church, where my grandfather had his ministry at the outbreak of the war. It was here that he had been seized from his parsonage on 7 December 1941. What I found was an empty lot surrounded by an old moss-covered stone wall—no parsonage. The original building, I learned, had become termite-ridden beyond cost-effective repair, so the church had been rebuilt on another site. Now renamed the Puna United Church of Christ, it is no longer the Japanese Christian church that served primarily Issei plantation workers, and although Rev. Watanabe's photograph appeared on the church's office wall on their roll of ministers, no one could tell me anything about him. The church's seventy-fifth anniversary history did devote five lines to him, some of them erroneous, so I shared with the minister and his secretary what little I knew at that point and later received a ninetieth-anniversary bulletin that included a line acknowledging my grandfather's experience during the war.

I began to understand on some level the distinction that Pierre Nora makes between history as a "reconstruction . . . a representation of the past" and memory as "always a phenomenon of the present," "in permanent evolution, subject to . . . remembering and forgetting, . . . and capable of lying dormant for long periods only to be suddenly reawakened" (1996, 3)—and the consequential fragility of that memory. Perhaps my brief visit had inadvertently caused Rev. Watanabe to take on a different presence from the faded photo on the wall or the forgotten lines in the previous church history; perhaps it had caused him to be remembered.

Thanks to friends, I was able to stay at the Kilauea Military Camp, a military recreation area on the Big Island prior to and since World War II. According to my grandfather's notes, it was the first facility where he and others from the island were locked up. During those clear, sunny days in February 2002, I felt the enormity of the freedom that I enjoyed to come and go as I pleased, in contrast to the confinement of the men who had been taken there by force more than six decades earlier. Of that time and place, Muin Ozaki had written:

> As if to relish
> Each step I take
> On this great earth,
> I walk—to the mess hall.
> The only walk allowed.
>
> (1984, 18)

Leaving the Big Island with little more than a vague sense of the places where my grandfather had been, I was, of course, disappointed but chose perseverance over discouragement. In March 2002, I planned a research trip to Santa Fe devoted to collecting whatever I could on the internment camp and the experience of the Japanese immigrants imprisoned there. Col. Ando of the SFIC Historical Marker Committee gave me helpful information, and we made plans to meet during that time. This fifth trip to Santa Fe became pivotal to my project and launched my study.

Carrie Vogel, a colleague and friend who supported my research, gave me a room in her cozy Santa Fe–style stucco home, and I worked for days in the New Mexico State Library, searching through vertical files and microfilms, and the adjoining New Mexico State Archives, which produced various files of correspondence from the governors who served during the war years. One document that chilled me to the bone was a letter from a man named Lloyd to Governor John E. Miles, advising him to "oppose with all the vim and vigor you posess [sic], the entrance of any Jap, born either in Japan or the U.S.A., into the State of New Mexico, either temporary or permanent." "All Japs are skunks," he asserted. "And no matter where a skunk is born, or under what star or flag, he is still a skunk—same stripe, same odor, same characterists [sic]." Lloyd underlined these words for added vehemence and closed with "Planting Jap colonies over this country would be worse than filling our water supply with Typhus germs" (n.d.). The abhorrence was itself abhorrent; I was in disbelief and could hardly contain myself, sitting there at the sanitized archival table with my sanitized white gloves.

I also found a petition of like-minded citizens with Anglo and Hispanic surnames affixed to the message: "We the people of Maxwell and vicinity do hereby petition the Honorable Governor John E. Miles that we . . . do not want a colony of Japanese in our peaceful community. As most of our boys are in the army fighting the Japs, we do not feel that we want the Jpas [*sic*] to take their place" (Petition [Negative] to Governor John E. Miles n.d.). In contrast, a counterpetition was signed by others in Maxwell, certifying that "we have no objection to the sale of land in said Maxwell tract to Japanese farmers who are American citizens now being evacuated from California and we feel that such sales will benefit the community." Most noteworthy of these signatures was that of F. A. Brookshier, who wrote, "During my twelve years of teaching school including nine years here as superintendent I have taught racial tolerance and the rights and duties of American citizens. This is a part of the democratic process" (Petition [Affirmative] to Governor John E. Miles n.d.). Finding citizenship and racial issues acknowledged in Brookshier's comment, I felt somehow reassured that there were compassionate voices to balance out the angry ones.

A tip from Col. Ando led me to seek out Thomas Chávez, the other cochairman of the marker committee and director of the of New Mexico History Museum's Palace of the Governors, whose 1997 newspaper article had drawn attention to the existence of the internment camp in Santa Fe. Also, in searching the files of the Fray Angélico Chávez Library at the Palace of the Governors, I happened upon a name and address in one of them—for Koichiro Okada, who had written a master's thesis titled "Forced Acculturation: A Study of Issei in the Santa Fe Internment Camp during World War II"; when I met with him, he kindly gave me a copy of this unpublished work, which gave rare attention to the Issei in the SFIC. Serendipity.

Finally, with Col. Ando's directions and the help of strangers, my friend and I were able to find the site of the camp, now a thriving housing development with attractive stucco houses reflecting a decidedly middle-class affluence. At this point, I had seen neither photographs nor paintings of the camp, so it was hard to imagine how it must have looked sixty years earlier. Driving up into the foothills just above the campsite one afternoon, though, I saw a high barbed wire fence silhouetted against the darkening sky, still ablaze with the intense pinks and oranges of a Santa Fe sunset. I imagined that Rev. Watanabe and his fellow prisoners might have seen many such scenes, gazing at the open sky through barbed wire fencing from the camp below.

The cumulative work—especially reading archival documents, book chapters, and journal and newspaper articles—established a foundation on which I could begin to construct scenarios of the Santa Fe internment experience. I also gained a sense of the past anti-Japanese attitudes in New Mexico, fueled by the large contingent of New Mexicans forced on the Bataan Death March in the Philippines, as well as an evolving sense of Santa Fe's community history. This was a history apparently plagued by divisions and conflicts brought to the fore by the

SFIC Marker project and eventually healed by the courage of a few civic leaders. While I could identify with the Issei as targets of hatred, I could also empathize with the New Mexicans' sense of loss. The only reference to Rev. Watanabe, however, was his name on a roster of SFIC internees that I found on microfilm.

As a result of my commitment to this research and being a family member of an internee, Chávez and Col. Ando invited me to attend the dedication of the SFIC Historical Marker just three weeks later. I was thrilled and honored to be invited, as it was a monumental privilege for a researcher in the early stages of a project to be included in an event of such community significance. Not only was it to be memorable historically as a gesture long overdue, but it was also of great social and political importance to Santa Feans, who had faced extreme discord around establishing the marker.

And it was indeed a special day. On 20 April 2002, on a hill overlooking the site of the internment camp in Santa Fe, I joined many who witnessed the coming together of people of different ethnicities, communities, and generations and their efforts toward common goals: to establish a stone marker at Ortiz Park that acknowledges the historical existence of the U.S. Justice Department internment camp during World War II on the site of the present Casa Solana neighborhood; to memorialize the experience of thousands of Japanese immigrants and American-born citizens of Japanese ancestry unjustly incarcerated there between 1942 and 1946; and to heal old wounds.

The intensely blue sky had the clarity of early spring, but the event became a baptism of wind and dust for some 250 participants and onlookers—and for the marker itself, a six-ton granite boulder with a bronze plaque engraved with the following statement:

At this site, due east and below the hill, 4,555 men of Japanese ancestry were incarcerated in a Department of Justice Internment Camp from March 1942 to April 1946. Most were excluded by law from becoming United States citizens and were removed primarily from the West Coast and Hawaii. During World War II, their loyalty to the United States was questioned. Many of the men held here without due process were long time resident religious leaders, businessmen, teachers, fishermen, farmers, and others. No person of Japanese ancestry in the U.S. was ever charged or convicted of espionage throughout the course of the war. Many of the internees had relatives who served with distinction in the American Armed Forces in Europe and in the Pacific. This marker is placed here as a reminder that history is a valuable teacher only if we do not forget our past. (Santa Fe Internment Camp Historical Marker 2002)

Fig. 1.1.   Santa Fe Internment Camp Historical Marker.

With loyalty and patriotism being so critically in question sixty years ear-lier—and those questions being renewed in post 9/11 America—the Pledge of Allegiance conveyed layers of unspoken meaning to me. Then, addressing the crowd of local residents, visitors from places as distant as Alaska, Hawai'i, and Washington, DC, and honored guests from the state and city, Chávez said, "We are here not to celebrate an event about which none of us is proud; we are here to commemorate an event that happened; it is our history" (2002).

The biting wind and dust we felt may not have been so different from the conditions experienced by my grandfather and the other men in the SFIC more than a half century earlier. Representing the internee families, Col. Ando com-mented on the self-censorship among these men: "In many Japanese American families across this country, our fathers never spoke to their children about their experiences in the camps. It was a shameful, it was a painful experience" (2002). This silence was itself an inheritance that bound many of us descendants together. But because of the original secrecy surrounding the Department of Justice facili-ties, such camps as the SFIC were grossly misunderstood.

Reading old newspaper clippings, I had learned that in the late 1990s, because of such historical misunderstandings, some World War II veterans had confused Japanese immigrants with the Japanese enemy and vehemently protested the proposed marker. The controversy split the Santa Fe community and its city council members. In the end, Santa Fe's mayor, Larry Delgado, broke the tie vote of the city council in favor of erecting the marker. As a cooperative effort of citizens of different ethnic and racial backgrounds, the establishment of the SFIC marker clearly represented a collective rather than a single ethnic triumph.

I was moved by the attendance of internee families from all over the country and the social, political, and spiritual significance of the event. At the luncheon reception following the dedication, Col. Ando asked me to speak to the crowd, and I surprised myself by overcoming my shyness and addressing the large audience as an intimate one, bound by the common inheritance of internment and, among non–Japanese Americans, the desire not to forget. The attentiveness of this audience brought the gravity of my project home to me. I began to realize my place and the place of my research in relation to the Japanese American community and the American public at large.

The Road Home: Archival Research, Personal Stories, and Communal Memory

Inspired, I returned to Washington, DC, where I was serving as a scholar-in-residence at the Smithsonian Institution. At fifty-nine, I was the same age as my grandfather was when he was arrested, and that fact took on a strange symbolism for me. One warm day in May, Franklin Odo, the founding director of the Smithsonian's Asian Pacific American Program, introduced me to veteran researchers Aiko and Jack Herzig, who had served as researchers for the Commission on Wartime Relocation and Internment of Civilians and who became invaluable mentors and friends. We talked for hours; I marveled at their expertise and was energized by their warmth and support. They gave me names of archivists at the National Archives, including Fred Romanski and Aloha South, and drew maps of buildings as they had for so many researchers before and after me.

Day after day, I dragged my computer bag with laptop and scanner over the rough sidewalks and grassy areas of the National Mall to the historic halls of Archives I in Washington, DC, or found a desk in the spacious second-floor Researcher Room of the contemporary Archives II in College Park, Maryland, and pored over hundreds of pages of typed memos and lists, mimeographed forms, and other reports, mostly carbon copies on aging onionskin. Months of work produced five files on Tamasaku Watanabe: one from the Immigration and Naturalization Service (INS, Record Group 85), one from the Military Government of the Territory of Hawaii (OMG, RG 338/494), one from the Department of Justice (DOJ, RG 60), and two from the Office of the Provost Marshal General

(OPMG, RG 389). Since I did not know my grandfather well, it was ironic that I began to know him through these files created by his captors. Although many documents overlapped, reflecting the multiple carbon copies produced by the government's bureaucracy, each file came to represent a different view of the man, a somewhat different personality.

The first time I encountered his mug shot in the INS file was especially distressing, as I imagined his humiliation. The degradation of knowing that the authorities would reduce him to two demeaning photographs showed in his hollow stare and grim expression. As I searched through his records and other more general files from the Office of the Provost Marshal General and the State Department, I discovered the names of hundreds of others like him—Fujitani, Hirano, Ikuma, Ishida, Kato, Kawasaki, Maehara, Matsumoto, Matsuura, Miho, Ohara, Otani, Tokairin—Issei men from Hawai'i, some his friends and acquaintances, many complete strangers, all locked up as he was. Eventually it became clear to me that these men were treated by the government as a discrete group and had a unique experience, having been shipped from the Hawaiian Islands over thousands of miles of ocean and land to frigid locations in the northern United States and arid deserts in the Southwest, separated from their families for as many as four years. Rather than studying the broader Department of Justice incarceration, which I saw by now was massive in scope, I would focus on Rev. Watanabe and the Hawai'i Japanese experience of removal and exile while maintaining my interest in literacy and cultural identity. From my office in one of the turrets of the Smithsonian's Arts and Industries Building, I made a phone call to a longtime friend and mentor, Tetsuden Kashima, at the University of Washington, who told me about his forthcoming book, *Judgment without Trial,* and encouraged me to pursue my line of thinking.

In the last months of my stay in Washington, DC, several incidents provided another dimension to my primarily text-based project. I met Marcia Mau, a Smithsonian volunteer and a grandniece of George Hoshida, who had been taken from the Big Island and who had sketched hundreds of people, places, and activities during his captivity. Marcia had found a sketch of my grandfather in her copy of her granduncle's memoirs. Rev. Watanabe's name, addresses, occupation, and age were written in his own hand next to his portrait. He was fifty-nine, it was October 1942, and other notes of his told me that he was in Lordsburg, New Mexico. This was the first visual image I had seen of my grandfather besides the single photograph of him with his barrack mates in Santa Fe found among his records. It was an astounding and precious gift. Knowing that the sketch existed, I could look for the original a year later at the Japanese American National Museum in Los Angeles, where the Hoshida family had donated their father's original artwork.

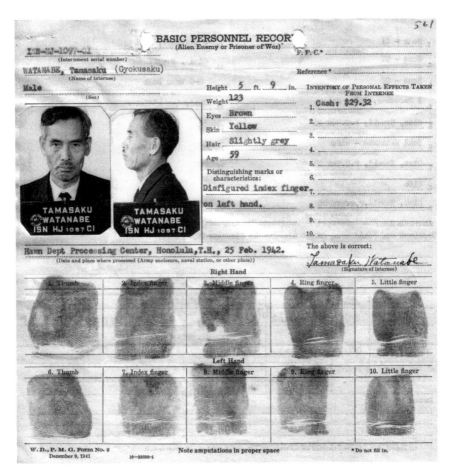

FIG. 1.2. Mug shot of Tamasaku Watanabe, Honolulu, Territory of Hawaii, 25 February 1942 (Santa Fe Evacuee Case File: Watanabe, Tamasaku, No. 1300/B-1970; Individual Case Files; Records of the U.S. DOJ INS, RG 85; NAB).

Marcia, an avid student of the internment experience, also introduced me to Reiko Odate Matsumoto, who lived in the DC area and whose father had been interned from the island of Kaua'i. Meeting Reiko over a lunch of noodles was another gift, for she not only granted me my first interview but also shared her father's camp writings with me, the writings of a Buddhist minister, Reverend Chikou Odate, who belonged to the Literary Society of Santa Fe. His calligraphy was breathtaking in its gentility and grace. Reiko, in turn, told me about Reverend Shingetsu Akahoshi, also a Buddhist minister, who, though not a resident of Hawai'i at the time of his arrest, was a survivor of the internment and was

F**IG**. 1.3. Sketch of Rev. Watanabe (*left*) by George Hoshida, Lordsburg Internment Camp, New Mexico, 8 October 1942 (George Hoshida Collection 97.106.2AU, Japanese American National Museum [Gift of June Hoshida Honma, Sandra Hoshida, and Carole Hoshida Kanada]).

visiting his children in Virginia. She invited me one day to accompany her to visit him, and although I wasn't prepared to conduct an interview in Japanese, I couldn't allow this opportunity to slip away. Rev. Akahoshi, a feisty man then in his early nineties, was amazingly clear in memory and articulate in speech. He not only remembered my grandfather in Santa Fe but vividly described a brief interaction that he had had with him, as I describe in chapter 4. It was a golden moment, more than I could have hoped for.

Another incident occurred at the National Museum of American History: During a presentation, I shared examples of key documents that I had found at the National Archives, among them a petition signed by about two hundred Hawai'i prisoners. As the documents circulated, there was a small commotion in one corner of the room, and a young woman exclaimed that she had found her great-great-grandfather's signature on the petition. Her father and grandfather would be very interested in speaking with me, she said. Serendipity again. This contact led to another interview two months later in Honolulu with the young woman's grandfather Edward Ikuma, then in his eighties and a veteran of the 100th Infantry Battalion, which had distinguished itself at the European front.

We talked at the 100th Battalion Clubhouse, replete with World War II memorabilia—portraits of Medal of Honor recipients, images in which history and memory fused. Ed Ikuma had a kindly, gentle manner. His rugged, sun-browned skin revealed his enjoyment of gardening and golf. Although I had hoped for letters, diaries, or other writings from his grandfather, Ikuma had only a photograph—Reverend Kinai Ikuma, a Shinto priest, in a large group of Japanese men—labeled "Grandfather Kinai" and "Albuquerque, N.M., Internment Camp"; the men stood in a setting, however, that I surmised was actually the SFIC, meaning that Rev. Ikuma had been imprisoned in the same location as my grandfather, at least for a while. I would learn later from a photograph and a list that both clergymen were actually on the same boatload of Issei prisoners, being shipped halfway across the Pacific to Angel Island in San Francisco Bay, and remained in the same camps throughout their internment. As our conversation came to a close, Ikuma commented thoughtfully, "There has been a lot of attention paid to the military veterans of the 100th and the 442nd, but what about the old guys locked up in camps?" (2002). His comment helped me to realize how important this research might be to others besides me and my family. He thanked me for doing this work, but his gratitude was most humbling for me and continues to inspire me to this day. Personal stories were surfacing, enriching my understanding of the deeper narrative: the unwritten and spontaneous recollections of such internee survivors as Rev. Akahoshi and the memories of internee descendants such as Reiko Matsumoto and Ed Ikuma.

Returning to Hawai'i from Ohio in January 2003, armed with various lists and files from the National Archives, I planned to seek out internee survivors who had made the same journey to the mainland as Tamasaku Watanabe, as well as the now elderly children of internees, who might have had recollections and documents from their fathers now gone. One way of learning my grandfather's story was to learn theirs. The question, of course, was how to find them.

I was housed in the University of Hawai'i at Mānoa's Center for Biographical Research (UHM, CBR) through the generosity of Craig Howes, its director, and Stanley Schab, its manager, having been introduced to them earlier by Warren Nishimoto, the director of the UHM's Center for Oral History. I marveled at the vitality and productivity of this place, crammed to the ceiling with books of people's lives. I could not have imagined a more inspiring academic home.

After I contacted George Akita, professor emeritus of history and a mentor of mine decades earlier, research opportunities snowballed. He introduced me to the UHM's Japan Collection librarian, who coincidentally was organizing an exhibit at Hamilton Library for the sixtieth anniversary of the 442nd Regimental Combat Team (RCT), the Japanese American unit celebrated for its heroism at the European front during World War II.[2] Seeing my artifacts—letters, Noh play librettos, a cross used in camp services—spurred her to invite me to participate in this exhibit and, having had some museum experience in a past life, I agreed to curate *Honoring Our Grandfathers: Japanese Immigrants in U.S. Department of Justice Internment Camps, 1941–45.*

Hours of curatorial work on Rev. Watanabe's papers and artifacts culminated in the following message in April 2003: "On this auspicious occasion, as we honor the sons of Japanese immigrants who served, fought, and died heroically in the U.S. military during World War II, let us also remember their fathers, grandfathers, and others who were concurrently incarcerated as 'alien enemies' in U.S. Department of Justice internment camps. The sense of duty and patriotism exhibited by the sons was often a reflection of the values of their elders" (Okawa 2003a). My words were meant as a reminder—to trigger Pierre Nora's dormant memory, to create or stimulate a consciousness. Like the memorial marker in Santa Fe established a year earlier, these artifacts could be a physical embodiment of cultural memory.

This exhibit led to an invitation to the library's opening reception for the anniversary festivities and the several-faceted exhibit that included the Japanese American National Museum's traveling installation about the Nisei World War II Medal of Honor recipients, a number of whom were being honored after earlier neglect. The event put me in the company of now elderly veterans of the 4-4-2 and the MIS (Military Intelligence Service), some of whose fathers had been interned. Their names were on one of my lists, and I would finally have the privilege of meeting them. On this occasion, I met Reverend Yoshiaki Fujitani, a retired Buddhist bishop, whose kind, unassuming manner defused my nervousness. He quickly introduced me to Katsugo Miho, a retired judge, and Akira Otani, a still-active businessman, both of whom agreed to speak with me about their fathers and their visits as young soldiers to them in internment camps such as Camp Livingston in Louisiana and the SFIC in New Mexico. With Rev. Fujitani, they were of my parents' generation, and I felt both awed and overjoyed at this stroke of luck. Each interview produced bundles like my grandfather's—varying numbers of old sepia or black-and-white photos, letters, and other memorabilia in time-weathered envelopes, albums, and cardboard boxes—as did subsequent conversations with other children of internees and the few surviving elderly internees themselves.

A week after the reception, I gave my first illustrated talk at the CBR, titled, "More than a Mugshot: Reconstructing Lives of Japanese Civilian Internees in U.S. Justice Department Concentration Camps." A large crowd squeezed skillfully into the center's space. Following the presentation, Susan Tokairin, also a granddaughter of an internee, came forward with photographs of the Santa Fe camp left by her grandfather, her memory prompted by my library exhibit. And Charlotte Nagoshi, a friend of newfound friends, told me about an internee survivor living in her hometown on Kauaʻi. Although a blurb on my project had appeared in a local community newspaper, yielding two very significant contacts, this word-of-mouth method understandably worked best in the Hawaiʻi Japanese community; it became a pattern at subsequent events in Hawaiʻi —relatives of those imprisoned coming forward or friends telling me about others. Despite my use of a formal protocol of questions, the interviews with internees and families of internees often settled into informal and comfortable conversations over sandwiches or ramen or bento. I found myself drawn into important relationships and began to feel that, more than being a researcher, I was involved in the recovery of my own community's history.

The highlight of this phase of my project was my interview with Kazumi Matsumoto (1902–2003), the hundred-year-old internee survivor on Kauaʻi. I spent a good portion of two days with him, speaking in Japanese both with and without a translator. He showed me a large pine trunk that he used to transport his possessions while interned and handed me a sheaf of photographs that reflected his many interests and memberships in different camp groups, including Japanese flute players, the camp theater group, and baseball teams. He gave into my charge purses of longleaf pine needles, beautifully and intricately braided and then sewn, as I describe in chapter 5. Most memorable were our last words: I wished him well and told him that I would see him again; cocking his head and smiling, he replied, "I'm one hundred years old, so there's no telling" (Matsumoto 2003). To my great sadness, he died within four weeks of our visit.

The audience interest in my topic led to several follow-up events in the islands, including "Memorials and Memories," a reception and update for the participants in my study and their families, and "Accessing Hawaiʻi Civilian Internee Files," a workshop for families, both events organized in 2004 to promote family research on the Issei prisoners, to reciprocate in some way their generosity toward me, and to develop a collective spirit around the project. Public lectures included "From Sand Island to Santa Fe" (2004), which drew a standing-room-only crowd at the Japanese Cultural Center of Hawaiʻi as part of its gallery exhibit and lecture series "Dark Clouds over Paradise: The Hawaiʻi Internees Story"; and "Through My Grandfather's Eyes: American World War II Internment from Kilauea Military Camp, Hawaiʻi, to Santa Fe, New Mexico" (2009) at the University of Hawaiʻi at Hilo because the Big Island had been home to a significant number of former prisoners.

A dynamic emotional energy seemed to prevail at these events and in the oral history conversations with internees and internee families, with talk serving

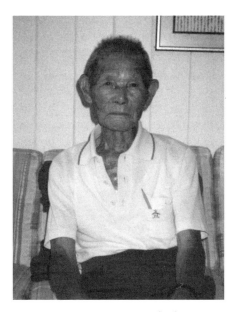

Fig. 1.4. Kazumi Matsumoto at his home,
Kalāheo, Kaua'i, July 2003.

often to "reawaken" memory. Treasured bundles—photographs, notebooks, letters, journals, plaited bags, paintings, and other artifacts—not only triggered but
also contained that memory, embodied meaning. Over the years, I had the privilege of interviewing four civilian internee survivors and members of more than
thirty-five internee families (forty-six family members), on O'ahu, Kaua'i, Maui,
and the Big Island. Some families who had hidden, forgotten, or simply laid aside
these stories began to come forward to tell them and, seeing artifacts valued in
exhibits and displays, began to appreciate what they still had. Others I talked
with had no writings, no photographs, no records, no memories of any sort, until
I provided them with copies of documents.

   But the story doesn't necessarily end with my return to the Hawai'i Nikkei
(persons of Japanese ancestry) communities, in which there may be a natural and
expected interest. I have told versions of this Issei internment narrative to mainland and international audiences, academic and community—from the West
Coast to the Southwest to the Midwest to the East Coast and in Alberta, Canada,
and Pamplona, Spain—hesitantly at first, not feeling sure of the interest among
people so far removed yet encouraged by their questions and compassion.

   Very gratifying for me has been the willingness of New Mexicans to "own" this
aspect of their history, reflected in Thomas Chávez's comment during the 2002

marker dedication, quoted earlier. Despite the controversy and confusion surrounding the original proposal to establish the historical marker, the late Vicente Ojinaga, an elderly survivor of the Bataan Death March, attended that event, a courageous act that helped to defuse the misdirected animus in the community.

After five years researching the Hawai'i Issei exile, one that for many internees, including my grandfather, culminated in Santa Fe, I made my way through a blizzard from northeastern Ohio to New Mexico once again in February 2007—a five-year pilgrimage of sorts to the historical marker. It had snowed the day before; my friend Carrie and I picked our way through the snow-soaked earth, hopping from grass clump to grass clump to avoid the mud. We left red asters. It was a small gesture.

But the illustrated talk that I gave at the time for the community opened another door, and the curators of the New Mexico History Museum again acknowledged New Mexico's role in World War II's internment history by requesting my family artifacts for the opening exhibition of the new New Mexico History Museum in 2009, an essay for their commemorative book *Telling New Mexico: A New History,* coinciding with that event, and a lecture in their inaugural lecture series in 2010. That I spoke to a sold-out house further reflected community interest in the topic. In 2011, I began the challenging process of organizing—from Hawai'i —a two-day symposium to be held at the museum in 2012. Titled "From Inside and Outside the Barbed Wire: New Mexico's Multicultural World War II Internment Stories," its main purpose was to mark the tenth anniversary of the SFIC marker dedication, commemorated on that blustery day in April 2002, but it was also to perpetuate the cultural memory of New Mexico's internment story. Ultimately, it was a community effort, involving interested Santa Feans—friends and colleagues,[3] strangers who had memories of the Santa Fe internment camp, related here in the epilogue, and the New Mexico History Museum director and staff, and supported by a grant from the New Mexico Humanities Council.

This is, after all, a story of the American past and the American present as we continue to grapple with questions of immigration, citizenship, discrimination, and conscience and to appreciate stories of survival in the face of great adversity. Besides being a personal, family, and Nikkei community recovery project, I have come to realize that the story touches the lives and hearts of many, as the following pages reveal.

CHAPTER 2

The Fate of the "Wingless Birds" I

Issei Immigration, Prewar Lives, Seizure and Arrest

Tamasaku Watanabe arrived in Honolulu, Territory of Hawaii, from Sacramento, California, in late November 1922, accompanied by my grandmother, Yuki, and three of their children.[1] They stayed for a few days at the Yamashiro Hotel, a lodging popular among Japanese immigrants, not far from Honolulu Harbor. My mother, Sumi, was only six but still remembered in her later years that as she walked with her father on a nearby wooden bridge, a child's pearl necklace that he had given her earlier broke and the tiny pearls scattered about. Her father was able to retrieve a few of them with the help of a passing stranger and eventually had the necklace restrung for her. A treasured family memento.

Through My Grandfather's Eyes

Seventeen years earlier, in 1905, Tamasaku Watanabe had immigrated to the United States from Hiroshima, Japan, a young man of twenty-two. He arrived in Seattle in February, then moved to San Francisco, where he was baptized as a Christian in September, months before the Great San Francisco Earthquake struck the city in 1906. The devastation that he witnessed made such a deep impression on him that although he had studied law in Japan, his new purpose became "learning [the] ministry of Christianity" (Watanabe 1945, 1).[2] In pursuit of this goal, he served as the secretary of the Japanese Young Men's Christian Association (YMCA), precursor to the Japanese Presbyterian Church, under Ernest Adolphus Sturge. A photograph of my grandfather, taken with Dr. and Mrs. Sturge and other Japanese Christians, captures a young man bound by earnestness and determination, ready to embark on a mission—to serve fellow Japanese immigrants and his Lord. In September 1912, he entered the San Francisco Theological Seminary to study the Christian faith formally. This he did with enthusiasm and commitment, as his notebooks reflect.

Fig. 2.1. Tamasaku Watanabe (*row 2, fifth from right*) and Japanese YMCA group, San Francisco, 1910 (Tamasaku Watanabe Collection).

Following his graduation and his ordination by the Presbyterian Church of the USA in April 1915, Reverend Tamasaku Watanabe began his ministry in Stockton, California, at the Stockton Japanese Presbyterian Church, and then in 1920 moved to Sacramento, serving at a Japanese Church of Christ, thus earning him a place in the 1922 edition of the Japanese *Who's Who*. With Yuki, the math teacher from Hokkaido whom he had married in September 1912 at the Japanese Presbyterian Church of San Francisco, he had four children. My mother related that the youngest, given the English name Ernest, possibly after Dr. Sturge, was struck by a Standard Oil truck and killed at the age of two in October 1922.

It must have been an agonizing time for my grandparents, a test of their faith and forgiveness. My mother recalled that the truck driver was so remorseful that her family felt sorry for him. In his pocket diary entry in English on 25 October, my grandfather notes simply, in words laden with sorrow, "Our dear Ishi departed from us." The next day, he writes, "Many friends called to console us. Went to Miller and [Sket——] to see dear Ishi. Thanks to God." A day later, again he writes, "Many friends came to sympathize us." And on the twenty-eighth, he records, "The funeral of my dear Ishi held at 2 p.m. at Japanese Church of Christ. Moon said 'goodbye to dear Ishi'" (Watanabe 1922).

Yet, Reverend Takie Okumura, one of the most influential Japanese Christians in the Hawaiian Islands, had spoken to my grandfather during an earlier visit to San Francisco about working with the Japanese in the territory, and when

FIG. 2.2. Watanabe family in California, 1919. *Left to right:* unknown, Yuki holding Shinichi, Sumi, Michiro, and Rev. Watanabe (Tamasaku Watanabe Collection).

the Hawaiian Board of Missions had called Rev. Watanabe to the islands earlier upon Rev. Okumura's recommendation, he had agreed to the transfer (Allen 1942, 2). The family had already moved out of the Sacramento church parsonage and was living in temporary quarters, recalled my mother. Now, two weeks after Ernest Ishi's death, my grandfather packed up his family—Grandma and the three remaining children, Michiro, age nine, Sumi, six, and Shinichi, four—"bought [a] ticket for Honolulu" on 14 November, and, beginning on 22 November, they made their way across the vast Pacific Ocean. "On account of Winter season," he writes, "sea was pretty rough"; much of the time, it was a "hard voyage" (Watanabe 1922).

That December, Rev. Watanabe moved his family from Honolulu to the island of Maui and began a long ministry at the Wailuku Japanese Christian Church. A photograph from that period shows him smiling broadly in the back row with a large group of Sunday school students, including his children, Grandma, and other adults—his "flock."

Despite his smile, he was undoubtedly working under the cloud of anti-Japanese prejudice and restrictionism developing in Hawai'i in the 1920s, extensively documented by Gary Okihiro.[3] As a Christian evangelist working with

Fig. 2.3. Rev. Watanabe (*top row, far left*), Yuki (*fourth from left*), Wailuku Japanese Christian Church Sunday School children, and others, Maui, ca. 1924 (Tamasaku Watanabe Collection).

Japanese plantation workers and others, Rev. Watanabe might have been aware of the 1920 strike on Oʻahu two years before his arrival,[4] but he most certainly knew of the U.S. Supreme Court's 1922 decision in *Ozawa v. United States,* which affirmed the denial of citizenship to Japanese immigrants like him, established by the Naturalization Act of 1790. The original act allowed naturalization only to "free white person(s)"—and later to "those of African birth or origin" (Daniels 2013, 3)[5]—designating other nonwhite persons as "aliens ineligible for citizenship" with permanent alien status. Such anti-naturalization laws socially and politically isolated the Issei, who were then accused by the haole (Caucasian) oligarchy of being unassimilable. My grandfather's mission had been to spread the Christian Gospel, thus aiding in the Americanization and assimilation of the Japanese, so he must have seen the contradiction and felt the insult. Meanwhile, efforts in the territorial legislature to regulate foreign language schools targeted the extensive *nihongogakko* (Japanese language school) system.

Besides ministering to his congregation in Wailuku, Rev. Watanabe became the principal and served as one of two teachers of a small *nihongogakko,* a wooden building with two classrooms, on the outskirts of Wailuku. My mother recalled having to walk to and from this school after a day at public school for the year that she was a reluctant student, wishing to play outside and get into mischief with her friends instead. Mrs. Sadayasu, the other teacher, lived with her son in a third room in the building and also taught cultural skills such as manners and Japanese sewing to the more diligent. This was one of some 163 such schools throughout the islands by 1920 that sought to maintain the Japanese language and culture among the Nisei (Kotani 1985, 49). First established as a school system in 1896 by Rev. Okumura in affiliation with the Japanese Christian movement, the language schools grew in number, as others were subsequently established by Buddhist temples and independent community organizations (50). On 13 December 1922, within two weeks of their arrival on Maui, my grandfather notes that he traveled to the adjoining town of Kahului to attend a Japanese language school teachers' conference (Watanabe 1922).

As the haole planter oligarchy grew more nervous about the organizational and community strength of the Nikkei following various labor strikes from 1909 through 1920, they sought first to abolish the Japanese language schools altogether, one argument being that they worked against Japanese assimilation into American society. When that effort failed, they disregarded the constitutional rights of Japanese families, whose American-born children were U.S. citizens, and went so far as to impose legal restrictions on Japanese school teaching personnel, curricula, and textbooks at a special session of the legislature in November 1920.[6] But leaders in the Japanese community, including Frederick Makino, recognized the violation of the citizens' constitutional rights and, with the Palama Japanese Language School and others, challenged this regulation in the territorial and federal courts.[7]

The U.S. District Court of Hawaii finally placed a temporary injunction on the legislation in July 1925 and referred the case, known as *Farrington, Governor of Hawaii, et al. v. Tokushige et al.*, to the Ninth Circuit Court of Appeals in San Francisco. The subsequent judgment of this court, on 22 March 1926, cited an earlier judgment against foreign language school laws in Nebraska, Iowa, and Ohio (*Meyer v. Nebraska*), stating, "the individual has certain fundamental rights which must be respected. The protection of the Constitution extends to all; to those who speak other languages, as well as to those born with English on the tongue. Perhaps it would be highly advantageous if all had ready understanding of our ordinary speech, but this cannot be coerced by methods which conflict with the Constitution—a desirable end cannot be promoted by prohibited means" (*Farrington* 1926, 714).

Referring to the Hawaiian territorial government's assimilation argument for imposing regulations on the Japanese language schools, the Ninth Circuit Court's judgment asserts that assimilation "is in part a matter of choice and in part a matter of necessity, *because one cannot assimilate alone.* No doubt the Japanese tongue will be spoken on the Islands for generations to come, . . . but we took the Islands cum onere and extended the Constitution of the United States there, and every American citizen has a right to invoke its protection. *You cannot make good citizens by oppression or by a denial of constitutional rights"* (*Farrington* 1926, 714; emphasis mine). Noting this tension between constitutionality and assimilation, I wondered what my grandfather might have heard and thought about these events as a Japanese and a Christian.

Losing this battle but remaining adamant, the territorial government took its case to the U.S. Supreme Court. But the Supreme Court, which then included William Howard Taft, chief justice, and Oliver Wendell Holmes Jr., associate justice, unanimously affirmed the judgment of the Ninth Circuit Court, upholding the Constitution and its protection of individual rights against infringement by government regulation. The day 21 February 1927 marked a triumph for the Japanese families, schools, teachers, and community. Okihiro calls it "perhaps the greatest achievement of Hawaii's Japanese in resisting cultural hegemony during the interwar period" (1991, 190). John Hawkins describes it as "an impressive example of a clearly subordinate group effectively mobilizing available resources, . . . and finally emerging victorious" (1978, 392).

Consciously or not, my grandfather had entered a world of considerable controversy upon his arrival in the islands, yet his faith in the American way seemed unshaken by such assaults on the Nikkei community. His diligence in his work was eventually rewarded in 1927—the same year as the *Farrington v. Tokushige* victory—when he was commissioned "Pastor-Evangelist" by the Hawaiian Evangelical Association. More telling, however, was the second- or thirdhand touring car assigned to him by the Hawaiian board. (A slight perhaps—it had no windowpanes. My mother recalled that when it rained, her father had to jump out and put up celluloid windows to keep the interior dry.) Nevertheless, according to a newspaper article written in 1957, upon his retirement years after the war, Rev. Watanabe had held the longest ministry in the history of the Wailuku church to that date, and the strength of his faith and leadership was reflected in the strong commitment of his parishioners (Nakamura 1957).

After a twelve-year residence as pastor of the Maui church, Rev. Watanabe was transferred to ʻŌlaʻa, island of Hawaiʻi, in early 1935 and began his fourth ministry at the Olaʻa Japanese Christian Church, serving Japanese laborers who worked on the nearby sugar plantations (Brazier and Thompson 2002). During

Fig. 2.4. Rev. Watanabe (*seated, far left*), and other Christian ministers, Honolulu, Territory of Hawaii, June 1931 (Tamasaku Watanabe Collection).

this time, the church authorities apparently had proposed an expansion of the parish, in response to which my grandfather wrote a short essay, discussing "the practical difficulties in working a larger parish plan." He candidly concluded his sociolinguistic argument with some pointed observations:

> I would like to ask as an actual matter whether *Haole* [Caucasian] people like to mingle with other nationalities and races and support one church? Some Haole like to teach but not mingle with others. The real difficulty I think is here. I know children in the public schools get along regardless of race or nationality, but I am told that it does not continue into the university. It seems to be natural for people to break up into such groups and anyway it is a fact at the present time. The church which does not take into account such practical realities cannot hope to be successful. (Watanabe, "The Practical Difficulties," n.d.)

Given the pressure of Americanization, especially that associated with the early Japanese Christian movement,[8] and the inclination among the haole authorities to racialize and politicize opposition in the prewar years, my grandfather's frank dissent on this issue and his brief explication of existing racial tensions and hypocrisies impressed me. During this time, too, the Japanese consulate appointed him to serve as its representative (*toritsuginin*, or subconsular agent) in this remote location of 'Ōla'a, keeping routine records, helping immigrants with affairs related to their Japanese citizenship, and facilitating the expatriation of American-born children of immigrants.[9] Little did he know that this humanitarian work would have ironic and dire consequences.

In late summer 1941, as political tensions between the United States and Japan intensified and assets of citizens of Japan were being frozen, Rev. Watanabe was asked by Norman Schenck of the board of the Hawaiian Evangelical Association to provide an affidavit attesting to "the ownership, purposes, activities, finances, and operations of the Ola'a Japanese Christian Church" (Watanabe 1941a, 1). So my grandfather was not entirely unaware of the events of the day but seemed to believe in the democratic process. He complied with the request on 9 August 1941 as the minister and head of his church. So dedicated was he to teaching his parishioners "the Christian Gospel and the fundamentals of Christianity; to train[ing] them in the fundamentals of the Christian moral and ethical code" and "the highest ideals of Americanism" (2), that he must have been shocked and confused by the events that soon unfolded.

(Pre)War Plans

Unbeknownst to my grandfather, as well as many other Issei fathers and grandfathers, the politicians and military leaders of various countries had been stirring the war pot and making plans for many years. In fact, coming of age in post–World War II America, I had held the naive belief, like much of the general American public, that the United States' involvement in World War II was precipitated by the Japanese attack on Pearl Harbor and that the question was how much knowledge the Americans had had of the impending attack. Yet reading government documents and the studies of various scholars over the years has continued to shed light for me on the extraordinary complexity of events in Hawai'i leading up to 7 December 1941.

In *Cane Fires,* for example, Okihiro describes pre-1920s military intelligence and haole perceptions of the Japanese "yellow peril" as well as those views of the 1920s and 1930s, when authorities construed labor issues as race issues to their own ends. During the labor strikes of the 1920s, the haole planter oligarchy and its allies specifically identified and vilified Japanese priests, newspaper editors, educators, and other "'subjects of the Mikado' as 'agitators' who had stirred up the placid waters of planter-worker relations" (Okihiro 1991, 78). This conflation of labor strife and anti Americanism/anti-Americanization by the planters in

Hawaiʻi would have clear consequences two decades later. When Kashima's long-anticipated *Judgment without Trial: Japanese American Imprisonment during World War II* came out in summer 2003, I found a meticulous documentation of the complex machinery and machinations of numerous government agencies in the U.S. War, Justice, and State Departments in what he terms "the imprisonment organization" (5), both well before and during World War II. Such descriptions dispelled any illusion that the incarceration of Japanese immigrants and their American children was a hysterical and mistaken response to the Japanese attack on Pearl Harbor.

Among Okihiro's findings is a chilling 1929 Military Intelligence Division report, one of "a long and continuous line of . . . intelligence reports and war plans emanating from the army's Hawaiian Department and high command in Washington" (1991, xi), reflecting an unmistakably anti-Japanese bias. Most shocking to me was the early conclusion that the Nisei were a liability and that all Japanese, including the American-born, should categorically be considered "enemy aliens" (123), the INS term designating only foreign nationals of enemy nations, in this case the Issei—in blatant disregard of the U.S. Constitution.

Six years later, in 1935, the same year that my grandfather went to serve the ʻŌlaʻa congregation on the Big Island, Lieutenant Colonel George S. Patton Jr. began serving as chief of U.S. Army intelligence in the territory. In "The Orange Race: George S. Patton, Jr.'s Japanese-American Hostage Plan," Michael Slackman describes a "secret plan" prepared by Patton between 1935 and 1937 with the purpose of "maintaining internal security" (1984, 1): Authorities would "arrest and intern certain persons of the Orange race who are considered most inimical to American interests, or *those whom, due to their position and influence in the Orange community, it is desirable to retain as hostages*" (Patton quoted in Slackman 1984, 25; emphasis mine). It is telling that "Orange" was used by American military strategists to designate Japan prior to World War II but that Patton uses it to refer to both resident aliens and U.S. citizens of Japanese heritage alike.

It is also telling that his purpose is to take hostages not because of any wrongdoing but for the destabilizing effect their absence would have on the entire "Orange community." He lists a total of 128 hostages, including such Christian leaders as Rev. Okumura, and racial prejudice underlies his assumptions—the belief that, as Slackman puts it, "ethnicity was the most important factor in assessing their [the Hawaiʻi Japanese] loyalty. Citizenship, length of residence, and other manifestations of loyalty to the U.S. [such as previous U.S. military service] counted for nothing . . . an outlook that elevated genetic accident to political principle" (1984, 16). To Patton, the Japanese were guilty by reason of their "race."

Patton was not alone in his racist assumptions among the U.S. military and leadership. In 1936, President Franklin D. Roosevelt wrote in a now infamous memo to his chief of naval operations that "every Japanese citizen or non-citizen . . . who meets these Japanese ships [calling at Hawaii ports] or has any connection with their officers or men should be secretly but definitely identified and his or her name placed on a special list of those who would be the first to be placed in a concentration camp in the event of trouble" (1936). The covertness of the president's order—five years before the outbreak of war—is stunning, as is his casual use of the term "concentration camp" in relation to Japanese immigrants, outlawed from American citizenship, and their U.S. citizen children. A few years later, on 28 June 1940, anticipating the "trouble" that FDR had mentioned, Congress instituted the Alien Registration Act (the Smith Act), requiring all aliens over the age of thirteen to register with the authorities.[10]

A draft of a report that I found in the National Archives on "Alien Control in Hawaii" (Morrison 1945c) under martial law reveals prevailing stereotyped views of the Nikkei similar to those of individual leaders. Although a draft, it was overseen by Brigadier General William R. C. Morrison of the Military Governor's Office of Internal Security (OIS) in August 1945, the last days of the war: the Japanese population is described as having "quaint oriental customs, [being] poorly assimilated into our western civilization" (8), especially "in Hawaii where the Japanese, an Oriental race, moved into so-called 'white man's' country" (12). This view led "those in authority who planned for an internal security program in Hawaii" to conclude that "the alien and dual citizen Japanese need the closest watching of all the races in Hawaii" (8).[11] Following an extensive discussion of "Japanese Community Life" and organizational activities, the report concludes:

> The effect which they [organizational activities] had upon the Japanese in Hawaii as individuals and as a community . . . was to hamper and retard the general progress of the local Japanese toward their Americanization. They were not engaged in espionage or sabotage, but by keeping alive Japanese nationalistic thoughts a potential fifth column was molded in Hawaii. It was this rise in Japanese nationalism, this slowness to become a part of the social community of Hawaii, this tendency to remain segregated and non-assimilated, this keeping alive of alien Japanese traditions and customs, which raised the question, what of the Japanese? How far can they be trusted? Are they truly loyal to the United States? (29–30)

Contemporary writers such as Kashima and Tom Coffman quite rightly acknowledge the difference in wartime treatment of the Hawai'i Japanese, selectively arrested, and that of the Nikkei on the West Coast, incarcerated en masse,[12] but it is undeniable that prejudices and suspicion, based on factors fabricated or real, were deep, broad, and directed at Hawaiʻi's Japanese at the territorial, federal, and military levels. It is also undeniable that the lives of hundreds of men, women, and their families were damaged by these fears and racist attitudes over the course of World War II.

Surveillance

In response to preconceived notions, impulses, and orders, the U.S. military intelligence organizations, as well as the FBI, had begun investigations and surveillance of selected Japanese individuals years before the attack on Pearl Harbor (Okihiro 1991; Kashima 2003). In 2002, I found myself searching through numerous files in the National Archives with great anticipation: What heinous act could my grandfather have committed? But in Rev. Watanabe's Department of Justice file, all I found was generic language describing his duties as a subconsular agent, which was recorded on a notecard on 9 April 1941: "[His duty as a consular agent] is primarily to aid eligible Japanese in filing their annual petitions for exemption from Japanese military service; to handle expatriation matters; to communicate with Japanese governmental agencies and businesses regarding the affairs of the Japanese who is incapable of attending to those matters himself and act in performing duties which may otherwise fall upon the Consulate" (U.S. Department of Justice; see "Names and Terminology" for use of *subconsular/consular agent*). This description was repeated verbatim in the FBI language used in a hearing for a group of forty-one subconsular agents in Līhuʻe, Kauaʻi, on 9 January 1942.[13] Such duties were primarily for the benefit of plantation laborers and others whose level of literacy in Japanese was inadequate for such tasks. Further wording in the Līhuʻe hearing states that "these Consular Agents are usually chosen from the Buddhist priests and the principals of the Japanese language schools in the Territory of Hawaii and from other Japanese, usually aliens, of more than ordinary intelligence" (Folder: Hamano, Sohei, n.d., 3).

In addition, the key accusation in Rev. Watanabe's file—that such consular agents "are chosen from the leading alien Japanese in the communities and *are believed* to act as espionage agents or observers" (emphasis mine)—appears to be based on pure speculation but is repeated in subsequent documents. This speculative language, by virtue of being used repeatedly, is eventually treated as "fact" and appears to be the only grounds for the arrest of my grandfather and, presumably, others like him. In a form memo to the chief of the Special Defense Unit dated 31 May 1941, more than six months before the outbreak of war, J. Edgar Hoover, director of the FBI, refers to "a dossier showing the information presently available in the files of this Bureau with respect to [Rev. Tamasaku Watanabe]," but this report about his subconsular agent status is the only "information" that predates Hoover's memo. On the strength of this report alone, Hoover writes, "It is recommended that this individual be considered for custodial detention in the event of a national emergency. The information contained on the attached dossier constitutes the basis for appropriate consideration in this regard" (Hoover 1941). This specious argument sealed my grandfather's fate and that of hundreds of other Issei.

As for Rev. Watanabe's Christian faith, while government officials were ostensibly suspicious of the Japanese in general because of their perceived slow assimilation into "American" society, the official view expressed by Brig. Gen. Morrison in the OIS "Alien Control" report mentioned earlier maintained a decided mistrust of the Japanese adherence to Christianity, implying a per-ceived Caucasian ownership of this religion: "There has even been found some Christianity among the alien Japanese, but whether or not this is a sincere adop-tion or not is hard to tell. It may be that Christianity has been adopted by some of the older aliens chiefly for business reasons or to enhance their social position among the Caucasian elements in the community" (1945c, 36). In his hearing held at Hilo, Territory of Hawaii, on 13 February 1942, Rev. Watanabe was asked repeated questions about his thinking as a Christian minister on matters of Japa-nese government and military actions, with insinuations that his faith was insin-cere. Rev. Watanabe and other Christians were damned if they didn't assimilate and damned if they did.

Although Patton's 1935–1937 report was "discarded as an operational plan" in 1940 (Slackman 1984, 6), shades of it appeared in the plan that did become operational in 1941. By 21 November 1941 a document titled "Memorandum: Seizure and Detention Plan (Japanese)" and stamped SECRET on each page had been drawn up by Lieutenant Colonel George W. Bicknell, U.S. Army, including extensive lists of Japanese immigrants and U.S.-born Japanese in Hawai'i who would be apprehended in case of war. This was a version of what was known as the "ABC List," a custodial detention list categorizing aliens by supposed levels of threat to national security.[14]

Bicknell's instructions prefacing the actual lists reveal that, among other things, the military preempted the FBI and other civil authorities prior to the declaration of martial law (Bicknell 1941a, no. 7, 2); that the stated intention regarding alien enemies was to "enjoin" them "to preserve the peace, to refrain from crimes against the public safety . . . and to refrain from actual hostility or giving information, aid, or comfort to the enemies of the United States." Moreover, it was to assure them that "so long as they shall conduct themselves in accordance with law, they shall be undisturbed in the peaceful pursuit of their lives and occupations and be accorded the consideration due to all law-abiding persons" (no. 8, 2). What happened to this intention, I wondered, considering subsequent events?

In this secret memorandum Bicknell determines that "the first group to be seized and detained will include all consular agents of Japan, certain known dangerous Buddhist and Shinto priests as well as other known dangerous Japanese aliens among the language school principals, merchants, bankers and other civilians" (Plan I, no. 2). The targeted groups, I found, were astonishingly similar to those vilified during the labor strikes of the 1920s. Rev. Watanabe's name appears in "Exhibit 'A,'" containing the names of "Japanese Consular Agents in the Territory of Hawaii as of 1 November 1941," including Seiichi Fujii, Naojiro Hirano, Kazumi Matsumoto, Reverend Chikou Odate, and ten other participants in this study.

Bicknell's memo also reveals the military's concern with its public image as a driving force behind the targeting of the subconsular agents as a whole group: "The non-inclusion of the members of this group in the initial seizure of enemy aliens would appear, to both the Japanese and American communities, as most illogical and inconsistent, and would be regarded by the former as a sign of weakness" (Plan I, no. 3). In the end, then, this would appear to have been a public relations move rather than one based on a real threat to national security.

The Roundup: Seizure and Arrest

The seventh of December 1941: in the early morning hours, navy planes of the Japanese Empire launched an attack on Pearl Harbor Naval Base and other military facilities on Oʻahu. Within hours, martial law was declared and the round-up of the Issei began.

In his weathered pocket diary for 1941, my grandfather's last entry—dated 7 December 1941—ironically reads in English: "Legend of the Wingless Birds," presumably the title or reference point of his sermon for that Sunday morning (Watanabe 1941b). Whether he actually delivered this sermon I have no way of knowing, but I did learn from one of his own documents that he was seized and arrested in his parsonage on that fateful day.

In keeping with Bicknell's pronouncement, the warrant for Rev. Watanabe's arrest, dated 7 December 1941, is a military and not a civil document, addressed to "any Sheriff; . . . any Police Officer within the Territory of Hawaii; or any Member of the Military Police; or any Member of the Corps of Intelligence Police; or any Officer of the Federal Bureau of Investigation; or to any Member of the Navy Shore Patrol." It is signed by Bicknell. These authorities were "commanded to take the body of TAMASAKU WATANABE on suspicion of being an alien enemy of the United States" (Bicknell 1941b). As sinister as this "alien enemy" designation appears, in fact, the racially biased Naturalization Act of 1790 prohibited Japanese immigrants from becoming U.S. citizens and makes this statement essentially a question of immigration status: the Alien Enemies Act of 1918, based on the Alien and Sedition Acts of 1798, declares that citizens from countries with whom the United States is at war become alien enemies upon the declaration of war (Kashima 2003, 25; U.S. Statutes at Large 1798). Thus, the accusation being made—possibly premature and illegal on 7 December but for the power of the president, given that Congress did not declare war until 8 December—was that Rev. Watanabe was suspected not of a crime but of being a citizen of an enemy nation, in this case Japan, an identity over which he had no control.[15] Surprisingly, no reference is made to his being a subconsular agent. Okihiro states that those arrested "were apprehended without warrants" because of the lack of bureaucratic timeliness of the U.S. Attorney General's office (1991, 209); this calls into question the 7 December dating—though not the date itself—that appeared on the warrant for Rev. Watanabe and others.

Furthermore, Okihiro also cites John A. Burns, then of the Honolulu Police Department, as recalling "that the group [Bicknell, Burns, and the FBI's Robert Shivers, who reviewed the FBI lists together] did not even bother to investigate consular agents, language-school principals and teachers, and other community leaders because 'they were aliens and they were prime and with very few exceptions they were picked up as a unit.' Whether these individuals were subversives was not the issue; they were interned because they were leaders" (1991, 209). Echoes of Patton's targeting of "those whom, due to their position and influence in the Orange community, it is desirable to retain as hostages" (quoted in Slackman 1984, 25). In Rev. Watanabe's diary on 7 December 1941, another sentence, written in Japanese at a different time, states rather matter-of-factly, "With the outbreak of war between Japan and the US, I went to the Volcano House" (Watanabe 1941b). This was to be the first of many stops in his journey of internment.

So, too, was it for other subconsular agents on the Big Island and elsewhere. In my search to understand my grandfather's experience, I have found a common story and a multitude of variations to it in talking with internee survivors and family members of internees. Naojiro Hirano had immigrated at age sixteen from Shizuoka, Japan, to Hamakua on Hawai'i Island, serving as a plantation worker, then a ranch hand, before moving to the Puna Plantation around 1908. Here he worked as a clerk for the plantation store and studied English at night school. On

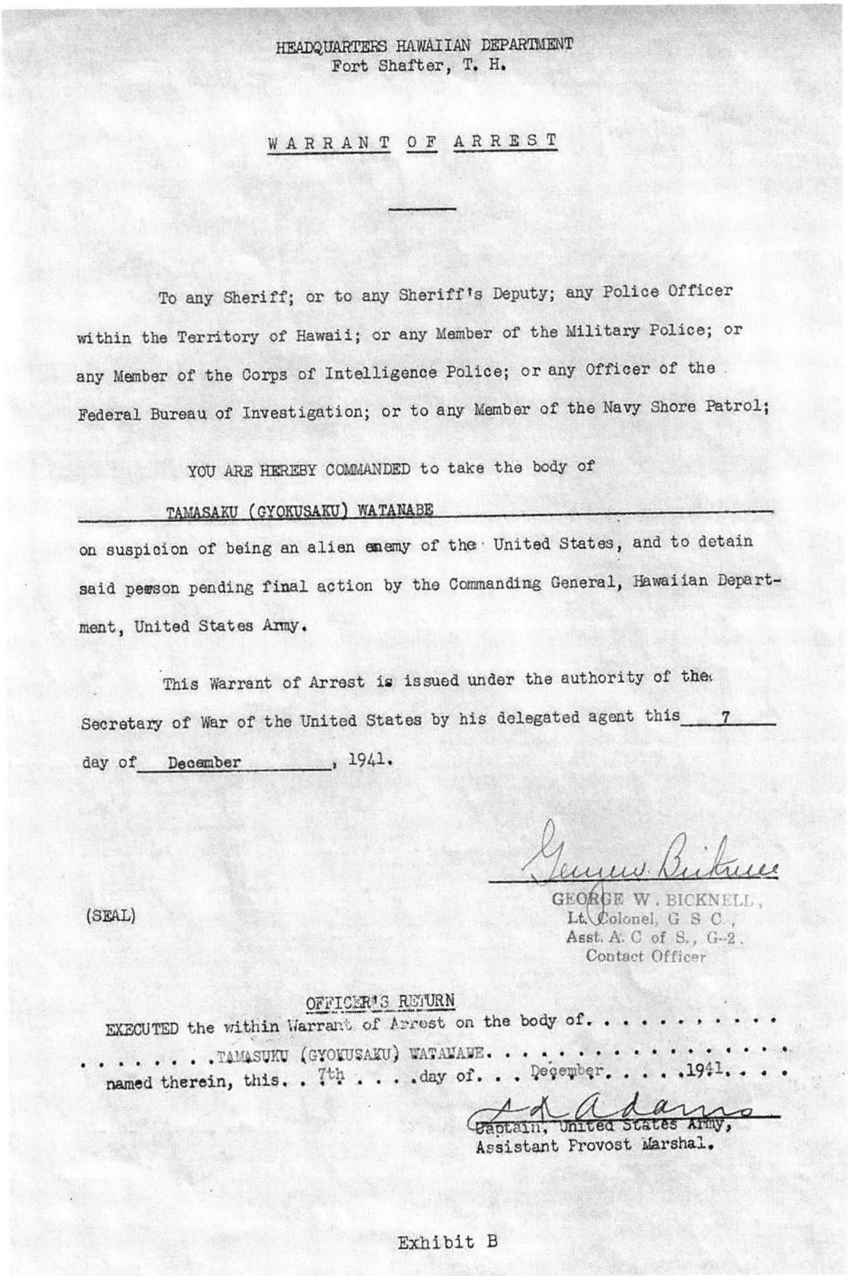

HEADQUARTERS HAWAIIAN DEPARTMENT
Fort Shafter, T. H.

W A R R A N T   O F   A R R E S T

_____

To any Sheriff; or to any Sheriff's Deputy; any Police Officer

within the Territory of Hawaii; or any Member of the Military Police; or

any Member of the Corps of Intelligence Police; or any Officer of the

Federal Bureau of Investigation; or to any Member of the Navy Shore Patrol;

YOU ARE HEREBY COMMANDED to take the body of

_____TAMASAKU (GYOKUSAKU) WATANABE_____

on suspicion of being an alien enemy of the United States, and to detain

said person pending final action by the Commanding General, Hawaiian Depart-

ment, United States Army.

This Warrant of Arrest is issued under the authority of the

Secretary of War of the United States by his delegated agent this___7____

day of___December_____, 1941.

GEORGE W. BICKNELL,
(SEAL)   Lt. Colonel, G S C.,
                                                Asst. A. C of S., G-2.
                                                Contact Officer

OFFICER'S RETURN
EXECUTED the within Warrant of Arrest on the body of. . . . .
. . . . .TAMASUKU (GYOKUSAKU) WATANABE. . . . .
named therein, this. . 7th . . . .day of. . . December. . . . .1941. . . .

Captain, United States Army,
Assistant Provost Marshal.

Exhibit B

FIG. 2.5. Warrant of arrest for Tamasaku Watanabe, Fort Shafter, Territory of Hawaii, 7 December 1941 (Hawaii-Civilian Internees, Valdastri to Wulff; Subject File 1942–46, Reporting Branch, Enemy POW Information Bureau; Records of the Office of the Provost Marshal General, RG 389; NACP).

occasion, as he walked past a local Christian church, which coincidentally became my grandfather's church years later, he heard hymns being sung and was so moved by this music that he became a Christian himself. He then moved to Mountain View to become the assistant manager of the Puna Plantation Store, before he opened his own Hirano Store in Glenwood in 1917. Becoming a leader in his community, he taught at the local Japanese language school and spoke at community gatherings. And because he was literate in English as well as Japanese, he also served as a subconsular agent. His reward for his level of literacy and humanitarian service? Like Rev. Watanabe, he was arrested on 7 December. His son, Wataru Hirano, told me that the local police chief and MPs came to take his father, who was "never so scared; he hardly talked" (2004). But he and my grandfather, being Christians in the Hilo area, knew each other and may have crossed paths more than once, so may have been of some comfort to each other while imprisoned.

Unlike many Japanese school teachers and principals such as Rev. Watanabe and Hirano, who came to teaching because of community needs in Hawai'i, Hiroshi Tahara was sent by the Mombusho (Japanese Ministry of Education) specifically to teach Japanese. He became the principal and a teacher at Papaikou Japanese Language School as well as a subconsular agent, until he, too, was arrested on the night of 7 December 1941.

On Maui, I learned, Katsuichi Miho, the owner of a small, family-run Japanese hotel in Kahului called Miho Hotel, was also arrested on 7 December as a subconsular agent. From Hiroshima Prefecture, he had immigrated to O'ahu as a Japanese language school teacher but left for California during the gold rush years. Eventually he returned to the islands, this time to Maui, where he served as a Japanese school principal before finally opening his hotel to house salesmen from Honolulu traveling through the outer island railroad town. One of his sons, Katsugo Miho, a retired attorney and family court judge when I met him, remembered that the FBI had come to their home—without a search warrant—as early as 1940.

Teiichiro Maehara was from a village in Hiroshima Prefecture, like Miho and my grandfather, and had immigrated to the islands in March 1904 to start a Japanese language school, this one in Kula, Maui. Settling eventually in "a home in the Alabama camp next to the Puunene Japanese School where [he] was [the] principal" (Maehara 1997), he and his wife, Yoshi, had six sons and three daughters. According to information collected by the Maui Nisei Veterans Memorial Center, the Maeharas lived across the street from a Congregational church that provided some assistance to the family, inspiring Maehara to become a Christian himself. His leadership in the Maui Japanese community led to his appointment as a subconsular agent in July 1941, whereby he greeted Japanese dignitaries and sailors visiting the islands, in addition to assisting less literate Japanese workers with their official paperwork. He was arrested on 7 December, detained at the Wailuku Jail, then transferred to Haiku Military Camp.

Also on Maui, Chiyoko Ohata Sue remembered her father, Seiichi Ohata, a physician, being at home when she left for church that December Sunday morning. When she returned, he was gone. Dr. Ohata had traveled to Hawaiʻi from Shizuoka Prefecture to intern at what was then the Japanese Charity Hospital (now Kuakini Hospital), then moved to Maui—to Lahaina and Wailuku and later to Pāʻia. He eventually established his own hospital, where he tended to Japanese and Hawaiian plantation workers. Chiyoko, who we discovered was a childhood friend of my mother, learned from her mother that Dr. Ohata's medical equipment and drugs as well as two swords were confiscated when he was arrested; this had upset her mother greatly, but she was able to visit her husband at the Maui County Jail and saw that he remained amazingly calm while imprisoned and was able to help others who were more distressed

On the island of Oʻahu, the central target of Japan's attack, Seiichi Fujii, a Japanese school teacher, was in the mountains collecting plant specimens with his students early that Sunday morning, indulging his horticultural hobby. When he returned home, he found the country at war, and that afternoon, according to his son Eugene, he was arrested as a language school principal, community leader, and subconsular agent. The FBI agent, who spoke fluent Japanese, searched the house for weapons but allowed Fujii to change his clothes and counseled his wife not to worry. Like Miho, Maehara, and Rev. Watanabe, Fujii was from Hiroshima Prefecture; he had immigrated to Hawaiʻi at age seventeen to finish his education and eventually started a Japanese language school on Libby Pineapple Plantation land at Kīpapa Gulch. Photographs show him accepting an American flag from a Caucasian official during the dedication of the school, and schoolchildren, with and without shoes, saluting the flag with their hands on their hearts, probably reciting the Pledge of Allegiance.

Fujii's colleague Masaichi Hirashima was born in Fukuoka Prefecture and immigrated as a teenager with his parents to Kohala on Hawaiʻi Island's west coast. He eventually became a teacher and the principal of the Japanese language school at Halemano, Oʻahu, in addition to being a subconsular agent. His son Craig was only two years old when the FBI arrested Hirashima on 7 December, so the father was gone during his son's formative years. Craig's lasting memory, however, is that after the war's end, his father returned to his family, which had moved to Hilo during the war, and bought a small store. When a devastating tidal wave hit Hilo six months later, on April Fool's Day 1946, he was out buying vegetables for the store and was killed; Craig was cheated of his father once again, and this time with an unkind finality.

Fig. 2.6. Seiichi Fujii accepting an American flag from a plantation official at the dedication of a new Japanese language school, Kīpapa Gulch, Oʻahu, prewar (courtesy Fujii Family Collection).

Fig. 2.7. Children at Fujii's Japanese language school, Kīpapa Gulch, Oʻahu, prewar (courtesy Fujii Family Collection).

On Kauaʻi, where there were only two FBI agents, the arrests went more slowly (Kashima 2003, 71). Kazumi Matsumoto, introduced in chapter 1, was picked up a day later, on 8 December. Also from Hiroshima Prefecture, he had immigrated as a seventeen-year-old in 1919 and, after various jobs as a carpenter, married into the Doi family and served as a *chumontori* (merchandise order clerk) for the Doi family's Kukuiolono Store in Kalāheo. In that capacity, he was in contact with and able to help plantation workers with their paperwork and was designated a *toritsuginin*. By 8 December subconsular agents like him were expecting to be detained. "There was no use in worrying," he told me (K. Matsumoto 2003). After his arrest, he was held in the Wailua Jail. Likewise from Hiroshima Prefecture, Reverend Chikou Odate was the second son of a temple priest and followed his father's path as a priest of the Higashi Hongwanji Shin sect in Waimea, Kauaʻi. There he also started a Japanese language school. His daughter Reiko, introduced in chapter 1, recollected that he "loved to write poetry"; in fact, she said, "he thought in haiku" (R. O. Matsumoto 2002). He was arrested on 8 December as a Buddhist minister, a Japanese school teacher, and a subconsular agent.

Regarding the subconsular agents as a "unit" (to use Burns's term), Kashima points out that "none in this group was ever charged with a criminal offense involving espionage or sabotage" (2003, 72). Yet, with the Japanese consulate located on Oʻahu, the need for subconsular agents to do the consulate paperwork was naturally far greater on the outer islands, and, as Kelli Y. Nakamura observes in her article " 'Into the Dark Cold I Go, the Rain Gently Falling': Hawaiʻi Island Incarceration," on islands such as Hawaiʻi, there was thus a higher rate of arrests relative to the population, and communities were more severely affected by the loss of their leadership as a consequence.

Others

Listening to different accounts, I found that not only subconsular agents and those in other allegedly "subversive" categories were targets of the initial roundup but so were individuals not necessarily even listed on Bicknell's November ABC List. On Oʻahu, businessmen such as Matsujiro Otani and Jinshichi Tokairin were also seized and arrested on 7 December. In his memoir, "Reflecting on My Eighty Years," Otani relates the story of his childhood in a fishing village in Yamaguchi Prefecture; his immigration to Hawaiʻi in 1909 at age eighteen; working various odd jobs; opening his first business, a small fish market; and the development of his business into a thriving enterprise that was to celebrate the last day of its grand opening on Sunday, 7 December 1941. Having witnessed the formation of Japanese planes and the black smoke over Pearl Harbor that morning, he writes, "Everyone was surprised [and] no one could believe that war between the United States and Japan had broken out. . . . What the Japanese in Hawaii had worried [about] for a long time had finally happened. . . . My longtime dream had been fulfilled and I was ready to embark on a new venture, but with the outbreak of the war . . . I was greatly disheartened" (Otani n.d.).

Late that Sunday afternoon, as his second son, Akira, remembers, his father was in his bedroom in a *yukata* (bathrobe) when FBI agents drove up to their Mānoa home. Accompanied by military police, an FBI agent pointed a gun at Otani and demanded, "Are you Matsujiro Ohtani? Do you know that the United States and Japan are at war?" Plagued with heart problems, Otani was not a well man, but the agent pulled him to his feet and began to shove him into the car, ignoring entreaties by Mrs. Otani to give him time to dress. Before they could drive away, though, she defiantly threw his coat and shoes into the car. Otani continues, "The car went directly to the Honolulu Immigration Office. We were taken up into a room on the second floor and they closed the iron door with a loud bang. This was December 7, 1941, 6:00 p.m." (Otani n.d., 21).

Born in Fukushima Prefecture in northern Japan, Jinshichi Tokairin immigrated to Hawaiʻi at age nineteen, the solitary adventurer among five friends who had vowed to make the trip. He worked various jobs on the Ewa sugar plantation, attending English classes at night school and forming a youth club, for which he was chosen to be the leader. He eventually became the owner of the Tohoku Inn, which took in boarders from all over Japan, especially the Tohoku region, and finally bought the Nuuanu Onsen (hot springs). He became a leader in the Japanese community, serving on the board of the Japanese Charity Hospital, as chairman of his prefectural association, and as president of the Honolulu Inn Association. In an interview with Kisaburo Ueda in 1970, three years before his death, he describes his anxiety and arrest on 7 December:

> My son [Hideo, who was in the U.S. Army] returned to his home unit right away. Since my son was in a Japanese unit I wondered whether he would be killed at the army barracks. I wondered whether I would be included and both father and son would be killed. . . . Around 4 p.m., my daughter said there was a call. . . . A Caucasian voice said, "Hello, Mr. Tokairin? You come down to your office right away." I answered, "Now?" and he replied, "at once, *wikiwiki.*" . . . I went to Tohoku Inn then to Beretania Inn. Then two Caucasian military police rode over in their jeep. . . . they asked, "You Tokairin?" When I answered, "Yes, sir," they said, "No talk." . . . They put me in the jeep and I was sent to the Immigration Station.[16]

The family would not hear from him for several months.

A businessman who did appear on Bicknell's ABC List, Koichi Iida, of an Osaka merchant family, became the owner of Iida Shoten, the Japanese curio and ceramic-ware shop that had become an institution on the corner of Beretania and Nuuanu Streets in Honolulu by my adolescent years. Taking over the family business when he was nineteen years old, he would make deliveries by bicycle over the Pali as far as Kailua on the other side of the island. By December 1941 he was a leader in the community, and on the night of 7 December, his youngest daughter, Laura, recalls, the family had "collected candles and thick cloth to cover up the windows" during the blackout. Their father, who had heard that many Issei leaders were being arrested, "was all dressed, nervously ready [for] any eventuality." At around 7:00 p.m. "there was a knock [at] the door and there stood two military policemen with rifles pointing at him. With no explanation or comment, they took him away" (L. I. Miho n.d, 2).

In 1907 Kyujiro Ishida had emigrated from Yamaguchi Prefecture to Oʻahu to work on the Kahuku Sugar Plantation, but not for long. He began working at the Iwakami Company, a Japanese trading company, and eventually ran a service station in Honolulu's Chinatown near River Street. On 7 December he was at home in Moiliʻili when FBI agents came to arrest him. Unlike Matsujiro Otani's experience, they allowed Ishida to change his clothes, but in his haste he took all of his keys with him, causing his son Hisao, who was left behind to mind the business, great consternation, an example of the immediate isolation of internees from their families.

Kango Kawasaki was born in Hiroshima Prefecture on 2 August 1882 and was left in Japan by his parents, who immigrated to Kauaʻi. Joining them in the islands when he was around thirteen, he attended school in Honolulu, graduating from Honolulu High School in 1902 as the first Issei graduate. His daughter, Sumie, told me that he learned to read English in high school and learned about writing by doing book reports. He must have been a promising student, for his principal, Mr. Scott, advised his parents to send their son to college; if they were unable to do so, he said that he would do so himself. Luckily, they managed to send Kango to the University of California, where he studied law and graduated in 1906; he moved to Sacramento and then to Hilo, Hawaiʻi. As an attorney in Hilo, limited in his practice because of his status as an alien, he worked with the independent Japanese sugar planters and the Japanese consulate and also met Japanese training ships and entertained their officers. He was arrested in the first "sweep" on 8 December 1941, at 8:30 p.m., taken to Kapiolani School, and imprisoned at Kilauea Military Camp (Miyasaki 2008), like my grandfather and others from the Big Island.

Later Arrests

Following this initial plethora of arrests, other Issei were picked up at different times, some more prepared than others for their imminent fate. Ichiji Kinoshita was a laborer on the Pepeekeo Sugar Plantation on Hawaiʻi Island, having joined his parents after they settled there. In time, he became a leader in his community, serving as parent-teacher association president at his children's school, making speeches at community events, and serving as a subconsular agent. According to a brief family history, "Whenever he received news of Japan, [Jiji (Grandpa)] would inform others, as well as post it at the community bath." A week after the war began, the FBI went to his house and interrupted his work in the cane fields. They took him for questioning but released him. "One week later, they returned in the middle of the night to arrest him. No one but his wife saw him leave. The bosses of the plantation . . . tried to get him released, saying that he was a good man, but to no avail" (Kinoshita n.d., 1).

Nearly a month into the Pacific War, on 6 January 1942, Okinawa-born Ryosei Aka went to work at the Waimanalo Sugar Plantation on Oʻahu and never returned home. Starting as a laborer in 1907 on various sugar and pineapple plantations on Maui, he eventually moved to the Oʻahu plantation and also taught at a local Japanese language school, replacing the Buddhist minister who had served as its principal. His daughter Janice recalled the closeness of the family—referring to *kokorohitotsu* (of one heart)—and how the children would sit and listen to their father philosophize (Okudara 2007).

Reverend Gyokuei Matsuura (1911–2008), a Buddhist minister, had traveled to Hawaiʻi from Yamagata Prefecture in 1936, when he was twenty-five, to serve as a missionary of the Soto Zen sect. When I met him, he was ninety-two and had retired as the bishop of Soto Mission in Honolulu but still taught Japanese archery to enthusiasts. As we talked, his calm and good-natured demeanor seemed to reflect his life's philosophy. His wife, Masue, a Nisei, related the story of their courtship before the war, when he was the minister at Hilo Taishoji, a Zen temple on the Big Island. At the time, he was also the principal of the Olaʻa Japanese School and remembered my grandmother Yuki, who served as a teacher there. On 17 January 1942 Rev. Matsuura was thirty-one years old with a young wife and baby daughter. He was home and ready when a police officer named Takemoto and two or three MPs arrived to arrest him as an "alien enemy."

In contrast, Reverend Kenjyo Ohara was a twenty-five-year-old bachelor, the youngest and most recent arrival among Buddhist ministers to the islands. From a farming family in Shimane Prefecture, he had arrived in April 1941 and was assigned to the Olaʻa Hongwanji (Pure Land Buddhist Temple) as the assistant priest in July 1941. He also became the principal of the Mountain View Japanese Language School. He told me in 2003 that, because of his late arrival, he apparently was not included on official lists and thus was not apprehended by the FBI until January 1942. In an interview with the Japanese Cultural Center of Hawaiʻi in 1993, he describes how the FBI came to apprehend Reverend Toda, the head priest at Olaʻa Hongwanji, only then becoming aware of him:

> I was quite disturbed . . . that we were at war. It was the following day when Rev. Toda and I were talking in the living room when the FBI came accompanied by a soldier wielding a bayonet-tipped rifle. He had come to arrest Rev. Toda. When the FBI [agent] saw me, he asked, "And who are you?" So I answered, "I'm a minister at this temple." And he immediately made a notation in his notepad. . . .
>
> I had my suitcase all packed. I was a bachelor and I thought being arrested would be exciting. . . . But no one came for me. The FBI finally came in January . . . at nine at night. (Ohara 1993)

Isoo Kato of Hiroshima Prefecture had relinquished his inheritance as the eldest son in his family to escape the drudgery of farm life and, in 1907, followed a fellow villager who had made his way to Kona on Hawaiʻi Island. Once there, he tried blacksmithing and later dairy farming with Thomas A. Jagger, a volcanologist well known for his research on volcanic activity on the Big Island. Kato eventually became a coffee farmer as well as a leader in the Kona community, serving on the board of the local Japanese school and the Japanese hospital. Recognizing the irony of the nation's ideals being compromised on Washington's birthday, his daughter Haruko told me that her father was arrested on 22 February 1942. In his unpublished journal, "Memoirs of World War II Internment," Kato describes his arrest and sad departure from his family:

> At 8:00 a.m. I was tending the garden when Chiaki [Kato's sixteen-year-old son] came running. "Police officer—— has come!" he blurted out. He seemed worried that I might be arrested. I told him not to worry as I had done nothing wrong. I asked him to help Mother, stay strong, and not be disheartened. I encouraged him to get along with the family and keep up the work on the coffee farm. Chiaki looked helpless but agreed. . . . Officer—— formally asked for my name, as if he didn't know. How haughty and officious he looked. . . . He searched me for unlawful possessions and ordered me to get ready as he was taking me to the marshal, and that I [was] not to take anything with me. . . . I was ordered to speak only in English. . . . Haruko carried Nobuko and Toshiko was in Chiaki's arms.

Shigeo was half crying. I reached out and clasped each child's hand in silent farewell. (Kato n.d., 10–11)

An Issei influential in the territory's Japanese language education program, Futoshi Ohama was a teacher who had been invited to the islands in 1913 by a Japanese language school principal on Kaua'i. At twenty-one, Ohama had just graduated from a Hiroshima teachers' college. He eventually taught at Fort Gakuen (institute) on O'ahu, until he was transferred to and became the principal of Palama Gakuen on 1 September 1927 (1960, 146–157), a few months after the U.S. Supreme Court handed down its judgment in *Farrington v. Tokushige,* the Japanese language school controversy described earlier in this chapter. Palama Gakuen had joined the Palama Japanese Language School several months after it initiated "the first test case on the constitutionality of the restrictions which had been imposed on the language schools" by the territorial legislature (Kotani 1985, 51). Ohama was arrested at school with no notification to his family, who naturally thought the worst; although his wife went to the military governor's office to inquire, her request for information was denied.

Reverend Kodo Fujitani of Shimane Prefecture had been assigned to the islands from Kyoto in 1920. By 1941 he had been the resident minister at the Moili'ili Hongwanji (Pure Land Buddhist Temple) in Honolulu for several years but had served from 1921 to 1934 on Maui as the minister of the Pauwela Hongwanji and the principal and one of the teachers at the Pauwela Japanese Language School. Although he had been spared immediate arrest, he was finally seized on 28 April 1942. His eldest daughter, Teruko Fujitani Yoshida, remembered that after 7 December, FBI agents and MPs "came several times" to their home. One night during a blackout, the children were sitting on the living room floor, listening to the radio, when the intruders startled them with their flashlights. Without removing their shoes, a well-known custom in Japanese homes, they stomped in. At another time, one of her sisters followed the men and saw them take books of matches. "Our father was picked up for questioning several times," Yoshida recalled, "but he returned each time, until April, when he never returned" (2003).

For those who were arrested in the days and weeks after the outbreak of war, the shock might have been less severe than for those taken initially, but the anxiety and suspense and torn loyalties might have been greater. Many internees were in their teens and early twenties when they left Japan and, like my grandfather, had lived more years in the United States than in their birth country. George Yoshio Hoshida, a resident of the Big Island, writes of this dilemma in his unpublished autobiography, "Life of a Japanese Immigrant Boy in Hawaii and America":

> More shocking was the fact that the enemy attacking his adopted country was his own country of birth! What will his position and others in [a] similar situation be? What will their relationship with people of other nationalities in this country be? Questions whirled dizzily in his mind but there were no answers!
>
> Yoshio, although raised here in Hawaii since [he was] four years old, was nevertheless without any citizenship. He was legally an enemy alien now because the law of this country had not allowed him to be a citizen. As a national of Japan born there, he was legally obligated and bound to Japan. However, of the 34 years of his life, he had lived here for 30 years and only 4 years in Japan of which he hardly could remember. He had his obligations toward this country for practically everything which he possessed now. Furthermore, his wife and their three children, being born here, were American citizens by their right of birth. But in spite of being husband and father to these citizens, this country [did] not recognize him as legally being a subject of [the] US and he was still an enemy alien. It was not his fault that Japan had chosen to attack this country. . . . Now suddenly he had become an enemy of the country which he had considered his only home. What was he to do? (245)

He was arrested on 6 February 1942, leaving behind his wife and three daughters, one of whom had been severely crippled in an auto accident.

A Dream

Twice now I've had a dream of capture
at home in Hawai'i—
the sound of helicopters
flying low in our back yard.
This time I stepped on the back porch
And saw one
spinning, hovering
And then men in combat gear crouching
transforming my father's mango trees and orchids
into a battlefield.
I watched afraid
Then tried to secure the screen door
To keep them out

To keep them away
To keep them from taking me
Away.

                    —Gail Y. Okawa, 2004

CHAPTER 3

The Fate of the "Wingless Birds" II

Issei Hearings, Internment, Exile

After their arrest by U.S. Army personnel, FBI agents, or other officials, the Issei prisoners were taken to various locations on the different islands and eventually interrogated, or, more euphemistically, given "hearings" before civilian hearing boards.

Hearings

My grandfather's notes reveal that on Hawai'i Island, he was taken to Kilauea Military Camp (KMC) at Volcano on the slopes of Mauna Loa but that he had his hearing in Hilo on 13 February 1942, almost ten weeks after his arrest on 7 December. Four men were on his hearing board: J. Frank McLaughlin, board president, Alex J. Porter, and Gavin A. Bush, all civilians, and Captain Lorenzo D. Adams, representing the military, as recorder. Capt. Adams was the officer who had signed off on Rev. Watanabe's arrest warrant, so his name was familiar to me. This composition and configuration of three civilians and one military officer seemed standard for the hearing boards, their purpose described as "the hearing of evidence and making recommendations as to internment of enemy aliens, dual citizens and citizens," clearly indicating the government's intentions to treat U.S. citizens in the same manner as aliens.

Tamasaku Watanabe was identified as "the internee" (even before being sentenced to internment), and the proceedings were prefaced by the following provisions: "Except when Government witnesses were being heard, the internee, TAMASAKU (GYOKUSAKU) WATANABE, was present during all open sessions of the Board, was afforded full opportunity to present evidence in his own behalf, to have counsel, to testify in person or submit a written statement, and to submit a brief" (OPMG 1942c, Watanabe hearing, 1). This statement, also standard in the hearing process, sounds generous but seemed problematic in a democratic society in which individuals ordinarily have the right to confront their accusers. Although Hideo Taguchi was "duly sworn as Japanese interpreter," Rev. Watanabe apparently chose to testify in his halting English, possibly reflecting his faith in his own ability and trust in the system.

Reading much like a play script, with people exiting and entering the room, the hearing was long and involved. The "government's evidence in this case" included what I found to be various errors and a questionable argument:

> Q. Case No. 83, involves an internee named Tamasaku Watanabe who lives at 9 Miles Olaa, is a Christian minister and 59 years old and a subject of Japan. As you are Dale R. Curtis, Special Agent of the Federal Bureau of Investigation, will you present the government's evidence in this case?
>
> A. Subject[']s education consists of eleven years in Japan and five in the United States in Hawaii, five on the mainland. Subject spent [twenty-] two years of his life in Japan and has been approximately 36 years in the Territory which includes the five years on the mainland. Subject is minister of the Olaa Japanese Church which has approximately 80 members. He was appointed Consular Agent on January 1, 1939 to act for a period of two years. (OPMG 1942c, Watanabe hearing, 2)

In point of fact, my grandfather had spent seventeen years on the mainland prior to his arrival in the territory, of which three were spent in the San Francisco Theological Seminary; he had ministered for nineteen years in the territory, making the source of the FBI's information questionable. This was the extent of the government's case and left me puzzled. Reading "Exhibit C" verified the parallels that I had noted between Patton's hostage plan and the internment of community leaders: "These Consular Agents are the real leaders in their respective communities and because of their extremely pro-Japanese sympathies are in an excellent position to constitute an espionage network and propaganda machine throughout the territory of Hawaii. In view of these circumstances it is believed that Consular Agent activities are inimical to the best interest of the United States, and that *their internment would prove most effective in controlling the actions of those of Japanese descent in the territory*" (emphasis mine).

In reading the transcript of Rev. Watanabe's hearing, I was especially struck by the attention paid to his subconsular agent status; whom he believed should win the war; what Japan was doing in China; the nature of his Christian beliefs; and the general subjectivity of the questioners (in the phrasing of questions, for example, little or no attempt was made to be impartial or objective). As Okihiro points out, "Internee case files revealed more of the hearing boards' prejudices than any danger posed by the accused" (1991, 245). This is not unlike Eric L. Muller's conclusion regarding what he calls the "system of legalized racial oppression" meted out by the "government's loyalty bureaucracy" (2007, 2, 4), which passed judgment on Nisei loyalty questions for the War Relocation Authority's incarceration agenda. To government officials, being a "consular agent" was highly sinister and suspect, whereas in my grandfather's view, it was a form of Japanese community service, his response to requests by his parishioners for help with expatriation and clerical reports. "In my real conscience," he said, "I am not the agent of the Japanese Consul of Japan because I don't get any reward even one cent" (OPMG 1942c, Watanabe hearing, 4, 5).

On the subject of the war, the questioning was grueling:

Q. Well, how do you feel now that your country and our country are at war?

A. I am very sorry. In my work as Christian minister, I say, I am very sorry.

Q. Yes, we are all sorry but we have to face the reality of the situation.

A. I don't like the war.

Q. But which side do you want to win, your country or our country?

A. No, I don't think such things, I don't like to think such things, only I want to come peace quickly. That is my desire. . . .

Q. But in the meantime we have to take sides and which side are you on?

A. . . . I like my country but I stay this country and my three children all graduate from University and I feel very thankful. I don't feel any bias even I don't like to think of that one moment. (6)

It was disturbing to me how the questioner (who remains unidentified on the record) insisted that Rev. Watanabe choose a country, though he later admitted, "Maybe it is not a fair question" (6). In a similar and related vein, the interrogators attempted to engage my grandfather in a rather simplistic discussion of complex political issues, making insinuations about his Christian faith:

Q. (By Mr. Porter). The Japanese army went into China to crush the Chinese. And Japan has no business doing that in China. What do you think about that? As a Christian minister what do you think about the behavior of the Japanese army and the Japanese government in invading China without any justification?

A. Well, I don't think that war—

Q. I am not asking you what you think about war. I am asking you what you think about the behavior of the Japanese Government and Japanese army in invading China without just cause. That is what I am asking you. As a Christian minister what do you think about that?

A. Well, it is a complicated matter and I do not know very well. I am not a good student of the politics.

In fact, they persisted in this line of questioning, becoming increasingly badgering and conflating their binary moral views of right and wrong with Christian morality:

Q. . . . Again, let me ask you as a Christian minister, as a devotee of Jesus Christ and his doctrine, particularly the doctrine of the Golden Rule, "Do unto others as you would have them do unto you," what do you think of the behavior of the Japanese army and Japanese Government upon the Chinese in China? As a Christian, can you have any opinion of the Japanese Government regardless of your race? What do you think about it? Do you think it is right?

A. No, I don't think it is right.

Q. Do you think it is wrong?

A. I have no suspicion of those things. Now, international matters—it is very complicated. I haven't sufficient knowledge. (7)

In reference to the diplomatic negotiations between Japan and the United States in Washington, DC, and the "absolute premeditated but unprovoked attack on Pearl Harbor and Honolulu," one interrogator asked, "As a Christian minister, what do you think of Japan acting on that occasion?"

A. Pardon me, I am Christian minister and I am preaching about the Christ and Savior and . . . about the ethical nature and the Christian legend of salvation. Christian[ity] is the legend of hope . . . but I don't like to speak about the international matter in the pulpit. I have no right. I don't know anything about it, but in my place as minister to speak those four points, that is the great help to American race. A great help to human beings. I have sense for that matter. I don't speak other matters. I don't say any politics or international matter in my pulpit because many ministers know but I don't know.

Q. Let me ask you this: Does your Christianity go far enough to enable you to choose between right and wrong regardless of the church? For instance, quite apart from international affairs[,] quite apart from what Mr. Nomura and Mr. Kurusu were doing in Washington while your government was preparing a vicious attack against the United States. If I were talking to you in the parlor of your house and my brother went around to the back door and smashed all the dishes in your kitchen what would you think of that? . . .

A. If just like you said, I think the Japanese Government is wrong way. But I don't know [what] I say. I have no sufficient knowledge enough so I don't like to talk about those matters. I don't like you to ask me such matters. I don't think that such matters matter. Only I am as minister I am doing my best. I am doing my very best for United States of America and that is good for Japan and that is good for human beings.

Q. But I am afraid that your Christianity is too elastic.

A. I am not politician. I am in the United States. (8–9)

After relatively extensive and antagonistic questioning and "having carefully considered the evidence before it," the board listed its findings:

1. That the internee is a subject of Japan;
2. That the internee owes allegiance to Japan;
3. That the internee's activities have been *pro-Japanese though not necessarily anti-American*." (emphasis mine)

The distinction made in the board's third finding is a significant one, reflecting a regard for intention rather than for activities alone. And considering these findings, the board made its recommendations: "Judge McLaughlin recommends that the internee, TAMASAKU WATANABE, be interned for the duration of the war; Captain Adams, Mr. Porter and Mr. Bush recommend that he be released" (11), with Capt. Adams supposedly reflecting the military viewpoint in his recommendation for release. Nonetheless, Rev. Watanabe was not released but was instead shipped to the Immigration Station in Honolulu on 23 February 1942, according to his notes.

Unlike Rev. Watanabe, who as a Christian minister was perhaps given some consideration along with equal distrust, Rev. Kodo Fujitani, as a Buddhist minister, was asked very few questions beyond those of an informational nature. The record of his later hearing, in Honolulu on 30 April 1942, was a perfunctory five pages long, reflecting its pro forma nature, as compared with the record of Rev. Watanabe's hearing of eleven pages, many reflecting the board members' efforts to challenge his Christian beliefs. Rev. Fujitani's hearing board on Oʻahu included

Lieutenant Colonel Edward K. Massee (U.S. Army, Retired), board president, other civilians, and the military representative and recorder. Perhaps the brevity and perfunctoriness of the questioning were related merely to the differences in board members and their personalities, but they are nonetheless noteworthy.

The government's case, for example, seems to be based largely on guilt by association and supposition, rather than on Rev. Fujitani's own actions: "Subject's brother and sister are living in Japan. . . . Subject has several nephews in Japan, who are probably serving in the Japanese Army. . . . Subject has many Buddhist priest friends now in custodial detention" (OPMG 1942b, Fujitani hearing, 2). The topics of the interrogators' questions: his marital status, his wife's birthplace, where he was married, the number of his children, their ages, their citizenship, whether he was a Japanese language school teacher and principal, for how long, whether he was a consular agent, for how long, his length of service as a minister, whether his congregation raised money for "comfort kits" for Japanese soldiers, whether he had brothers or sisters in Japan or "relatives in the Japanese Army or Navy" (4), whether he himself served in the Japanese military. The last question, voiced by the recorder, echoed one of those in my grandfather's hearing, as did the answer:

Q. Whom would you like to see win the war between the United States and Japan?

A. It is a very big question and I, myself, could not answer it. The only thing that I can hope for is peace.

This board did not badger Rev. Fujitani to provide a more specific answer; however, the findings stated:

1. That the internee, KODO FUJITANI, is an *enemy alien.*
2. That he is loyal to Japan and *not to the United States.*
3. For about a period of ten (10) years the internee acted as Consular Agent in the Island of Maui.
4. For a period of fourteen (14) years he was Principal of a Japanese language school.
5. One child was born in Japan, one child was not registered and six children were registered and have not been expatriated.
6. He has been a Buddhist priest in the Island of Oahu since 1921. He stated that money was raised by his congregation to buy articles to send to the Japanese Red Cross. (4–5; emphasis mine)

Based on these findings, where the language itself is prejudicial, as in findings 1 (note the difference in implication from Rev. Watanabe being described as a "subject of Japan") and 2 (the conclusion being drawn that he is not loyal to the United States), or erroneous, as in finding 6, in which *1921* should have read *1934,* the unanimous recommendation of the board was that "KODO FUJITANI be interned for the duration of the war" (5).

Isoo Kato, from Kona, on the western side of the Big Island, was taken with others by car from one side of the island to the other. In his journal, he describes their approach to Hilo: "Mauna Loa was visibly raining, and through Ola'a it poured heavily. At Volcano there were nearly twenty army trucks parked on both sides of the road. Alongside the road among trees and foliage were numerous tents, and the entire place seemed alive with soldiers. We drove into Hilo and were directly taken to a second floor room at headquarters" (n.d., 14). Reading his account, I imagined a similar arrival for my grandfather from 'Ōla'a many weeks earlier.

On 15 April 1942, Kato stood before the same hearing board in Hilo as my grandfather—with the exception of the recorder, Lieutenant Colonel Victor Woodruff. These proceedings differed from those of the two ministers in that Lieutenant Farrell Copeland, the army officer representing the G-2 (military intelligence) and the government's case, submitted an accusatory letter, written in Japanese, as "Exhibit A." This letter is not included in Kato's hearing file, but members of the board spent considerable time questioning Lt. Copeland, who concluded his remarks with the statement: "In my mind, there is a lot more of this man than I am able to present because from the investigation of that letter, *there must be something to cause people of his own race to write a letter like that* and *I am sure that that letter was written in good faith*" (OPMG 1942d, Kato hearing, 4; emphasis mine).

In hindsight, the use of the letter reveals the government agent's gullibility and/or culpability in such matters. It also reveals the divisiveness in the Japanese community incited by the government's targeting of individuals versus the mass incarceration on the West Coast (Odo 1994, 6–9). In his journal, Kato contemplates the vindictiveness of his accuser: "There was a Nisei 'dog' [*inu,* the Japanese term describing one guilty of duplicity] who wrote a letter in Japanese reporting me to the authorities. . . . On one occasion in the past, he gave me a bad time, maliciously accusing me of tax fraud. . . . Upon investigation, . . . I was totally cleared of the charge. . . . He had failed to do me in at that time, and now this must be his way of getting back at me" (n.d., 7).

In the hearing itself, Kato is asked numerous questions in a straightforward manner and then is given the opportunity to make a case for his being "released from protective custody" as the "subject of an enemy nation," to which he responds with a compelling argument:

I have resided in this country for 35 years and I like this country better than any place else. I have worked hard during these years but did not make much of a success and I did not have the means of owning my own home but I finally accumulated enough money to buy some land in 1937 and in August, 1941, when Mr. Shivers an army officer and Mr. Warner of the University of Hawaii arrived in our district, they spoke on the position of aliens in this country and I was very much impressed with their talk and I was appreciative of the fact that the United States government was giving us full protection and I have endeavored to work hard since that time to help in small way the United States of America. By help, I mean anything I can do for the industry . . . is a help to Uncle Sam. I have with the aid of my children cleared some land in Kona and have proceeded to plant coffee and vegetables for defense up to February 22, at the time I was interned. I sympathize with my wife who has to take care of 6 children and I do not wish to have my family be a burden to the community. I would like very much to be released so that I can keep up my family and also I wish to state that I have absolutely no anti-American feeling. In fact, why should I have such a feeling when I am given an opportunity to make a good living in this country. (OPMG 1942d, Kato hearing, 7)

The board's findings are very similar to those for Rev. Watanabe:

1. That the internee is a subject of Japan;
2. That the internee owes allegiance to Japan;
3. That the internee's activities have been pro-Japanese, though *not necessarily subversive.* (10; emphasis mine)

However, the recommendation of the board mirrored that for Rev. Fujitani: "isoo kato [should] be interned for the duration of the war" (10).

Held at the Wailua Jail, which Okihiro refers to as "the Wailua military prison" (2013, 249), Kazumi Matsumoto attended his hearing in Līhuʻe, Kauaʻi, on 17 January 1942. The interpreter was Lieutenant Bert N. Nishimura, who later became a leader in the famed 442nd Regimental Combat Team and the first Nisei to be promoted to full colonel on active duty in the regular army. The hearing was relatively brief, but questions focused on Matsumoto's subconsular agent status:

Q. Are you a consular agent of the Japanese government?

A. I have not done work very often but I have been acting as one.

Q. You have your certificate now?

A. The F.B.I. has taken my papers. . . .

Q. What kind of work were you doing as a consular agent?

A. I used to help people when they came for help; that was very seldom. I assisted with expatriation, only expatriation.

Q. How many people did you help?

A. About three or four. (OPMG 1942e, Matsumoto hearing, 2–4)

The interrogators also attempted to implicate him and others in the community—echoing FDR's infamous 1936 memo:

Q. Did you ever go aboard any of these Japanese ships that come in here?

A. When the Taisha Maru was in I visited, I made a short visit.

Q. Did you entertain any of the officers or men in your own home?

A. No.

Q. Did you see any of the other Japanese citizens here entertaining any of these Japanese officers or men?

A. Just about that time I was not feeling well so I don't know, I was ill. . . .

Q. Is there a very large Japanese Association at Kalaheo?

A. Not very large.

Q. Who is the most active one in that organization?

A. I don't know very well.

Q. You know of any Japanese who are intensely loyal to Japan in that neighborhood?

A. No. (4–5)

The findings of this board seem quite factual:

1. That the internee is a subject of the Empire of Japan.
2. That the internee is apparently loyal to the Empire of Japan.
3. That the internee is *not engaged in any subversive activities.* (5; emphasis mine)

Yet the recommendation, like Kato's, is that "the internee, KAZUMI MATSUMOTO, be interned" (5). Regardless of their being cleared of subversive actions, the result was the same.

Although I did not obtain the hearing record of Rev. Ohara, the young Buddhist priest at Olaʻa Hongwanji whom I interviewed, in a 1993 interview at the Japanese Cultural Center of Hawaiʻi, he describes his interrogation in Hilo:

I was held at the detention center, but every day I was taken to Hilo to be interrogated at the FBI office on the second floor of the Post Office. I must have gone there at least ten times escorted by a bayonet-tipped rifle wielding soldier to respond to the same question: "Are you a spy?" "You must be a spy!" And I would say, "No, no, I'm not a spy." . . . I told the interrogator that a Japanese minister would never serve as a spy. There is no connection between those two occupations. But he wouldn't believe me, and took me everyday for interrogation. The interpreter, who looked Japanese but had a Caucasian name, told me, "Why don't you say you're a spy. Then you won't have to come day after day." But I couldn't agree with him because I wasn't a spy after all. . . .

Finally, after many days the interrogator accepted my position and stopped coming to get me for interrogation. . . . I was the last minister to come, so they took it for granted that I must have come to spy. But I would think that a spy would be better equipped than a fellow like me. They wouldn't be asking a guy like me who doesn't even know English to be a spy. I was incarcerated for three months at Kilauea Detention Center. (n.p.)

The fates of hundreds were sealed regardless of the hearing boards' findings on subversive activities. Like those imprisoned at KMC on the Big Island, those arrested on Kauaʻi were held at such facilities as the Kalaheo Stockade and Wailua Jail and on Maui at the Maui County Jail and Haiku Military Camp. Other temporary holding facilities also existed on Lānaʻi and Molokaʻi.

Departures

Those from the outer islands who were not released, including Rev. Watanabe, Kato, and Matsumoto, and those from Oʻahu, including Rev. Fujitani and Fujii, ended up being sent to the INS Immigration Station in Honolulu. Although, as attorney Kango Kawasaki writes, families on Hawaiʻi Island were "allowed to come up to the Camp [KMC] to say Aloha" (1941–1945[1]), each internee had to suffer the pain of departure from the safety and familiarity of home. Kawasaki mentions that his wife and daughter, Sumie, visited him; I hope my grandmother and others bade farewell to my grandfather. On the afternoon of Saturday, 21 February 1942, 106 men from the Big Island left for Honolulu. Kato of Kona, leaving his infant twins and other young children, poignantly describes scenes from the ship: "I saw the sugar plantation coastline of east Hawaii for the first time from the sea. . . . I saw sections of what must have been Hamakua and Kohala. I could only see the big sky over Kona. My heart was full. Way yonder somewhere below the sky was my home and my family. If I had *half a seagull's wing*, I would fly to Waimea and beyond to my wife and children. The sun set beyond the mountains in the west, but I gazed on and on and on" (n.d., 53; emphasis mine).

Hoshida of Hilo, in his unpublished autobiography, uses his artist's eye and writer's pen to describe his parting view:

> The ship sailed on its way to Honolulu about 4 PM. As it glided out through the channel between the breakwater and the Coconut Island, the town of Hilo spread out along the cresent [*sic*] waterfront across the bay. Above the town, the emerald green of the cane fields spread upward to the dark rain forest of ohia trees and rose up towards the peaks of Mauna Kea to the right. To the left, the lava flow, invisible under the lush tropical growth, meandered up to Yoshio's home village of Kaumana and then onto the smooth peak of Mauna Loa. . . . Will he ever come back or will he ever see his family again? They were only about a mile away in distance from here but how infinitely apart they seemed. (284)

As he departed from Hilo on 23 February 1942, it is very likely that my grandfather saw a similar scene, but at age fifty-nine, he had adult children, so it is also likely that he had somewhat different apprehensions.[2]

Without diary entries from Rev. Watanabe following 7 December, I must rely in part on U.S. Signal Corps photos of the Honolulu Immigration Station setting to imagine the internees' experience there. These photos depict Issei men, some dressed in hat, coat, and tie, standing in army chow lines or standing, sitting, and waiting to be called for processing or questioning. Many were quite expressionless, with emotions, I suspect, hidden just below the surface. There, the authorities at the Hawaiian Department Alien Processing Center took my grandfather's mug shot and vital statistics.

Matsujiro Otani, arrested on 7 December and imprisoned immediately at the Immigration Station, writes about an attempted suicide that he witnessed as well as his early days there: "I realized this was another [person] sacrificed because of the war. From the night of the . . . outbreak of the war every day, more and more Japanese were taken to the Immigration Office and soon the Immigration Building was filled with Japanese" (n.d., 22). Hundreds of prisoners were held there until March 1942, when they were transferred to the Sand Island Internment Camp, where eventually all of the internees were locked up.

Internment and Exile: Where, What, and How They Were

Sand Island today is largely a state recreation area in the western section of Honolulu Harbor, with few traces of its past use as a concentration camp. Large open grassy areas dotted with occasional young trees divulge its history of wartime occupation. On 8 December 1941, the day after Pearl Harbor was attacked, five acres of it became the Sand Island Detention/Internment Camp, eventually complete with two rows of barbed wire fencing, a hospital tent, and rows of smaller floorless, open-air tents to house prisoners, erected by the first internees removed to Sand Island under army orders. Okihiro points out that "the army had planned to use Sand Island as a concentration camp since April 1941 because the island could be easily guarded to prevent escapes, it was adjacent to Honolulu but separated from it by water, and it was near the Office of Military Governor yet isolated from strategic targets" (1991, 214).

In his journal, Kato describes the hard labor imposed on the "first group of internees . . . elderly men of the clergy and educators and other professional men who had never done such physical work." They were forced to "cut kiawe trees to

FIG. 3.1. Sand Island Internment Camp tents (photo no. 137296, W-HD-[1-13-42]-C; "General view of Internees Camp, Sand Island, Honolulu, T.H.," 13 January 1942; Records of the U.S. Signal Corps, RG 111 SC; NACP).

make fence posts, clear all the fallen trees, dig all the holes for the fence posts and help to make the barracks" (61). This group may have included Oʻahu's subconsular agents, who were among the first to be picked up, as well as other established leaders in the community such as Tokairin and Iida.

The men themselves, according to Franklin Odo, were "treated as criminals or prisoners of war." His description is brief but vivid: "They slept, crowded together, in tents on the sand; and . . . the wind and rain or blistering heat were difficult to endure. They faced a daily regimen with a few articles of clothing, no privacy, isolation from family and businesses, no recreation or diversion and constant humiliation" (1994, 6–7). Otani in his memoir describes what has become the infamously humiliating spoon story, in which a spoon went missing from the mess hall, leading the camp commander to demand that internees—even those hospitalized—stand naked in the hot sun for body searches. Some collapsed from sunstroke. "The spoon in question," Otani reports, "appeared a few days later" (22), found in a completely different location, such that the Issei internees interpreted the affair as purposeful harassment.

Like Odo, Kashima refers to the internees as "civilian prisoners of war" (2003, 75). The official term eventually applied to the prisoners was *civilian internee* (CI), and those from Hawaiʻi were given the designation "HJ" (Hawaiʻi Japanese) as a prefix to their number. Hence, Rev. Watanabe became number "HJ-1097-CI," and Kazumi Matsumoto became number "HJ-1770-CI." In time it became glaringly apparent to me that this status, while demeaning, eventually carried with it the protections of the Geneva Convention—a controversial and significant factor in this human drama of internment.

Considering that some Issei were arrested and taken with only the clothes they were wearing, I wondered how it was that some of them wore three-piece suits in photos taken later in their imprisonment. Relating his experience, Otani writes, "The biggest problem that we had there [at Sand Island] was the washing place. We had been relocated with only our clothes on our back[s]. Our private property like pencils, papers, and money had been confiscated by the Immigration Office. The only thing that we could wash was our top and bottom underwear but the people who were ill, like myself, could not even do this." He describes the kindness of a fellow internee who was willing to wash his clothes and the clothes of other sick and elderly prisoners, and the relief he felt on a day in January: From "the night of 7 December [until] the 45 days that we were kept on Sand Island we had only one set of clothing but on that day [21 January] we received many clothes from my home and now we were able to change into [other] clothing" (23).

Perhaps unknown to the internees, nearly a month earlier, on 26 December 1941, Headquarters Hawaiian Department, Provost Marshal's Office, Fort Shafter, had sent a memo to the family of Seiichi Fujii, Kīpapa, Oʻahu, and other "Friends and/or Relatives of Detainees at Sand Island Detention Camp or U.S. Immigration Station, Ala Moana, Honolulu, T.H.," ordering:

> You are hereby notified that you are now authorized to send a certain amount of clothing to detainees for their comfort.
>
> The clothing will be limited to necessary articles, and such underclothing and socks as may be required for proper sanitary changes and laundering.
>
> The following list of clothing is authorized and recommended:

1 – Hat	2 – Trousers, outer
1 – Raincoat	4 – Underwear, shirts
2 – Shirts, outer	4 – Underwear, drawers
2 – Shoes, pair	1 – Sweater
6 – Socks, pair	2 – Suits of pajamas
1 – Slippers, pair	1 – Bathrobe

> Such clothing must be clean, and in a serviceable condition.

A mixed blessing, addressing the needs of the men, albeit in a condescending and disrespectful tone, the memo continued:

> All clothing to be delivered, will be properly marked with the detainee's full name printed legibly on the bundle or tag attached thereto; and delivered to a representative of the Department Provost Marshal's Office at the U.S. Immigration Station . . . where all packages will be thoroughly inspected prior to delivery to the detainee. (Provost Marshal's Office 1941)

Then, a month and a half later, on 15 February 1942, the same office sent a second memo to the families:

1. You are hereby notified that you may send additional warm clothing to Detainees for their comfort.
2. The following list of clothing is authorized and recommended:

(a) 1 Suit Case, Large

a. 1 Overcoat

b. 1 Raincoat

c. 3 Shirts, Dress

d. 2 Suits underwear, heavy

e. 2 Suits underwear, light

f. 12 Socks, pair (6 wool; 6 cotton)

g. 2 neckties

h. 1 Hat

i. 6 Handkerchiefs

j. 2 Shoes, pair

k. 2 suits of clothing (including coat, trousers and vest).

l. Toilet Articles: including comb, tooth-brush, tooth-paste, toilet soap; 2 bath towels and 2 face towels.

m. 1 Bathrobe

n. 1 Slippers, pair. (Provost Marshal's Office 1942)

The same instructions followed regarding cleanliness, delivery, and inspection. The overcoat, wool socks, and heavy underwear hinted at the internees' removal to colder climates. Since few prisoners may have already possessed such articles in their wardrobes at home (unnecessary in the warm island climate), the expense to their families, many struggling without them as heads of households, must have caused great hardship. I wondered about my grandmother having to gather such things. Were my mother and her brothers there to help? Photos of imprisoned men in three-piece suits are indeed curious; these lists explain why with a strange irony.

Among my grandfather's papers, however, I found a related handwritten document of confiscated items, namely, "A Claim of Tamasaku Watanabe," which verifies Otani's reference to confiscation:

These articles had been taken away by an officer at the entering examination to Detention Camp, Sand Island on March 4, 1942

1 toilet brush	.65
2 of cuffs buttons (gold)	10.00
1 fountain pen (Waterman)	5.00
1 purse for currency	1.50
1 student bag	.50
1 English dictionary	.50

These articles I could not find on May 11 (Monday) when I was permitted to look in my two baggages.

1 shaving bowl	.50
1 needle set	.35
1 nail cutter	.15
1 nail file	.15
2 pencils	.10
1 shoe black	.15

1 bottle of ink	.25
1 soap box	.15
1 shaving cream	.25
1 tooth paste	.15
3 of white collars	1.00
1 pair of gloves	.15
1 pair of garter	.25
1 neck tie	1.00

Total $29.75

(Watanabe, "A Claim," n.d.)

On 12 April 1942, more than a month after Rev. Watanabe arrived at Sand Island, a military intelligence board—presided over by George Bicknell, Military Intelligence; I. H. Mayfield, Naval Intelligence; and R. L. Shivers, FBI—overturned the decision of the civilian hearing board, which had recommended my grandfather's release, and stated, "it appearing necessary, it is ordered that TAMASAKU (GYOKUSAKU) WATANABE be interned." His experience contradicts Kashima's assertion that the military intelligence board preceded the civilian/military review board (2003, 73–74). I was shocked by the flagrancy with which the democratic majority decision of the civilian hearing board was ignored, couched in the passive language "it is ordered," but, after all, Hawai'i was under martial law.

Pawns

While these Issei were being seized and shunted around physically, their fate was being determined at various levels of government as well. Kashima and the Commission on Wartime Relocation and Internment of Civilians (CWRIC) separately describe such machinations in great detail; perhaps most impressive was the complex role of Lieutenant General Delos C. Emmons, the second military governor of the Territory of Hawaii. Like other members of internee families who know only *the fact* that their fathers and grandfathers were interned on the mainland, I was haunted by one question: Why? Why was imprisonment itself not punishment enough for what they were alleged to have done or been? Why were they *exiled* from Hawai'i to the mainland?

A series of personalities and events seems to provide some explanation.[3] On 9 December 1941, Secretary of the Navy William Knox visited Pearl Harbor to examine American losses. Despite extensive intelligence to the contrary, provided by the Munson and Ringle (Naval Intelligence) reports and the FBI, he claimed on 15 December, upon his return to Washington, that "the most effective Fifth

Column work of the entire war was done in Hawaii" (quoted in Kashima 2003, 75; also CWRIC 1997, 55). Three days later, Knox and Secretary of War Henry Stimson recommended "that enemy aliens be removed and placed on an island other than Oahu" (Kashima 2003, 76), a recommendation accepted by President Roosevelt. By casting aspersions on Hawai'i's Japanese immigrant and American-born population, concluded the CWRIC, Knox and his recommendation "for the removal of all Japanese, regardless of citizenship, from Oahu" constituted "one of the first calls for mass racial exclusion." The dire consequence of this claim was the mass incarceration two months later of the mainland Japanese immigrant and American citizen population under Executive Order 9066. "Nothing was promptly done at the highest level of the government to repudiate Knox's initial statement or publicly to affirm the loyalty of the ethnic Japanese, even though Munson (through Carter) emphasized Knox's inaccuracy and urged that such a statement be made by the President or Vice President" (CWRIC 1997, 56–57). This is one clear example of the "failure of political leadership" cited in the Civil Liberties Act of 1988 (see 56–60).

In the meantime, also on 18 December 1941, Lt. Gen. Emmons had replaced the discredited army commander Lieutenant General Walter C. Short. On 22 December, in his first public radio address,[4] Kashima tells us, Emmons "acknowledged the particular and peculiar status of those individuals [interned at Sand Island] and assured their families that the internees would not be mistreated": "These people are not prisoners of war and will not be treated as such. . . . There is no intention or desire on the part of the Federal authorities to operate mass concentration camps" (2003, 75). Emmons is further quoted as saying, "While we have been subjected to a serious attack by a ruthless and treacherous enemy, we must remember that this is America and we must do things the American Way. We must distinguish between loyalty and disloyalty among our people" (CWRIC 1997, 265).

Amid the controversy among his superiors as to whether all Japanese—aliens (now with the immigration status "alien enemies") and American-born citizens—or select Japanese and Japanese Americans were to be interned on other Islands, Emmons, in early February, argued against the feasibility of such a mass incarceration plan. He asserted that "the Japanese provided irreplaceable labor for the war effort and bluntly advised that the Japanese security problem 'should be handled by those in direct contact with the situation'" (CWRIC 1997, 270). The CWRIC concluded that "Emmons effectively scuttled the Hawaiian evacuation program that Washington sought to pursue in 1942" (269). Under continued pressure from Washington, however, Emmons finally recommended that select Issei prisoners be transported to the mainland on returning freighters and transport ships and was granted permission to "send those Issei he deemed dangerous to the mainland" (Kashima 2003, 76–77).

Even after this authorization was granted, disagreement continued among the president, Knox, and others in Washington. Secretary of War Stimson and Assistant Secretary John J. McCloy came to have grave legal reservations about such a plan. Stimson, in fact, noted privately in early April 1942, "As the thing stands at present, a number of them [Japanese] have been arrested in Hawaii without very much evidence of disloyalty, have been shipped to the United States, and are interned there. McCloy and I are both agreed that *this was contrary to law,* that while we have a perfect right to move them away from defenses for the purpose of protecting our war effort, *that does not carry with it the right to imprison them without convincing evidence.*" Moreover, he advised the president about the constitutional question of "the *President's own attempt to imprison by internment some of the leaders of the Japanese in Hawaii* against whom we however have nothing but very grave suspicions" (CWRIC 1997, 271; emphasis mine).

The number and nature of those to be evacuated continued to be debated well after the transfer boats began transporting their prisoners in February 1942. Despite his reservations, Stimson reassured Roosevelt in the fall of 1942 that "all persons of Japanese ancestry resident in the Hawaiian Islands who are known to be hostile to the United States have been placed under restraint in internment camps either in the islands or on the mainland." Emmons also chose to define "future evacuees" as "those residents who *might be potentially dangerous* in the event of a crisis, yet [who] have committed no suspicious acts. . . . In general the evacuation will remove persons who are *least desirable* in the territory and who are *contributing nothing to the war effort*" (CWRIC 1997, 273, 274; emphasis mine)—rhetorical ploys, possibly meant to placate the powerful.

Thus, Emmons's attempt to divert or subvert the FDR-Knox idea regarding mass incarceration of Hawai'i Japanese immigrants and American-born citizens to the outer islands resulted in select Issei being exiled to the mainland. The Issei exile, then, became a trade-off, a concession in the face of power. According to the CWRIC, quoting a memo to Colonel Karl Bendetsen, "The move to the mainland was 'primarily for the purpose of removing non-productive and undesirable Japanese and their families from the Islands' and 'largely a *token evacuation* to *satisfy certain interests* which have strongly advocated movement of Japanese from the Hawaiian Islands'" (1997, 274; emphasis mine).

In addition, Michi Nishiura Weglyn discusses the result of the extreme and continued pressure on Emmons by those "certain interests" still advocating mass evacuation: even McCloy, who had legal reservations about such action, told Emmons that he "had better work out some alternative evacuation plan . . . to satisfy the President and Mr. Knox." Emmons's "alternative" was a "voluntary evacuation" plan, which included the families of Issei internees like Rev. Matsuura kept in limbo in WRA camps for months, waiting for reunification with husbands and fathers. Weglyn characterizes this process as "a surrealistic tale of chicanery and duress, deplorable for its official use of mendacity to abrogate the rights of ordinary citizens blameless for wrongdoing" (1996, 88).

So, as the proverbial pawns in a political chess game, the Issei civilian internees continued to be shipped out from Sand Island to the mainland in ten boatloads over twenty-two months. One of the documents lent to me by Henry Kuniyuki, the son of internee Aisuke Kuniyuki, a Honolulu businessman, is the official listing of internees on the ten transfer boats that crossed the Pacific from February 1942 to December 1943.[5] The accompanying tables list those from my study according to transfer boat—the internee survivors themselves or the fathers of the sons and daughters with whom I had spoken—along with their civilian internee numbers (useful for family research), their residences at the time in the islands, and their principal occupations.

Lists of Issei Civilian Internees in This Study by Transfer Boat*

Transfer Boat 1
Number of men: 172
Date of departure: 20 February 1942

Name and CI no.	Hawai'i residence	Occupation
Seiichi Fujii HJ-9-CI	Wahiawā, O'ahu	Japanese school teacher
Masaichi Hirashima HJ-20-CI	Wahiawā, O'ahu	Japanese school teacher
Koichi Iida HJ-145-CI	Honolulu, O'ahu	Import-export store owner
Kyujiro Ishida HJ-143-CI	Honolulu, O'ahu	Gas station owner
Muneo Kimura HJ-31-CI	Honolulu, O'ahu	Movie theater operator
Jinshichi Tokairin HJ-172-CI	Honolulu, O'ahu	Small hotel owner
Ryosen Yonahara HJ-83-CI	Waimānalo, O'ahu	Japanese school teacher

Transfer Boat 2
Number of men: 166
Date of departure: 20 March 1942

Name and CI no.	Hawai'i residence	Occupation
Ryosei Aka HJ-74-CI	Waimānalo, O'ahu	Plantation worker, Japanese school teacher
Itsuo Hamada HJ-1526-CI	Kahului, Maui	Businessman, community theater director and performer

Transfer Boat 2 *(cont.)*

Name and CI no.	Hawai'i residence	Occupation
Naojiro Hirano HJ-1008-CI	Mountain View, Hawai'i	Store owner
Kazumi Matsumoto† HJ-1770-CI	Kalāheo, Kaua'i	Merchandise order clerk
Gyokuei Matsuura† HJ-1106-CI	Hilo, Hawai'i	Buddhist priest
Katsuichi Miho HJ-1519-CI	Kahului, Maui	Small hotel owner
Seiichi Ohata HJ-1512-CI	Pā'ia, Maui	Physician
Masaichiro Shinoda HJ-1079-CI	Hilo, Hawai'i	Automobile salesman
Hiroshi Tahara HJ-1085-CI	Pāpa'ikou, Hawai'i	Japanese school teacher

Transfer Boat 3
Number of men: 109
Date of departure: 23 May 1942

Name and CI no.	Hawai'i residence	Occupation
Kodo Fujitani HJ-421-CI	Honolulu, O'ahu	Buddhist priest
Kinai Ikuma HJ-179-CI	Honolulu, O'ahu	Shinto priest
Ryuten Kashiwa HJ-274-CI	Honolulu, O'ahu	Buddhist priest
Isoo Kato HJ-1140-CI	Kona, Hawai'i	Coffee farmer
Kango Kawasaki HJ-1027-CI	Hilo, Hawai'i	Attorney
Ichiji Kinoshita HJ-1031-CI	Pepe'ekeo, Hawai'i	Plantation worker
Aisuke Kuniyuki HJ-413-CI	Honolulu, O'ahu	Businessman
Yasuyuki Mizutari HJ-1047-CI	Kaūmana, Hawai'i	Japanese school teacher
Kinzaemon Odachi HJ-1155-CI	Hilo, Hawai'i	Tenrikyo priest
Futoshi Ohama HJ-343-CI	Honolulu, O'ahu	Japanese school teacher
Shigeo Shigenaga HJ-336-CI	Honolulu, O'ahu	Restaurant owner
Tamasaku Watanabe HJ-1097-CI	'Ōla'a, Hawai'i	Protestant minister

Transfer Boat 4
Number of men: 39
Date of departure: 21 June 1942

Name and CI no.	Hawai'i residence	Occupation
Hisato Isemoto HJ-1014-CI	Hilo, Hawai'i	Businessman
Chikou Odate HJ-1791-CI	Waimea, Kaua'i	Buddhist priest
Kenjyo Ohara† HJ-1176-CI	'Ōla'a, Hawai'i	Buddhist priest
Matsujiro Otani HJ-206-CI	Honolulu, O'ahu	Businessman

Transfer Boat 5
Number of men: 48
Date of departure: 6 August 1942

Name and CI no.	Hawai'i residence	Occupation
Teiichiro Maehara HJ-1540-CI	Pu'unēnē, Maui	Japanese school teacher
Shinjiro Yoshimasu HJ-1560-CI	Pā'ia, Maui	Railroad worker

Transfer Boat 6
Number of men: 28
Date of departure: 16 September 1943

Name and CI no.	Hawai'i residence	Occupation
Ichiji Adachi HJ-1117-CI	Kona, Hawai'i	Bookkeeper/accountant
Seisaku Aoyagi HJ-1208-CI	Hilo, Hawai'i	Junk/salvage businessman
Ryozo Izutsu HJ-1840-CI	Makaweli, Kaua'i	Shopkeeper

Transfer Boat 7
Number of men: 23
Date of departure: 10 October 1943

Name and CI no.	Hawai'i residence	Occupation
Shigeji Terada HJ-1603-CI	Lahaina, Maui	Hospital chief cook, kendo teacher

Notes: CI, civilian internee; HJ, Hawai'i Japanese.

The three remaining boatloads did not include internees from my study; they departed on 2 March 1943, with 43 men; on 1 July 1943, with 34 men; and on 2 December 1943, with 29 men.

Transfer Boat 1 also included Kumaji Furuya, a businessman and poet from Honolulu; Transfer Boat 2 included Otokichi Ozaki, a Japanese language school teacher and poet from Hilo, Hawai'i; Transfer Boat 3 included George Yoshio Hoshida, a salesman and artist, also of Hilo; and Transfer Boat 5 included Yasutaro Soga, a journalist and editor of *Nippu jiji* (Japan Times) from Honolulu; these men were not in my study, but all are quoted or cited in this narrative.

* For a complete list of civilian internees from the Territory of Hawaii, see Soga 2008.
† Internee survivors interviewed by the author.

On Transfer Boat 1, for example, 172 men were shipped out on 20 February 1942, among them seven Issei related to this study, from different occupations and locations on O'ahu. On the second boat, departing on 20 March 1942, were 166 internees, including two survivors and seven other Issei in the study.

The ocean journeys were arduous, as Kato describes in his journal:

The anchor lifted, and the ship started to rock. I felt totally helpless as I couldn't get out and thought this to be my final farewell to Hawaii. . . .

There were three or four guards stationed outside our room at all times. We needed a permit for each time we went to use the bathroom. . . .

Treatment on board ship was bad. We submitted what we thought was [a] legitimate complaint to the officer in charge, but he was mean and uncaring. The treatment worsened. . . . He called us low-down scoundrels. The colonel above the lieutenant threatened us that our complaining will only make matters worse for us. He [would] see to it. He was mean, this colonel. (n.d., 63–65)

One of Kato's shipmates, departing on Saturday, 23 May 1942, on Transfer Boat 3, was my grandfather; both men from the Big Island, along with Kango Kawasaki, Rev. Fujitani, and Ichiji Kinoshita, introduced earlier, were in good company. In addition to these men were seven others in my study who, along with others, totaled 109 men. In his scrapbook record, Kawasaki reports the "sea quiet" on Monday, but notes the next day that "a man overboard" was "lost" (SB).

In his memoir, Otani writes about the deception involved in the departure of the fourth transfer boat on 21 June, a few weeks after Kato and my grandfather left Sand Island:

At 6:00 a.m., we were ordered to line up in a row and roll call was taken. Captain Eifler came in and said, "We have good news for you. Tomorrow is Father's Day and so you will be able to meet your loved ones, your wives, your parents and your children, so you should wear your best clothes and greet them with a smile." We were overjoyed that we would be able to meet our family the next day, so from the previous day we shaved and we prepared ourselves. The following 21st day the designated hour was 1:00 p.m.[;] we were all deciding what we would say to our families and we anxiously waited for the hour. It was 1:00, then 2:00, then 3:00, but no family member appeared. We waited most anxiously. We had lost hope and it was already 4:00. What came was the order for us to relocate to the U.S. mainland. . . . The order was that we would leave at 4:20 so we had to prepare for it. Receiving this opposite news, we were all disheartened but because it was war we could do nothing about it. At 4:30 we were put on a small boat from Sand Island.

We were sent to the U.S. mainland on a military ship . . . but we were not allowed to go on the deck. We could not look at the Island of Oahu nor could we express our feelings [about] departure. (n.d., 23)

FIG. 3.2. Internees from Transfer Boat 3, SFIC. *Left to right: row 1*: Ichiji Kinoshita (3); *row 2*: Rev. Kinai Ikuma (1), Kango Kawasaki (3), Yasuyuki Mizutari (9), Rev. Tamasaku Watanabe (14); *row 3*: Futoshi Ohama (5), Shigeo Shigenaga (7); *row 4*: Isoo Kato (5), Rev. Kodo Fujitani (12) (courtesy Kato Family Collection).

He was accompanied by three other Issei from my study, including Rev. Ohara of 'Ōla'a, whom I interviewed as one of the youngest men arrested, with others totaling thirty-nine men. Transfer Boat 5 departed on 6 August 1942, with two Issei from this study and forty-six others. Transfer Boats 6 and 7 also carried men from my study in September and October 1942, but there were none from my study in the last three boatloads, which had 1943 departures.

After noting who among the internees traveled on the same transfer boats and comparing their itineraries, I could surmise that those who were shipped out together usually traveled as a group and followed the same path of internment sites, at least initially. All internees were shipped from the Sand Island Internment Camp, across the Pacific, to the Immigration Station and Fort McDowell on Angel Island in San Francisco Bay. From this mainland entry point, there were three main routes (see Maps 1–4), which generally concluded at the Santa Fe Detention Station / Internment Camp in Santa Fe, New Mexico:

> Route 1 (see Map 1)—North–South Route: Camp McCoy, WI → Camp Forrest, TN → Camp Livingston, LA → Santa Fe Internment Camp, NM
> Route 2 (see Map 2)—Southerly Route 1: Fort Sill, OK → Camp Livingston, LA → Santa Fe Internment Camp, NM
> Route 3 (see Map 3)—Southerly Route 2: Fort Sam Houston, San Antonio, TX → Camp Lordsburg, NM → Santa Fe Internment Camp, NM

Yet a fourth route was followed by a composite group from various transfer boats, but heavily from Transfer Boat 1 and Transfer Boat 2, as well as mainland internees, being diverted from Camp Livingston, Louisiana, to Fort Missoula, Montana, before being shipped to Santa Fe:[6]

> Route 4—Northern Loop Route:
> Transfer Boat 1 Group (see Maps 1, 4)—Camp McCoy, WI → Camp Forrest, TN → Camp Livingston, LA → Fort Missoula, MT → Santa Fe Internment Camp, NM
> Transfer Boat 2 Group (see Maps 2, 4)—Fort Sill, OK → Camp Livingston, LA → Fort Missoula, MT → Santa Fe Internment Camp, NM

The U.S. Interior Department study by Burton and colleagues, *Confinement and Ethnicity: An Overview of World War II Japanese American Relocation Sites,* clearly documents the existence of these War and Justice Departments prison camps for civilian internees in different parts of the country. And meticulous government lists, typed in multiple copies at the time, confirmed the transfers of internees from camp to camp to camp to camp—the fate of the wingless birds.

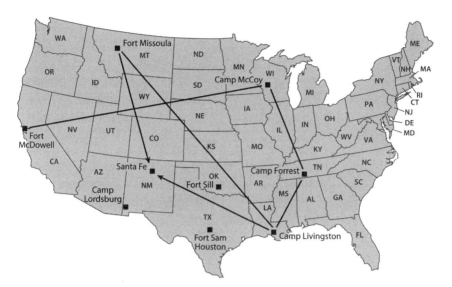

Map 1. Route 1: North–South Route. Transfer Boat 1 internees were sent from Sand Island to at least five camps, with a subgroup being sent to Montana before joining the main contingent at the SFIC, New Mexico.

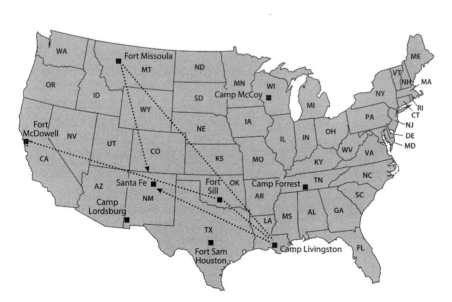

Map 2. Route 2: Southerly Route 1. Transfer Boat 2 internees were sent from Sand Island to at least four camps, with a subgroup also being sent to Montana before Santa Fe, New Mexico.

Map 3. Route 3: Southerly Route 2. Transfer Boat 3 internees were sent from Sand Island to at least four camps, the last, for many, in Santa Fe, New Mexico. Those on Transfer Boat 4 were sent directly to Lordsburg, then Santa Fe.

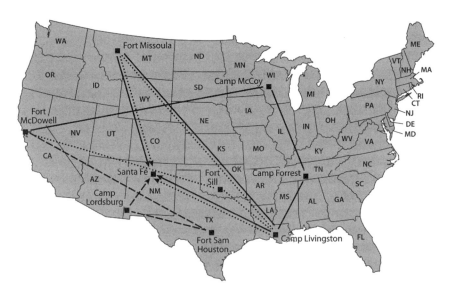

Map 4. Combined Routes. This map reflects the extensive use of transportation resources; some Hawai'i internees were paroled to WRA camps, repatriated to Japan, or reunited with their families at the Crystal City Family Internment Camp, Texas. After the war, many were returned to Hawai'i through Seattle, Washington.

CHAPTER 4

In Exile I

The Journey, a Captive Life, and Issei Resistance

From the cabin window
I bid farewell
To this fair island,
My home of fifty years,
Until its shadow disappears.
—Keiho Soga (1984, 28)

My grandfather, Rev. Watanabe, along with many hundreds of Issei men had to bid farewell to their island homes as they were transported from the outer islands to Honolulu's Immigration Station and Sand Island Internment Camp, but being removed forcibly and completely from their families and "home[s] of fifty years" to unknown locations over the Pacific Ocean and in remote areas of the U.S. mainland was nothing short of exile. And it was this "constant awareness that one is not at home" (Barbour 2008, 1), in addition to imprisonment itself, that continued to plague many of them, to dampen their spirits, to appear in their writing. But it also inspired them to resist.

To Angel Island

Isoo Kato, we know, had been shunted from his coffee farm in Kona to Volcano and the Kilauea Military Camp on the opposite side of the Big Island, where he was interrogated. Then, with my grandfather from ʻŌlaʻa and scores of other Issei men, he was shipped to Honolulu and, months later, on 23 May 1942, shunted farther over the ocean on Transfer Boat 3 to another immigration station, this one on Angel Island in San Francisco Bay. Most Hawaiʻi Issei imprisoned on the mainland followed a similar path to this point. While the men naturally differed in personality and perspective, their individual impressions of the journey into exile give us insights into the experience of the larger Hawaiʻi internee group.

In his journal, Kato describes their ship dropping anchor on 1 June 1942, near "the world renowned Golden Gate Bridge"; he calls it "a thing of beauty," describing it in detail (n.d., 66), while George Hoshida, who accompanied him, terms it "a thrilling sight . . . a refreshing treat after the long miserable voyage" (n.d., 291). In another contrast, Hoshida describes the internees' "miserable" appearance: "Going without bathing and . . . not being allowed to shave, . . . we had our suits on but they were all wrinkled and soiled. With army duffle bags on our shoulders, marching single file down the plank, guarded by soldiers with fixed bayonets, we must have appeared like real prisoners of war criminals. It truly was humiliating" (292).

Kato reports being taken by a small boat to Angel Island, where the internees followed in the footsteps of thousands of Asian immigrants entering the United States but now were greeted by "dozens of bayoneted guards" standing on either side of them (n.d., 66): "We headed for the Immigration Center up a hill. An iron gate opened and we filed into a room. I heard the steel gate clang shut and locked. . . . Again we were stripped naked and put through another inspection. When will this ever end, I wondered" (67). I wondered, too, how my grandfather, in his fifty-ninth year, endured this indignity. I also wondered how he felt returning to San Francisco a prisoner when he had left California for Hawai'i with his young family in 1922 a free man, looking forward to his third ministry in the islands.

Despite the initial strip search—and the discomfort of 109 of them crowded into two rooms, Kato writes of humane experiences as well: "It is different here from Hawaii in that we are enjoying more privileges. We are free to bathe and use the toilet at any time. All accommodations are comfortable. . . . The dining room is new and the food preparation is sanitary and tasty. The cook and kitchen helpers are all military men and they treat us kindly" (n.d., 67–68).

The beauty of the island itself was not lost on these men either. Itsuo Hamada, a businessman and poet from Pa'uwela and Kahului, Maui, who had arrived on the second transfer boat in mid-March, writes in "Bearing Pineapple" that "Sahohime, the god of spring, was singing for the arrival of spring, and flowers were in bloom, which made us forget about our predicament for a short while."[1] Kato's description of Angel Island allows us to imagine it in May and allows me to imagine what my grandfather saw as they arrived together: It is a "small mountain. Down to the foot of the mountain it is lush and green with trees. There are pine trees, cherry-like trees, and other deciduous trees. . . . Small chirping birds are plentiful" (n.d., 68). Hoshida observes "a tiny hummingbird for the first time with its blurring wings. It darted among the branches, stopping motionless for a few seconds at some flowers" (n.d., 292). Kato's keen powers of observation capture other creatures of the area as well: "Many small fish abound in San Francisco Bay in front of the Immigration

Center. It seems they are attracted to gushing water from the aqueduct. They are a thick, black school of fish near the water conduit which in turn attracts the sea birds to feed on them. With fish in beaks, the gulls soar upward, the fish glistening like silver" (n.d., 69). Matsujiro Otani, who arrived on the fourth transfer boat in June also appreciated this "beautiful island within San Francisco Harbor. Flowers were in bloom, birds were singing, and it was a small island like heaven" (n.d., 24).

But they were, after all, prisoners. Kato relates yet another inspection:

> On the third day here, everything in our possession and every piece of garment on us were recorded. . . . I had no money to hand over, so my few pieces of clothing and the statistics of name, age, and such things were recorded. On and on as we are inspected we have less and less things to call our own. We are left with only the clothes on our body. I was given a certificate of claims stating I had no money. . . . This was the first time in my whole life that I was ever given a receipt or statement for having no money. A receipt for something non-existent struck me as utterly funny. (n.d., 70)

So anxious were some prisoners to express themselves, to record their transient presence in that place, that they carved inscriptions into the Immigration Station walls. Scholar Charles Egan has reproduced and translated these inscriptions. For example, Takuji Shindo, a druggist from Hilo, Hawaiʻi, arrived at Angel Island on the same transfer boat as Kato, Hoshida, and my grandfather and simply wrote:

> June 4th
> As a prisoner.
> Hilo City Shindo
>   (n.d., 85)

Another internee, possibly also on Transfer Boat 3, anonymously inscribed a more poignant message:

> Evening.
> The expectation that one day
> Will bring escape—
> Cold, bleak.
> June 4th
>   (n.d., 86)

On that very day, at 6:30 p.m., however, Kato records, "We boarded a train," and he wrote this poem, concluding his journal about the first months of his internment:

I'm headed for [a] destination I know not where,
Over thousands of miles of mountains and oceans I've come.
I gaze at the stars in exile,
In dreams I fly the Hawaiian skies.
Left behind are my wife and children
In native Kona that is much too far.
I think of home and I cry sad tears,
Thoughts of loved ones bring on sadness.
When again, when again
Will I see them all?
I do not know,
I do not know. . . .
                    (n.d., 71)

In prose, he is resolute—"I am fully reconciled to hard times ahead of me in the weeks and months, and years to come"—but his poetry reveals his real anguish over the separation from his family and home place and the powerlessness of not knowing or being able to determine his own fate. I suspect many others, including my grandfather, who shared space with him on that third transfer boat across the Pacific, also shared his sentiments.

To Fort Sam Houston and to Lordsburg

While the internees on the first and second transfer boats were eventually sent to Camp Livingston, Louisiana, via other camps, my grandfather along with Kato, Shindo, Hoshida, and more than a hundred other men from Transfer Boat 3 were sent by train on a southerly route of imprisonment, first to Fort Sam Houston in San Antonio, Texas. Hoshida's writing and sketches document their passing from Oakland and its slums through various towns in Nevada, through the Nevada desert, past the Great Salt Lake in Utah, through Utah towns and Colorado canyons and towns, to the Rio Grande, and to Texas. Here he is fascinated by the arid sun: "The sun was so different from [the] one I had been [used to] seeing back in Hawaii. It looked so fierce and wild in this barren wasteland that a sense of awe assailed me. Not a shade of cloud appeared in the awakening sky and the sun's ray[s] already had the warmth and promise of a fierce summer heat" (n.d., 302). A strange familiarity in a contrasting landscape accelerates his feeling of exile:

> Abruptly, the barren ridges fell away and golden rays of the sun flooded across a wide open farmland. . . . Houses dotted the acres of farmland, and small towns and villages whirled by. As the train stopped briefly at one of these towns, we could see people raking their front lawns and workmen with lunch pails exchanging greetings. They brought back memories of those peaceful days back in Hawaii only a few months ago and made this sight here so unreal.
>
> The houses with green turfs and shady trees were homes to these people here. But to me who had been forced to travel so far from our homes thousands of miles away, the sight of children playing in the lawn awakened in me a sudden longing for my own home and children. (302–303)

Kango Kawasaki's notes verify their route, noting the distance from Angel Island to be "about 2,672 miles, [the] total from Hilo about 5,022 miles" (SB) and the duration to be about four days to San Antonio, where they arrived on 8 June at 10:00 a.m.

At Fort Sam Houston, they were housed in pyramidal tents and suffered 120-degree heat, sweltering in their undershirts and shorts. Hoshida writes not only of the unbearable "searing heat" and humidity but also about their human ability to adapt—and in some way conquer—that "hellish" environment, even in whimsical ways: "To us Hawaiians, coming from the temperate climate cooled by the northwest breeze, this heat was really hellish. . . . But as time passed, we got used to the heat and during the morning when it was cooler, we amused ourselves looking for fossils of shells and pretty stones" (n.d., 306–307).

Kawasaki, who was designated "commander of HJs," was completely bilingual and kept thorough and copious records in English throughout the entire internment, often with notes in Japanese. He titles his scrapbook "Internment Records (Dec. 8, '41–Dec '45)" and inscribes on the cover the following lines in flowing Palmer method penmanship:

> In a violent storm
> The tallest trees are hardest hit.
> Are the trees to blame?

Upon their arrival at Fort Sam Houston, Kawasaki notes that there were Alaskan and mainland Japanese already imprisoned there, in addition to Germans and

FIG. 4.1. Cover of "Internment Records" kept by Kango Kawasaki, December 1941–December 1945 (courtesy Kawasaki Family Collection).

Italians. On 9 June, he formed three companies of "the 109 HJ" and notes the captain for each one with a listing of the tents under his charge. On 12 June, he writes, there was "continuous thunder and lightening [*sic*] almost every night. rain downpour. leaking single tents. sleep under cots" (SB). Hoshida describes these as "fierce storms": "The fierceness of the thunder storms really surprised and shocked us. Back in Hawaii when it thundered, they came in long intervals but here the lightening [*sic*] came every few seconds on all sides followed by ear-splitting thunder-claps which chilled our hearts.... This experience was repeated quite often wherever we were sent until we became used to it and felt less fear" (307–308).

A trip to the Fort Sam Houston Museum in 2002 helped me to imagine the setting decades earlier: Although there were pleasant areas with flowers and green grass in administrative and living sections of the camp, some six rows of tents among hundreds were designated as the "concentration camp / POW camp" on the very bleak Dodd Field.

For the Hawai'i Issei, the U.S. Army seems to have changed its mind after ten days and sent them to Camp Lordsburg, New Mexico, on 17 June 1942. Although this was another army camp like Fort Sam Houston, it must have been perceived as something else, as a weathered cardboard box from the camp attests: Among my grandfather's internment possessions, this was clearly labeled "Lordsburg/Rosubagu" in Japanese by Rev. Watanabe's hand. Contained in it were found wood objects of different shapes that must have attracted his attention. But the box itself has the more telling label "Enemy Concentration Camp Lordsburg" scrawled boldly on its side by someone else's common perception. So to New Mexico they went, first to Lordsburg in the southwest corner of the state, 764 miles away from San Antonio by Kawasaki's precise calculation.

When they arrived at Lordsburg the next day at 3:00 p.m., Kawasaki writes, the "first in Camp. Bks. [barracks] inside covered with inches of dust. Wash everything. Toilet facilities incomplete" (SB). Completing those chores, the men immediately elected officers for Company 10: Kawasaki as vice mayor and Hoshida and Shigeo Shigenaga as barracks captains 4 and 5, respectively. All three men had been shipped on Transfer Boat 3, along with Rev. Watanabe. Lacking my grandfather's diaries or notes, by association I could understand more clearly the day-to-day occurrences in his internment life.

FIG. 4.2. Box labeled "Enemy Concentration Camp Lordsburg," containing Rev. Watanabe's wood artifacts, Lordsburg Internment Camp, New Mexico, 1942–1943 (Tamasaku Watanabe Collection).

THE GENEVA CONVENTION OF 1929

Curiously enough, a few weeks earlier, on 28 April 1942, the Philadelphia office of the INS had produced a critical ten-page document: "Instructions Concerning the Treatment of Alien Enemy Detainees." I consider it one of my more significant discoveries in the National Archives in that it reflects official intention and policy (or lip service), in contrast to the reality of practice. Its author, Lemuel B. Schofield, was special assistant to the U.S. attorney general and was consolidating various instructions, dating back to 12 December 1941, concerning the "treatment of alien enemies in the custody of the Service and the standards of custodial care adopted for all detention facilities" (1942, 1). Each district director was thus ordered to disseminate these instructions to all employees who had duties connected with the detention of alien enemies, making the scope broad and binding.

The "minimum standards of treatment" were based on the Geneva Convention of 1929, known as the "Convention between the United States of America and

Forty-Six Other Powers . . . Relating to the Treatment of Prisoners of War." The U.S. government, it states, had "agreed with the belligerent powers to apply these provisions to *civilian alien enemy internees* wherever applicable." Schofield stresses that the "basis underlying our treatment of alien enemy detainees is *reciprocity,*" referring to the corresponding treatment of American prisoners (1942, 1, emphasis mine). In addition to its covering twenty-one topics as far-ranging as work, food, sanitation, religious services, censorship, and death and burial, I noted especially passage 1 on "Humane Treatment": "(See Article 3—Geneva Convention) Detainees must at all times be humanely treated and protected, particularly against acts of violence, insults, and public curiosity. Physical coercion must not be resorted to and, except in self defense, to prevent escape or for purposes of proper search, no employee of this Service under any pretext shall invade the person of any detainee. No measures calculated to humiliate or degrade shall be undertaken" (2).

Schofield concludes with the statement that "the spirit of the Geneva Convention, as well as the letter of these instructions, must be carefully followed at all times. The first duty of this Service [INS] in connection with the detention of enemy aliens entrusted to its custody [is] their safekeeping. Next, but fully as important, is the obligation to treat them fairly and humanely in accordance with the principles of treatment to which the United States Government is committed" (1942, 10). The fact that instructions dating to December 1941 needed to be consolidated and reissued in April 1942, however, reflected to me a lack of compliance with those initial instructions by members of the INS and their military counterparts—as seen clearly in examples of the internees' experiences.

Despite official intentions, which were motivated more by fears of retaliation against American prisoners perhaps than by altruism, the spirit of the convention prevailed neither at Sand Island nor at Lordsburg nor at other camps, especially in the early days of internment. Firsthand accounts attest to mistreatment. In addition to psychological manipulations and abuse such as the Father's Day incident at Sand Island, described by Otani (see chapter 3), there were repeated strip searches, including the spoon affair reported by Otani and those mentioned by Kato, as well as other degrading actions by authorities. According to Kashima, mainland Issei received particularly harsh treatment, including severe physical abuse and solitary confinement, at the Fort Missoula, Montana, internment camp in the early months of the war, until the Japanese ambassador to the United States, Kichisaburo Nomura, learned of it and "protested to the State Department," after which "agents of the Justice and State departments flew to Missoula . . . to investigate" (1991, 55). It is safe to assume that the resulting investigation precipitated Schofield's reissued instructions, given its 28 April 1942 date.

In New Mexico, the venomous racism of some of its citizens toward the Japanese is starkly represented by a letter quoted earlier, from "Lloyd" to John E. Miles, then governor of New Mexico. In it, the writer labels "all Japs" as "skunks" and asserts that "*no matter where a skunk is born, or under what star or flag, he is still a skunk,*" underlining his words for emphasis. Similar attitudes may well have motivated camp administrators such as Lieutenant Colonel Clyde A. Lundy, camp commander at Lordsburg, in his dealings with labor disputes and other conflicts following the Hawai'i internees' arrival.

Schofield's instructions had little effect on Lundy's practice—at least not until, as Kawasaki reports, "eighty-six Seattle and Tacoma men arr. from Missoula, Mont.," at which time, "Genji Mihara of Seattle, leader, brings copy of GENEVA CONVENTION" on 26 June 1942 (SB). According to Reverend Yoshiaki Fukuda of San Francisco, a minister of the Konko Church of North America, who was there at Fort Missoula, Schofield himself had given copies of the convention document to Fort Missoula internee representatives during the dispute there, with Genji Mihara possibly among them (1990, 40–41). This document thus appeared in Lordsburg in Mihara's hands, giving the civilian internees there some leverage for a collective self-advocacy. Besides the individual belief in self-expression reflected in Soga's and Kato's poems, these men clearly believed in the power of words contained in legal documents as well.

The day after Mihara's arrival, the internees called a general meeting, at which Kawasaki reports in his scrapbook, "all agree not to work outside of compound," based on the "Provisions of Geneva Convention." Lundy, the "CO," responded to what he considered a "work refusal" by confiscating the internees' canteen tickets and closing the canteen, relieving the company mayors of their rank, ordering a reelection, confining the men to their barracks, and guarding the yards. A few days later, the company mayors negotiated with Lundy: Their men would go out to work if he would "wire Spanish Consul to come here." (As Spain was the protecting power for Japanese interests on the U.S. mainland, the Spanish consuls from various offices visited and inspected the internment camps on behalf of the Spanish ambassador and reported their observations to him.) Lundy agreed to this and "some men [went] outside to work," while the canteen reopened and canteen tickets were returned (SB).

At around this time, as tensions began to intensify, Otani and others from Transfer Boat 4 arrived by train on 5 July, directly from Angel Island via Los Angeles and Phoenix. In his memoir, Otani recalls stopping en route "for 30 minutes and at the train station shop [seeing] a giant watermelon which had the price tag of only 25 cents. For us [internees] who did not own a single cent we just simply gazed at the watermelon but could do nothing to purchase it" (n.d., 25).

Yet the fact that the men of the previous transfer boat were there in Lordsburg to greet them was encouraging to Otani and his comrades.

Less than a week later, on 9 July, Kawasaki writes in his scrapbook, "2 PM temp. 110 degrees. hot like hell. heavy sand storm again. Lt. Mitchell brings detail list, requiring AM: 100 men, and PM: 80 men, to work outside of compound; refusal to be considered disobedience to orders. Our reply: 75 men for AM only until Spanish consul arrives." Two days later, they "sent out 75 men for AM, none for PM." And when the lieutenant gave them an ultimatum to work outside in the afternoon, "our reply: No." That led to a lights-out at 8:00 p.m. instead of 10:00 p.m. and confinement to the barracks after 8:00 a.m. Subsequently, the mayors of Companies 9–11 were segregated in a house and all men were confined to their barracks. On 16 July, a "telegram sent to Sp. Embassy to send representative right away" (SB).

On 23 July at 1:00 p.m., Lundy posed a question to the internees in the different companies, demanding a yes-or-no answer by 3:00 p.m.: "Are you willing to work, 8 hours per day, when necessary both inside and outside of compounds, as stipulated in Internment Regulations and the Geneva Convention?" (quoted in SB). Kawasaki reports the following outcome in his scrapbook: "Cos. 9 and 11 answer 'yes,' without consulting my Co. 10. Co. 10 replied: Under the Geneva Convention, CO [Lundy] has no right to demand forced labor outside of the Compound. Until the matter is passed upon by the Spanish Embassy, as charge for J. interests, we cannot reply." The CO's response was retaliatory; according to Kawasaki, "Cos. 9 and 11 may remain as they are, but Co. 10 men, exclusive of old and sick men, are ordered to remove to Prison Camp. Kompound [sic] 2. total 176 men, forming Co. 5. Mayor Mihara of Co. 9 and Mayor Kasai of Co. 11 also. Under bayonet guard. All bks. doors closed" (SB).

Much of this mistreatment came to a head four days later, on 27 July 1942, with the controversial shootings of two sickly mainland internees, Toshiro Kobata and Hirota Isomura, part of a group of 147 Issei prisoners who had arrived from Fort Lincoln, Bismarck, North Dakota. Although the guard who shot and killed them claimed that they were trying to escape, the fact that they were too ill to walk several miles from the train depot to the camp and were waiting to be transported by vehicle calls that story into question. John J. Culley (1985) has written extensively, analyzing the implications of this incident, raising questions about U.S. Army administrative ability and practice as well as the nature of the government's policy regarding alien enemies.

Equally important was the response of the internees themselves regarding the incident. Some officially questioned the circumstances and the government's response to the shootings and requested an autopsy, a request that was denied.

Kawasaki, as a civilian internee leader, expressed the condolences of the men in (the new) Company 5 at the prisoners' services for Kobata and Isomura on 2 August 1942. Rather than speaking to the attendees in the audience, he presumably faced and addressed the deceased with the following poignant and telling words in Japanese:

> Our two brothers, who arrived at this camp from North Dakota, ailing in poor health, and who didn't even have the opportunity to become acquainted with the other internees here, sadly disappeared from the earth along with the desert dew. It is to be regretted to the utmost.
>
> The authorities tried to justify their action and claimed that they shot you because you tried to escape when told to stop, but that you, who were seriously ill, could have escaped is questionable. Common sense prevents us from believing so. Unfortunately, there was not a single eye witness, and the incident was buried exactly as the authorities claimed. On Judgment Day, the person responsible will surely receive his due.
>
> Although we are utter strangers to you [both men were from California], we of Co. 5 send you our most sincere condolences. We wish that you would accept them. (SB, trans. Rev. Y. Fujitani)

Finally, on 9–10 August 1942, José M. de Garay, the long-awaited Spanish consul, arrived from New Orleans to visit the internees in Lordsburg, accompanied by a State Department representative. Related to this visit is an undated secret memo sent by FBI director J. Edgar Hoover to Adolf A. Berle Jr., assistant secretary of state, marked "PERSONAL AND CONFIDENTIAL" and "BY SPECIAL MESSENGER." Enclosing a translation of de Garay's seventeen-page report made to the Spanish ambassador, Hoover writes, "This material became available to this Bureau through a highly confidential source, and it is requested that it be held in the strictest confidence" (n.d.).

Dated 14 August 1942, the report covers the Spanish consul's visits to other camps holding Japanese internees, with pages 10–15 concerning Lordsburg. In these pages, de Garay describes the population, location, and organization of the camp. More significantly, he refers to such topics as the poor condition of the camp upon the internees' arrival and the labor dispute, both cited earlier from Kawasaki's notes, as well as complaints about funds, clothing, and cooking and cleaning utensils—the lack thereof—and requests for improved living conditions, including a library. Further, de Garay writes, "Among the internees, there are some teachers who would like to establish a school for their comrades; Lieutenant Colonel Lundy has promised me that they will be given facilities for the acquisition of books and necessary material for the school" (1942, 12). In a reference to a separate report on the "treatment given to the internees from Hawaii," he mentions that "Matsujiro Otani lost his valise on [their trip from Honolulu to San Francisco and Lordsburg], and it has not yet been recovered" (13). He also reports difficulties in the Hawai'i and Alaska internees' communication with their families due to language, the system of censorship, and distance. He registers with the ambassador the internees' desire to have "a copy of the text of the Geneva Pact of 1929 in Japanese" (14).

Lastly, de Garay makes reference to the establishment of a family camp, since "the majority of the internees do not wish to be repatriated." The Spanish consul also offers the following observation on the shootings of the two mainland internees:

> All the internees appeared worried about the incident which occurred on July 27, 1942, and which caused the death of two internees. In attachment #16, Your Excellency will find the report of the incident according to the opinion of the internees. Lieutenant Colonel Lundy advised me that the sentry who shot the two Japanese was prosecuted and exonerated of all blame since it was proved that the prisoners had tried to escape. According to the Japanese some of the soldiers have a great animosity for them, and for this reason it would be desirable that future transfers of internees be made during daylight hours. They told me that when they were walking with their luggage the six miles which separate Lordsburg from the Camp an empty Army truck passed and they requested the driver to carry some of the bags which they were carrying; this was firmly refused. The two who were later shot were left behind in order to be carried in a truck due to the fact that, being ill, they were not able to walk. (de Garay 1942, 15)

For Kawasaki personally, August 1942 was a good month, for he received not only the first letter from home, along with a photo of his daughter, Sumie, but also the first package from home, consisting of "1 pr. pants, 2 shirts, 3 towels, 3 tooth brushes and 1 paste, 1 carton Luckies and 4 pr. socks," as well as the first remittance from home in the amount of one hundred dollars. In September, he reports that he received another package from home, which contained "1 suit, 1 doz. hdkfs, ½ doz. socks" (SB). Being bilingual in English and Japanese, he translated and broadcast the news of 8 September in Japanese for his Company 5 community.

Several months later, on 21 November 1942, Alfred Cardinaux of the International Committee of the Red Cross, the organization closely associated with the Geneva Convention, visited Lordsburg, an English translation of his report (possibly from French) appearing in State Department records without an attached Hoover memo. Cardinaux covers topics as various as buildings and facilities, including the hospital and library, food, education, religion, clothing, and mail. On the subject of work, he provides an extensive discussion on the disagreement between internees and camp commander Lundy, concluding with the following observation: "The Commanding Officer of the camp, a colonel, adheres literally to the regulations and does not succeed in obtaining the collaboration of the internees. The greatest defect of the camp is the lack of remunerated work. Idleness, on the one hand, and the necessity of doing certain work without payment . . . on the other, makes the internees bitter and discontented. The Commanding Officer could make the internees more tractable if he granted them $0.80 when they are working to improve the roads and [install drains] outside of the [internee compound]" (1942, 10).

A few weeks later, in early December, F. de Amat, the Spanish consul at San Francisco, also visited the camp, accompanied by State Department personnel. I did not find Hoover's secret translation of his report, but as was typical, the State Department representative, Bernard Gufler, provided documentation of the visit for the record on the usual subjects and summarized the internees' requests and complaints. I found the following sections of Gufler's report revealing in light of the internees' previous assertions about their emotional and physical well-being:

c. Reuniting the Families.
The internees expressed the hope that families would be reunited as speedily as possible in family internment camps or if possible by parole of the fathers to relocation centers and that in the establishment of the basis for family reunion all unmarried members of the family regardless of age be considered members of the family unit.

j. Guards.
They stated that the guards sometimes are intoxicated and threaten to harm them. On Thanksgiving Day some guards under punishment were put into the compound with the internees and one of the guards who was drunk stabbed an internee.

k. The Shoot to Kill Order.
They stated that adequate warning is not given before the guards shoot to kill. They stated that they were told that they would be informed of the report given on the fatal shooting on July 27, 1942 but that they have not received information on this report. (1942, 2–4)

Although Gufler's report maintains an appropriate degree of objectivity, his comments seem critical of the army's practice:

> The mistake had been made of placing some guards who had got drunk in the stockade with the internees. . . . One of them who was still drunk took occasion to go on a "Jap hunt" during the course of which he stabbed one of the internees. The internees preserved commendable discipline but the incident left a considerable bitterness behind it that came to the attention of the Spanish representative and spoiled the very good impression that he had at first made of the camp and its commander. . . .
>
> As a footnote to the shooting incident that happened at this camp, it should be noted that the soldier who shot the two Japanese was after his acquittal by the court martial promoted to the rank of corporal and became the recipient of a purse of $75 made up for him by the citizens of Lordsburg. He was given a two weeks furlough to spend the purse. (1942, 4)

These visits resulted in negotiations for what eventually became the family internment camp at Crystal City, Texas. A multifaith petition, requesting that officials make culturally sensitive revisions in determining who would populate such a family camp, was signed by Rev. Fukuda, the Konkokyo minister introduced earlier; my grandfather Rev. Watanabe, a Christian; and Reverend Hosho Kurohira, a Buddhist, on 9 December 1942, and presumably presented to officials at the time (see Okawa 2015a). The internees' concerns regarding unruliness and violence also precipitated at least one military inspection into the incidents.

Despite Schofield's seemingly fair-minded official policy and despite the orders to post the text of the Geneva Convention for all internees to view, true communication with and among the inmates could not occur until the document was actually translated into Japanese. This formidable task was taken on by Rev. Fukuda, Shigeru Nozaka, and other companions. After completing the translation of the convention document, Rev. Fukuda and his colleagues distributed twelve hundred mimeographed copies to the internees, and, "Upon request," writes Rev. Fukuda, "I gave explanations on the Geneva Convention agreement and its regulations and applications at various barracks. This knowledge of the convention helped us immensely" (1990, 43–44). This controversy over internee rights illustrates in no uncertain terms how literate some of the Issei were, how aware they were of their legal rights, and how they used that knowledge and literacy to better their circumstances through overt forms of resistance.

On 17 December 1942, Lt. Col. Lundy was replaced by Lieutenant Colonel Louis A. Ledbetter with apparently very positive results, according to a 2 June 1943 report by Alfred Cardinaux:

The difficulties about the maintenance of work of the camp, which existed at the time of my last visit, have been entirely eliminated. All the work which is not clearly related to the upkeep of the internees' camp is paid for at the rate of $0.80 a day. There are no longer any armed soldiers to guard the internees who work outside the gates. Not only has the number of these soldiers been reduced, but they now carry only a police stick. . . .

The relations of the internees with Col. Ledbetter . . . are very cordial and this fact is expressed very frequently at the camp. The Colonel lunched with the internees and [Cardinaux]. He has conferred with the officers in charge of administration and has explained to them the spirit and application of the Geneva Convention. He has particularly stressed the fact that he would not permit acts of animosity. He is also interested in all the activities of the internees and the latter told [Cardinaux] that they greatly appreciated what the Colonel was doing for them. (1943, 2–3)

Another one of the highlights of December 1942 was the first meeting of the Hiroshima Kenjinkai (prefectural group), which made up nearly half of the total internee population at the time. The group elected a chairman and different men spoke, representing the cities, sections, and islands in Hawai'i from which they had come. Rev. Ikuma, a Shinto priest from Daijingu Shrine in Honolulu and Ed Ikuma's grandfather, led the banzai for long life. Then, on 31 December, as 1942 came to a close, Company 5 held a *mochitsuki* (rice cake pounding) to celebrate the coming of the New Year with all of the officers—Kawasaki was now the mayor—and barracks captains present.

From Angel Island and Other Camps to Camp Livingston

While the men in Transfer Boats 3–7 were settling in at Lordsburg and, by 27 November 1942, had been accounted for on an official list, their fellow prisoners in Transfer Boat 1 had been shunted from Hawai'i and Angel Island to Camp McCoy, Wisconsin, and Camp Forrest, Tennessee, before settling temporarily at Camp Livingston in Louisiana.[2] Patsy Saiki in *Gambare!* relates stories of Camp McCoy and the kind camp commander, Lieutenant Colonel Horace Ivan Rodgers, who, upon a request from one of the internees, allowed the Issei prisoners to celebrate Hanamatsuri in honor of the Buddha's birthday and also introduced them to the northern lights; who told his successor at Camp Forrest that "this group of men were gentlemen and asked that they be treated as such"; and whom the internees honored with the shout of "Banzai!" when he left them in Tennessee (Saiki 1982, 90).

Peggy Choy, however, characterizes Camp McCoy as "a bastion" of a "dominant racial order" that "threatened to dehumanize these men" (1991, 88), point
ing out that the internees' journey "was shrouded in secrecy" and "heavily
guarded." Her discussion of anti-Japanese attitudes in the surrounding community, stoked by the media, offers us a reality check about the conditions the men
were forced to endure. Although they no longer were subjected to the extreme
heat and overt mistreatment of Sand Island, the internees were housed in Depres-
sion-era Civilian Conservation Corps barracks and had to suffer the extreme
cold of Wisconsin's winter upon their arrival in March. Choy relates an interview with a former internee, who remembered that "toilets located in an enclosed
outhouse were long wooden benches with holes" (90). She also describes internal
friction among the prisoners and labor disputes; rather than attributing positive
changes to administrative altruism, Choy makes a case for the internees' initiative, especially their developing "constructive activities of their own choosing"
(93)—this being consistent with my observations regarding Issei assertiveness
and advocacy in other camps. At the next stop, Camp Forrest, Saiki relates, the
food was "good and plentiful," and the Issei were allowed "self-rule, attended
classes, could engage in hobbies, and could receive money and letters from
home" (1982, 88); both of these camps seem to have been quite an improvement
over Sand Island.

The prisoners in Transfer Boat 2, including internee survivors Kazumi Matsumoto and Rev. Gyokuei Matsuura, whom I interviewed in 2003, were sent from
Angel Island to Fort Sill, Oklahoma, then to Camp Livingston. Fort Sill appears
to have been quite a contrast to Camp Forrest. Otokichi Ozaki, a Japanese language school teacher and poet, describes in postwar radio scripts the experience
of the Transfer Boat 2 internees sent from the lushness of Hawai'i and Angel
Island to the desert at Fort Sill, the contrast in climate not unlike that experienced by the men in Lordsburg:

Here at Fort Sill, Oklahoma, where glittering heat waves rise and peak as
far as the eye can see, the jumbled sound of machines and hammers can
be heard, triggered apparently by the sudden need for more barracks.
There is not a tree to be seen. Tents stand in rows. The heat. As though the
wind is dead. . . .

No soap rations. No toothpaste. No hair oil for the past two months.
Even my one-and-only suitcase, containing my entire fortune, and my
bag—I have not seen them since February, March, April, May. What
money we had was taken from us, so we have none. Inside the barbed
wire fence, there is nothing we can buy anyway.

We become irritable. Eat. Sleep. Wake up. Eat. Sleep. Wake up. A life cut off from everything in the world. The unbearable monotony of a life without variation seems to slowly warp our minds. The crazy weather and the tent life—one cannot help but begin to lose one's mind. . . . Are we not becoming like leaking balloons—ambitionless, lethargic and apathetic? (2012, 66–67)

In "Bearing Pineapple," Hamada confirms Ozaki's perception: "The weather changed suddenly from cold winter to hot summer. At times, wind storms raised yellow sand all over the place and thunder roared. Life in the suffocating tents was dull and tedious."

It was here at Fort Sill that Kanesaburo Oshima of Kona was shot and killed on 12 May 1942 while climbing the barbed wire fencing, the story told from different views by Saiki and by Ozaki, who knew Oshima because both their names began with O and they found themselves together on the ships from Hilo to Honolulu and from Sand Island to the mainland. Ozaki relates the report conveyed by Minoru Murakami, also of the Big Island, who was one of the leaders of their company:

At about seven o'clock this morning, Mr. Oshima clambered up the barbed wire fence on the left side of the main entrance to the compound. Surprised fellow internees tried to pull him down, but he was too fast. He jumped down on the other side of the ten-foot high inner fence. A guard on duty standing nearby ordered him to stop, but he ran southward. The guard gave chase, pistol in hand. Seeing this, fellow internees ran along their side of the fence shouting, "Please don't shoot! He's gone crazy!" The guard seemed to hesitate for a second, then fired two or three shots, none of which hit Mr. Oshima. Startled by the gunshots, Mr. Oshima ran to the end of the fence, reaching the foot of a guard tower, where machine guns were positioned. He scaled one of the barbed wire posts at the bottom of the tower. When he reached the platform jutting out about three feet, he hesitated, and at that moment, a pursuing guard fired a shot. It pierced the back of [his] head and exited his forehead. He fell backward, having died instantly. . . . Let us not forget Mr. Oshima's death. Regulations prohibit us from approaching the barbed wire fencing, but shooting a man just for climbing over the fence is not justified. What sane person would even attempt to escape through the main gate in broad daylight? (2012, 68–69)

Internees first from Fort Sill and then from Camp Forrest eventually were moved to Camp Livingston, near Alexandria, Louisiana. In what appears to be a notepad of his uncensored drafts of letters, on 19 June 1942, Ryosei Aka writes to someone at home, "We [were] removed to Camp Livingston from Fort Sill Oklahoma, late 30th of May [1942]" (DL, 11).[3] He describes passing an extensive forest of tall trees on the way, an apparent change of landscape. Upon arrival, Hamada writes that "the surrounding scenery reminded us of ancient times. It was a dense forest of huge pines. Sprinkled maples were opening fresh green leaves as if they were welcoming us" (n.d.).

Aka notes that the internees are "well-treated" and calls Camp Livingston a "very nice place[,] better than Oklahoma" (DL, 11). In a subsequent letter, he informs his family that he has "gained about 15 to 20 pounds" and that "everything's O.K. now. So you do not need [to] worry about [my] well being." He also refers to the question of repatriation, one that plagued many an internee:

> There has been talk for long and now it is probable that we will be sent to Japan (repatriation). Of course this will be in exchange with the American detainees in [the] orient. . . . But if we wish to stay here we can. So I made up my mind [to] stay here.
>
> I feel that we lived so many years in T. Hawaii. And all our child[ren] are American citizens. They were educated and [are] working faithfully [in] America. So we ought and better to stay in America. So I answered not to return back [to] Japan. . . . I am living for over thirty five years under the star[s] and stripe[s] and feel proud to work for this country. (12–13, 16–17)

Still at Livingston, he tells his family, "We see fireflies flying every night. It is beautiful to see their flying. I did not expect to see fireflies here" (14–15). "We see many tall pine trees near the camp and the cool wind passes through the woods always" (16).

Having moved with Aka and Hamada from Fort Sill to Camp Livingston, Rev. Matsuura recalls in a 2004 interview with the Japanese Cultural Center of Hawai'i that the internees organized and took classes, studying various subjects rather than remaining idle. For some classes, they ventured into the pine groves, finding various fauna such as turtles and snakes, according to Saiki (1982, 120). She relates that they also organized theater productions and played softball and golf, as they did at other camps (120–123). More experiences of internees at Camp Livingston will be related in chapters 5, 6, and 7, respectively—of Kazumi Matsumoto and his remarkable braided purses and other handicrafts; Rev. Matsuura and his letter writing; and Jinshichi Tokairin and Katsuichi Miho and the visits of their soldier sons to the Louisiana army camp.

It was at Camp Livingston in fall 1942 that Kyujiro Ishida had a stroke that paralyzed him for the duration of the war. According to an official report, dated 20 October 1942, "This morning at 8 AM while doing muscular exercise [he] felt dizzy so went back to barrack & lied [sic] down in bed. Gradually left lower extremity became numb & weak & then left upper extremity became involved. Hemiplegia developed & became semi-conscious. Signature of official [illegible]."[4] A later note indicates that Ishida was not hospitalized until ten days later, on 30 October 1942, with "apoplexy. Paralysis left side of body. . . . Physical condition at the moment fair but general situation is precarious because he will probably suffer another stroke eventually which will likely cause his death. He is helpless to do anything for himself. No civilian nurse could be had for $100 per month. Initialed by Sgt. Turchetti." And on 4 March 1943, the ward surgeon, Major Edwin Rypins, wrote a memo certifying that Ishida "requires a special night nurse," with an added handwritten note: "at the patients [sic] expense" (Ishida Family Collection, n.p.).[5]

To Points North

Conditions at Camp Livingston were apparently so miserable for some of the internees that "after enduring Camp Livingston for about a year, seventeen of the Hawaiian [sic] Japanese internees volunteered for the Kooskia Internment Camp" (Wegars 2010, 16), an experimental work camp located in the "Idaho wilderness" (xix).[6] Although the seventeen were not Issei from my study, I mention them here because they were from the major Hawaiian Islands and represent a variety of occupations (201–213); their story is therefore part of the larger Hawai'i Issei internment narrative. At this "highway construction camp," Japanese civilian internee volunteers were used to construct the Lewis and Clark Highway, arduous and dangerous work for which they were paid fifty-five dollars a month (Okihiro 2013, 236). This work began as a choice and thus reflected some agency for the prisoners, yet the camp shared many of the same characteristics as facilities that were not voluntary, including mail censorship and the regulations of the Geneva Convention.

According to archival lists and personal records, another contingent of internees was sent from Camp Livingston northward twenty-eight hundred miles, to Fort Missoula, Montana, in June 1943, and not reunited with fellow Hawai'i internees in Santa Fe until early April 1944 (Fujii n.d.). Included in this group were Ryosei Aka, Seiichi Fujii, Naojiro Hirano, Masaichi Hirashima, Koichi Iida, Kazumi Matsumoto, Katsuichi Miho, Jinshichi Tokairin, and Ryosen Yonahara—Issei in my study from both Transfer Boats 1 and 2. Why these particular internees were selected is unknown. In a letter to his family in early June, Aka gives his first impressions:

> We were moved to Missoula, Montana, arriving on 6th of June. We left Livingston five o'clock in the morning, and the trip took four days. I am very happy that I had a joyful trip and everything was nice with me.

We still see the snow on the mountain tops near our camp. It is a very beautiful sight which I never saw before in my life. (DL, 76)

Several weeks later, on 30 June 1943, he provides more details about the camp's location to his son Lee: "Now, I am living northern part of America, near Canada. Our camp is surrounded by the Rocky Mountains and the city of Missoula is . . . about two miles away from our camp. We are able to see the neon signs in Missoula City.—These phenomena are [a] comfort [to] us in the day and night" (80).

It is possible that Aka includes such details in this letter because it is an uncensored draft, but it is also possible that rules restricting specific topics had been relaxed to some extent by summer 1943.[7] In contrast to the harsh treatment of mainland Issei at Fort Missoula during the early months of the war, witnessed by Rev. Fukuda of San Francisco (1990) and discussed by Kashima (1991) and Fiset (1997), living conditions for the Hawai'i Issei seem to have been far less contentious. Photos and other writing show that Hawai'i internees at Fort Missoula made their way and lived their lives, posing, like Fujii and Yonahara, for individual photos in deep snow during the Montana winter and forming baseball teams and playing on open fields during warmer weather, as did Matsumoto and Miho.

FIG. 4.3. Kazumi Matsumoto and Katsuichi Miho (*row 1, second, sixth from left*) with baseball team, Fort Missoula, Montana, 1943–1944 (courtesy Kazumi Matsumoto).

Although the community surrounding Fort Missoula reflected some anti-Japanese sentiment, along with detractors among federal government officials and the national media, to his credit, French T. Ferguson, the editor of the local *Missoulian,* at least initially urged restraint against racism and hysteria in a 10 December 1941 editorial: "There is no excuse for anti-Japanese hysteria in this part of the United States, far away from the scene of action, removed from any properties or positions of great military importance. There should be no threats or actual violence against harmless Japanese hereabouts. . . . We are not going to win this war by losing our heads" (quoted in Van Valkenburg 1995, 41).

Despite this admirably sane attitude, public opinion toward the Japanese fluctuated from reasonable to hostile. Yet several months after the Hawaiʻi Issei arrived in Missoula, an incident occurred one spring day that restored their faith in Americans: Saiki relates a story by an internee who, with some companions, was permitted to leave the camp to shop in town and discovered the gravestones of fifty Japanese from the early 1900s: "The site of their graves was clean. Someone had mowed the grass, cleared the weeds, and even scrubbed the mold from the tombstones. Later, 24 priests received permission from the camp commander to hold Buddhist services for the deceased. They burned incense at each grave. Their tears fell, not for the young men who had died . . . , but in gratefulness that the town residents had cared for the graves for so many years, and especially now, knowing the ethnic origin of those buried below" (1982, 133). In his memoir, Furuya lists the names of those men, whose ages ranged from eighteen to sixty-three, adding that "the story warmed my heart" (2017, 138).

To Santa Fe

Throughout June 1943, the Hawaiʻi men from the army camps at Livingston and Lordsburg were transferred by train to Santa Fe, New Mexico, and to the Santa Fe Detention Station / Internment Camp (SFDS/SFIC), which was overseen by the Justice Department and administered by the INS and the Border Patrol. Seisaku Aoyagi of Hilo, a relative latecomer to Lordsburg, having been shipped out on 16 September 1942 from Sand Island on the sixth transfer boat, relates basic details of the trip to Santa Fe: "At 6:00 a.m. on [June] 14th I left the Lordsburg camp with 350 compatriots, and under heavy guard of military police, we . . . arriv[ed] at the El Paso, Texas, railway station at 11:15 a.m. We stopped there for about an hour and . . . arrived at the Albuquerque railway station at 5:30 p.m. . . . At about 11:30 p.m. we arrived at the Santa Fe railway station and got off the train. Then we boarded a truck and were taken to the Santa Fe camp under heavy guard" (n.d., 3). My visits to Santa Fe more than half a century later revealed the train station, dating to 1909, appearing much the same as it must have appeared to the Issei: a small stucco building alongside the train tracks, framed by clear azure skies. As I mentioned earlier, however, there was no trace of the concentration camp.

The prison camp site itself, like Camp McCoy, was a former Civilian Conservation Corps camp built in 1933, so buildings were ready-made for large numbers of men and renovated to hold more (Kashima 2003, 110). In fact, barracks were eventually spread out such that the Issei referred to one section as *shitamachi* (downtown) and the other as *uramachi* (uptown). In his memoir, Otani describes Santa Fe as being located on "a high plateau, 5,000 feet above sea level," with the camp itself "at the foot of the mountains about three or four miles north of the town." He continues: "We were surrounded by barb wire.... [T]here was an office, a hospital, eating hall, storage, and over 10 barracks. This was not a desert.... It was a wonderful location.... [T]he air was dry and thin but it was a healthy place" (Otani n.d., 26).

My grandfather wrote to my mother on 24 July 1943 about his first impressions of Santa Fe: "A month ago I moved [to] this new place . . . located in the really best climate. Rain comes often . . . not so hot as [Lordsburg]" (Watanabe 1942–1945).[8] And the next spring, as the war wore on, he writes, "Here there is snow on the high mountains, but it feels as though summer is near. The naked trees have begun to dress themselves in green. But I miss Hawaii, which is always lush and green and the flowers bloom ceaselessly" (12 May 1944),[9] his words in Japanese reflecting the longing of the exile.

In contrast to Fort Missoula, the Hawai'i Issei faced a different reversal in Santa Fe. In mid-March 1942, about four hundred mainland Japanese had arrived as the first wave of internees at the Santa Fe camp. An article from 14 March 1942 in the *New Mexican,* the local newspaper, reports that their arrival was "calmly accepted" by Santa Fe residents, who were assured that the internees were not "dangerous" and who generally "regarded the camp as an asset."[10] By the time of the Hawai'i men's arrival more than a year later, however, the feelings of animosity toward the Japanese had increased, as the news of the Bataan Death March in the Philippines in April 1942 reached the southwestern towns, home to many members of the New Mexico National Guard, some of whom had been victims of Japanese military brutality. In fact, this reaction was the result of American confusion and conflation of the Japanese enemy with the Issei "alien enemies." INS official Jerre Mangione relates a situation that he encountered on a visit to the SFIC in 1943: "I had barely arrived when a three-member committee representing the two thousand Japanese in the all-male camp presented Loyd H. Jensen, the camp commander, with a petition asking that the barbed-wire fence

FIG. 4.4. Internee group, SFIC. *Left to right: row 2:* Rev. Chikou Odate (*1*), Matsujiro Otani (*7*), and Rev. Kenjyo Ohara (*8*) (courtesy Otani Family Collection).

FIG. 4.5. Detail of Santa Fe Internment Camp painting, color rendered by Rev. Gyokuei Matsuura, SFIC, ca. 1943–1944 (courtesy Matsuura Family Collection).

surrounding the compound be made at least a foot taller. The petition was motivated by the fear that the residents in the surrounding area might become incited by recent reports of heavy American casualties in the Pacific and try again to storm the camp, as they had the year before" (1978, 337).

Regarding tensions within the camp, Rev. Akahoshi, the Buddhist minister and first internee survivor whom I was privileged to interview, related a story of his encounter with my grandfather in Santa Fe, which revealed some of those differing views:

> At a gathering in Santa Fe, a driver for someone appeared half intoxicated and created an incident by throwing his *geta* (wooden clog) at someone who happened to be sitting in front of me. I stood up and grabbed this guy's arm, and escorted him to bed in his barracks. When I returned, I was asked to appear at the office of the person in charge of the group. At that time, Watanabe-san was a witness and said, "You did a good job." This incident was [described] by Mr. Soga as an incident of pro-Japanese against pro-American sentiments in origin. I know that this was not so, and Mr. Watanabe knew that this was written up falsely by Mr. Soga. (2002)

As it turns out, this story from one of my early interviews was the only firsthand recollection of my grandfather that I was able to gather and has become all the more precious to me in strangely actualizing Rev. Watanabe's presence there. I can almost see my tall, thin grandfather quietly praising the younger man so that it still made an impression on him decades later. Rev. Akahoshi's memory of that chance encounter has given me a memory in the sense of Pierre Nora's "phenomenon of the present," cited earlier: "in permanent evolution, subject to . . . remembering and forgetting, . . . and capable of lying dormant for long periods only to be suddenly reawakened" (1996, 3).

CHAPTER 5

In Exile II

Battling "Barbed Wire Disease": Strategies for
Survival and Resistance

As time in any given prison camp increased from days into weeks and months into
years, captivity tested the endurance of even the most stalwart of internees. In the
binder where he kept notes of all sorts and subjects, Naojiro Hirano, the shop
owner from Hawai'i Island, writes, "It has been said that an internee is most likely
to succumb to the discouragement and depression known as 'barbed wire disease'" (1944, n.p.)—this condition being the result of the "unbearable monotony"
that Ozaki described when he was at Fort Sill. "To keep myself out of the disease,"
Hirano continues, "I am participating in many activities at this camp" (n.p.).

And he was certainly not alone. Like Hirano, Rev. Watanabe and his fellow prisoners also developed patterns of life—adapting existing prewar practices and habits
and cultivating new ones, employed even on the transfer boat crossings and in earlier
camps—to help them cope with the isolation and tedium of captivity and feelings of
exile, to ensure that they did not surrender to the overwhelming forces of prison life.

In *Voices of the Vietnam POWs,* Craig Howes illustrates how long-term captives
often employ universal human strategies to cope with the deprivation of freedoms
and the malaise of boredom, citing John Laffin's four main methods: "the physically creative, the physically active, the intellectual, the imaginative" (Howes
1993, 120). To Laffin's methods, I would add spiritual and ritual strategies for survival among the Hawai'i Issei. They employed all of these practices, some of
which, naturally, overlapped; how they employed them was, of course, highly specific to the internees individually and to their culture as Hawai'i Japanese.

While these men felt the oppressiveness and loss of control of wrongful imprisonment, in addition to their using negotiation and the Geneva Convention, I identified their greatest forms of resistance to oppression in their deliberate efforts to
maintain their cultural and personal equilibrium and balance. Such efforts were
supported by the Japanese value of *gaman* (stoicism, internal control, dealing with
adversity with dignity) and an attitude of *shikattaganai,* referring in this context to
a realistic recognition of circumstances and an attempt to cope with them.

As language teachers, Buddhist, Shinto, and Christian clergy, journalists, businessmen, and other leaders of the Hawai'i Japanese communities, many of the Issei were educated and highly literate and understood the significance of the written and spoken word. One internee referred to this unusual gathering as a "cultural heaven," a rare, albeit compulsory, assembly of what I call the immigrant intelligentsia. In a similar vein, my grandfather writes of his appreciation for this stimulating collection of individuals in a letter to my mother: "Every Sunday [a] different minister takes [the] pulpit and deliver[s] a good sermon. So I can get many instructions from various standpoints. Also there are other religious sects holding their meetings according to their principles. So I am learning many things which I can never meet again in my life perhaps" (29 February 1944).

The leadership, intellect, emotions, and creativity of these men were often manifested most profoundly in writing and other forms of cultural literacy performed in the camps, such as theater, music, art, Noh chanting, and funeral services. They used language, Japanese and English, to maintain connections with communities outside the camps, predictably with home, and to create different communities within camp society. I believe these media served not only as forms of expression but also as forms of resistance, both overt and covert. As John J. Culley points out, "The Issei . . . were not just inert material that was acted upon. A behavioural approach would recognise that they were actors who helped shape the internment experience. Their response helped determine what the internment experience would be for themselves at that time, as well as what role it would assume in their lives in later years" (2000, 151).

While noting the "many activities" that Hirano mentions, I have observed a dovetailing of the universal and cultural strategies practiced by the Issei prisoners in this study. As subjective and imperfect as this classification may be, its variety and breadth, as illustrated by the individual narrative examples that follow, nonetheless display the ingenuity of the human spirit under duress.

Physically Creative Activity

Physically creative activity among the internees took both two- and three-dimensional art forms. Two-dimensional art included *shodo,* traditional calligraphy enjoyed by Issei such as Rev. Fujitani, whether he was copying a libretto for a Noh play or adorning a fellow internee's brush painting. It also included painting in a Japanese or Western style, as practiced by Rev. Akahoshi, the Buddhist minister who served as the camp art teacher on occasion. Rev. Akahoshi's family shared with me two of his Western-style paintings, one of the camp buildings, complete with guard tower, barracks, and barbed wire fencing, the other a barrack scene with a potbellied stove in the foreground and men on their bunks in the background. Rev. Fujitani's family shared a Japanese brush painting of vibrant red maple leaves in autumn, also painted by Rev. Akahoshi, on which their father had inscribed a poem:

> Those who renounce the world
> And take refuge in the forest
> Transcend the realm of honor and disgrace.
> —K. Fujitani (n.d., trans. Rev. Y. Fujitani)

So serious and adept were some of these artists in their work that they displayed their creativity in camp art exhibitions to be viewed by fellow internees and camp staff. In one photo, Reverend Ryuten Kashiwa sits and Jinshichi Tokairin stands with their respective paintings in front of a sign, "Exhibition Pictures." And Rev. Akahoshi showed me a guest book for a camp exhibition, which he had saved through the decades, displaying hundreds of his fellow internees' signatures.

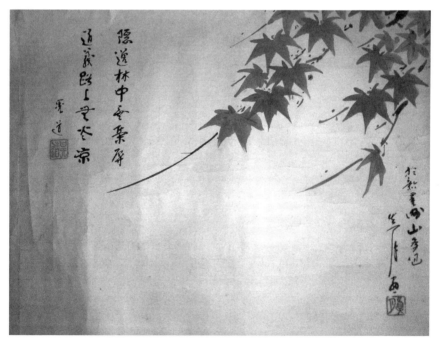

Fig. 5.1. Calligraphy by Rev. Kodo Fujitani, painting by Rev. Shingetsu Akahoshi, probably SFIC (courtesy Fujitani Family Collection).

FIG. 5.2.   Rev. Ryuten Kashiwa and Jinshichi Tokairin (*third, fourth from left*) display their artwork, probably SFIC (courtesy Tokairin Family Collection).

Among the unique traditional art forms that reflect both creativity and imagination based on visual and auditory memory is the *oiwake* in Isoo Kato's internment collection. Originally folk songs by packhorse drivers and fishermen from northern regions of Japan, Kato's *oiwake* consist of lyrics written in the calligraphic style called *sousho* (grass writing) on watercolor paintings of Japanese style and subjects—with some adaptations from the Hawaiian landscape. In one, the artist includes a lauhala tree, typical of island foliage, along with large rocks interrupting ocean waves. These images serve as the background on which the artful and floating *sousho* is written with the following lyrics:

Ukiyo no aranami kogi ide mireba
Adaya orokani sugosarenu
Uku mo shizumu mo mina sono hito no
Kaji no toriyō to kaze shidai

Arai nami demo yasashiku ukete
Kokoro ugokanu oki no ishi
Nami ga kudakenu isobe no tsuki mo
Midare nagara mo maruku naru

Sailing out on the rough sea of transient life
You cannot maneuver your life care-lessly—
Floating or sinking depends on how you steer
And how the wind blows.
Set your mind/heart easily and securely
Like an offshore rock in the ocean unmoved by even rough waves;
The moon reflecting on the shoreline waves, continuously changing
    its shape,
Eventually grows round.
                —Anonymous (n.d., trans. T. Hayashi)

Could these words express the internment life and predicament of the writer and his fellow prisoners and advice on how to cope with them? Suikei Furuya, in his 1964 memoir, *Haisho tenten,* mentions that an *oiwake* club formed at Camp Livingston, the instructor being a Panamanian Japanese, and his first students included Hawai'i Issei such as Otokichi Ozaki (1964, 177–178). It is possible that similar clubs formed at Lordsburg and Santa Fe and that Kato belonged to one of them. Such visual and oral art forms in themselves reflect the profound yet adaptive cultural literacy of the artists.

One of the most prolific Hawai'i Issei artists was George Yoshio Hoshida of Hilo, introduced earlier, who recorded his entire Hawai'i internment experience in pen-and-ink sketches and pastel drawings (Nakano and Nakano 1984, 11)—from the Kilauea Military Camp, where he was first incarcerated, along with my grandfather and other Big Island men, to DOJ and army camps in Hawai'i and the mainland, as well as WRA camps, where he was finally reunited with some of his family. He also served as an art teacher. In my observation, his drawings constitute the best extant visual documents of the daily Hawai'i Issei DOJ internment experience; they create an invaluable visual record of people, places, and activities, for Hoshida often named individuals and dated the events that he was sketching. According to Karin Higa, a curator at the Japanese American National Museum, Hoshida "was fully aware of the importance of recording his experiences through his pen and ink drawings. . . . He drew on loose leaf binder paper that he had requested from his wife upon arrival at Kilauea and carefully compiled the drawings into binders" (1992, 41). Among his most prominent sketches

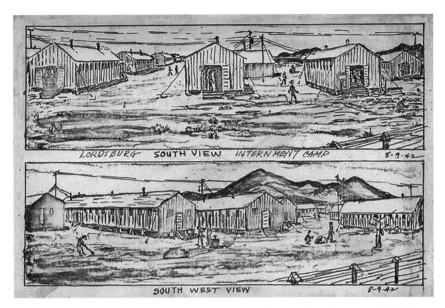

FIG. 5.3. Sketches of Lordsburg Internment Camp, south views, by George Hoshida, Lordsburg, New Mexico, 9 August 1942 (George Hoshida Collection, 97.106.1EK, Japanese American National Museum [Gift of June Hoshida Honma, Sandra Hoshida and Carole Hoshida Kanada]).

are scores of drawings of his fellow internees—their individual portraits with their birthplaces; addresses in Hawai'i, the mainland, or elsewhere; occupations; ages; and signatures, all in each man's handwriting. As I described earlier, Hoshida's grandniece Marcia Mau discovered and shared my grandfather's portrait with me in the early days of my project and helped to launch my study. It became compelling evidence at the time of a somewhat distant reality.

Physical creativity also took less traditional, though no less inspired, forms: the three-dimensional shell and coral art that brought some beauty and ingenuity to the bleakest of tent camps at Sand Island; Ryosen Yonahara's photo album decorated with pressed wildflowers; and Kazumi Matsumoto's intricate plaited purses and cigarette cases of longleaf pine needles from Camp Livingston, Louisiana. During my interview with him, Matsumoto brought out a box filled with purses of different sizes, one as large as a briefcase, made with a braiding technique that he had learned as a child in Hiroshima. The plaited strands were stitched together with incredible precision and patience into functional art. Rev. Matsuura also mentions to his wife in a 21 December 1942 letter, written in English, that he "completed a nice purse which was made from pine leaves." During

FIG. 5.4. Internee coral and rock art (photo no. 137298, W-HD-[1-13-42]-A; "Designs made by the Japanese Internees around their tents, Sand Island, Honolulu, TH," 13 January 1942; Records of the U.S. Signal Corps, RG 111 SC; NACP).

FIG. 5.5. Album page with family photos, pressed flowers, and stamps of Taos Pueblo by Ryosen Yonahara, probably SFIC (courtesy Yonahara Family Collection).

Fig. 5.6. Longleaf pine needle craftwork by Kazumi Matsumoto, Camp Livingston, Louisiana, 1942–1943 (author's collection).

an interview with me, a daughter of internee Ryosei Aka brought out examples of plaited purses made by her father, who accompanied Matsumoto and Rev. Matsuura on Transfer Boat 2 and then was with Matsumoto throughout their internment at Fort Missoula and finally Santa Fe. I wondered who taught whom or if they all had brought the skill with them from their childhood homes.[1]

The old cardboard box labeled with the telling words "Enemy Concentration Camp Lordsburg," mentioned earlier, contained numerous found wood objects that had attracted my grandfather's eye. Some, he must have found recognizably animal-like, with a head, four legs, and a tail, while others were more naturally abstract; some were varnished or polished, others in a natural state. In a letter to my mother on 8 October 1942, he tells her about creating "handiworks from Sagebrush," which he displayed at an "art exhibition in my camp," calling collecting "a good merriment." A few months later he refers to collecting and pressing Lordsburg flowers—probably quite rare in the desert—which he sent to her

(1 February 1943), and "carved Lordsburg wood work and stones," sent to my uncle (7 April 1943). Later that year, in Santa Fe, he mentions varnishing his "own [hand]made wooden curios" (16 August 1943). Rev. Fujitani also found petrified wood pieces that he fashioned into bookends and polished, which are still in the possession of his family. And Alfred Cardinaux of the International Red Cross notes that "the internees make a great number of objects of wood, especially small low tables which . . . are very pretty and the internees send them as presents to their families and to friends" (1942, 9).

As for rock collecting, which was apparently a favorite pastime for internees, INS official Mangione describes a humorous theatrical sketch performed in his honor during one of his visits to Santa Fe:

> The . . . presentation was pure farce, a spoof that demonstrated the prisoners' ability to laugh at themselves. The war has ended and as the curtain rises we see two Japanese returning from an internment camp, lugging heavy valises. Their wives receive them with shouts of joy that become even more jubilant when they are told that the valises are filled with presents for them. On opening them, the wives find they contain nothing but rocks that the husbands had collected during internment. The curtain falls as the disgusted women begin pelting the men with the rocks. There was . . . wild applause for this sketch. As [someone] pointed out, the audience could easily identify with this theme since rock collecting was the favorite camp hobby. (1978, 340–341)

In an interview with me, a daughter of Jinshichi Tokairin recalled that her father had brought home "lots of rocks" and felt insulted by his family's making fun of his treasures, verifying the message of the skit. In one of his letters, my grandfather mentions finding "a good sized Quartz in my camp yard," one he polished for about two weeks. "But dear Sumi," he writes to my mother, "stone polishing is very hard work, because many people like to start it but quit it before long. But character building," he moralizes, "is the most hard work" (14 August 1944).

Physical Activity

Although the median age in the internment camps is said to have been fifty to fifty-five, many men sought to remain physically active, participating in organized sports, such as baseball, boxing, sumo, golf, and tennis. At Fort Missoula, both Matsumoto and Miho played for the Hawai'i team in the baseball league (see photo, chap. 4) and reportedly won the camp championship during their imprisonment there. One photo shows the whole team wearing ball caps sporting an *H,* while another captures a different group of teammates wearing sweatshirts with *Aloha* emblazoned on the front. For some of the internees, participation in such organized sports was a new experience. In another photo, both Iida and Yonahara are seated with boxing gloves on the floor in front of them, and in yet another, Rev. Ohara is pictured holding a tennis racket. There were also regular chores such as KP, washing, and latrine duty that kept them busy and active. In a small notebook that he kept while he was the captain of his barrack, Rev. Watanabe notes that he and/or his barrack have KP more than forty times over the course of a year. On 7 September 1944, he writes: "K.P. Morning washed pans, afternoon washed pots, evening washed pans" (1944–1945, 5b–20b). Kawasaki also mentions it in his scrapbook; it was apparently a democratic duty.

Hiking was tremendously popular, for obvious reasons. As the conflict wore on, camp rules in Santa Fe were relaxed, and groups were allowed to go beyond the camp borders. In his pocket notebook, my grandfather writes that he "went to the mountains from 1 p.m. to 4:00" on 26 September 1944, and again on the afternoon of 1 October, as well as on 4 February the next winter (Watanabe 1944–1945, 14a, 15b). A photo captures a group of men, including Matsujiro Otani, after they arrived at the Cross of the Martyrs several miles from the Santa Fe camp site. It is clearly winter, as they are bundled up to their ears and the first row of men in the photograph is kneeling in snow. In modern-day Santa Fe, I found it is no small feat finding this huge stone cross obscured by condominiums, but in the 1940s it was a landmark "commemorat[ing] the deaths of the 21 Franciscan friars at the hands of the Pueblo Indians in the revolution in . . . 1680," a native effort "to regain control of their homeland" from Spanish colonialists (Anders 1996). I wondered if the hikers appreciated the irony of their being prisoners in temporary freedom at the foot of a monument to colonials killed by those whom they had colonized.

Gardening and farming, both physically active and physically creative tasks, no doubt allowed the gardeners and farmers some tangible satisfaction during their captivity. Reports from the internees themselves and local observers as well as official sources verify the Issei to be "expert" productive gardeners. Rev. Matsuura writes to his wife about the "many kinds of beautiful flowers planted by my brother Gempei . . . in full bloom in front of our barrack" in Camp Livingston, Louisiana (18 October 1942). Otani notes that there were many farmers among them in Lordsburg, some of whom "went outside and started farming, planting melons, watermelons, vegetables, and fruits and the produce [was] excellent. . . . It surprised our Caucasian guards how resourceful we were" (n.d., 25), especially because the desert soil had seemed to be so unproductive. In the report of his visit to Lordsburg in late November 1942, Cardinaux of the International Red Cross observes:

FIG. 5.7. Koichi Iida and Ryosen Yonahara (*row 1, first, second from right*) with boxing group, Fort Missoula, Montana, 23 January 1944 (courtesy Yonahara Family Collection).

Gardening is the principal occupation of the internees. On the land, which is difficult to cultivate, they have laid out striking decorative gardens and very fertile vegetable gardens. . . .

The internees have laid out a very beautiful rock garden in a courtyard of the hospital. There is mostly cactus and a kind of small palm which they found in the vicinity of the camp. Nearly every barracks has its small flower garden. Vegetable gardens in which the vegetables grow so fast that the officers of the camp are astonished lie between the barracks. The internees manifest an unceasing zeal in their efforts to impart a more pleasant aspect to their camp which previously lacked all vegetation. (7)

In Santa Fe, my grandfather records in his notebook on 24 August 1944 that he received a cucumber from Miho Yoshida (Watanabe 1944–1945, 14a). Seiichi Fujii, who had a passion for plants and horticulture before the war, appears in a group photo of the "College of Horticulture, Santa Fe D.S., New Mexico 1944," documenting the widespread interest in the subject among his fellow internees.

Fɪɢ. 5.8. Hikers, including Matsujiro Otani (*kneeling, far left*), at the Cross of the Martyrs, Santa Fe, New Mexico, ca. 1943–1945 (courtesy Stanley Toyama).

Creative/Physical/Imaginative Activities

According to various reports, among the most popular forms of entertainment were live theater performances on stages built by the internees in different camps. In Lordsburg, Cardinaux notes that by late November 1942, "the internees have built an outdoor stage" (6), where a small acting group performed nearly every day before dinner. In June of the next year, Cardinaux writes, "This stage is decorated with much taste and the internees showed [him] the large collection of costumes which they had made" (1943, 2). In Santa Fe, photographs and Hoshida's sketches show the theater as a separate building that faced a large open area for expanding or contracting audiences. By July 1944, the State Department representative notes that "outdoor theatricals are presented fortnightly or perhaps three times each month" (Eberhardt 1944, 2). Reflecting the physically creative, physically active, and imaginative strategies, theatrical performances provided great satisfaction for both the performers and their audience, who practiced the Japanese custom of giving sponsorships to their favorite actors. A photo shows strips on which were written barrack numbers and names of individuals from that barrack who were inspired to support a particular actor. Mangione reports that "the camp's acting company . . . was the most popular of the camp's cultural activities; not even the movies were as well attended. Many of the actors were professionals; several had been in Hollywood movies. The theater group was held in such high esteem by all the prisoners that by common consent the actors who played female roles were exempted from all menial camp chores that might roughen their hands" (1978, 339–340).

Kazumi Matsumoto did not recall such exceptionalism when I questioned him, but for at least one *shibai* (play, performance) in 1945, undoubtedly in Santa Fe, he learned to play an *onnagata* (woman's role) in a Japanese theater tradition in which men, as a rule, played all roles, including those of women. In the same photo, he sits demurely among elaborately costumed lords, ladies, and warriors, wearing headdresses and kimonos that the internees had made themselves, together with the *gidayu* (narrator/singer), who chanted to the accompaniment of a shamisen player. In this case, the narrator is Itsuo Hamada, from Maui, who, as Rev. Fujitani remembers, both directed and performed in community theater groups in Pa'uwela before the war (Y. Fujitani 2004). Hamada wrote a play at Camp Livingston, according to Saiki (1982, 104), and served as a director of the SFIC theater group, appearing in numerous photos.

Fig. 5.9. Theater performance with Kazumi Matsumoto (*seated on dais, far right*) and Itsuo Hamada (*at lectern*), SFIC, 1945 (courtesy Kazumi Matsumoto).

Fig. 5.10. Theater group, including Muneo Kimura (*row 3, with hat*), Itsuo Hamada, and Kazumi Matsumoto (*back row, second, fourth from right*), SFIC, 1945 (courtesy Kazumi Matsumoto).

As popular as such historical/period pieces were, so also were the variety shows in which the internees performed skits or the hula, reflecting their acculturation into island culture. In summer 1944, my grandfather reported to my mother: "Other day we enjoyed dramatic performances. Some acted very splendidly. And in the middle of this month, I saw Bon festival dances just as we saw in Hawaii . . . but all dancers are old folks, so the view is entirely different from Hawaii's" (22 July 1944).

As Mangione mentions, the movies were outdone by theatrical performances in popularity and attendance. To enhance the experience of the American movies for the internees, Muneo Kimura, who had run the Nippon and Kokusai movie theaters in Honolulu, served as the *benshi,* where he assumed the speaking roles of various characters after translating the English dialogue into Japanese. My interview with his family members and research by Chie Gondo reveal that after Kimura immigrated to Hawai'i, he worked as a laborer on a plantation but wanted to be an actor and performed with a group at temples in Honolulu before there was a theater building. He soon became a *benshi* in the era of silent movies and toured many of the plantation camps. With the advent of talking movies, he shifted his focus to importing Japanese films and other entertainment from Japan (Gondo 2004). But his previous experience as a *benshi* made him a valuable asset to his fellow internees' enjoyment of American films.

In the *utaikai* (chanting societies) sketched by Hoshida, the men in these groups, like my grandfather and Rev. Fujitani, diligently copied *utaibon,* the vocal books or librettos for Noh plays, probably from circulating master copies, sometimes several in a day. Noh theater has been traced back to eighth-century Japan, portraying classical stories in a highly esoteric formal style sometimes compared to classical Greek drama. For some men in Lordsburg and Santa Fe during World War II, this was an absorbing way to pass the time and reflected their high level of cultural literacy. Yasutaro Soga, the journalist and editor of the *Nippu jiji* (Japan Times), so valued this pastime before the war that he "hid a tiny book containing the *noh* song 'Yoroboshi' (Blind Priest)" in one of his pockets on the night of his arrest (2008, 25). Among my grandfather's internment papers, I found an *utaibon* of *Tohsen* and another of *Kurama Tengu,* which he had copied in Lordsburg, while Rev. Fujitani returned with seventy-eight *utaibon,* among them *Takasago, Matsukaze, Funabenkei,* and *Sotoba Komachi.*[2] Soga writes in his memoir that there were "no less than three noh clubs" at Lordsburg (2008, 111). According to Rev. Akahoshi in our conversation that day in Virginia, the *utaikai* performed their chanting not only for themselves but for other internees, and he noted that he had "painted the backdrop for the stage" for one of their performances (2002). Not only were these men practicing an activity that many of them had enjoyed before the war, but in their chanting, I imagine that their voices blended into a single chorus, reinforcing the communal spirit of unity in adversity.

As a granddaughter who had been captivated by the Noh theater decades later, in the 1970s, but also decades before learning of this pastime in the internment camps or my grandfather's great interest in it; who had studied Noh plays and was familiar with such titles as *Matsukaze, Takasago, Funabenkei,* and *Sotoba Komachi;* and who had fleetingly practiced *utai* and *shimai* (Noh dance) in Kyoto, I found an unexpected connection with my grandfather but also a sadly missed opportunity.

Another photo shows a large group of internees who gathered to play the *shakuhachi* (Japanese flute), including Kazumi Matsumoto. When I visited him in his Kaua'i home, he offered to show me one he had made himself in one of the camps, but we ran out of time, and I told him I would return and see him again. Sadly, he died four weeks later, and the fate of his *shakuhachi* is unknown.

Spiritual and Ritual Activities

Accounts by internees and photos from internee families reflect another cultural strategy that aided the Issei prisoners' survival in confinement: spiritual and ritual activities, especially funeral or memorial services for those who died during internment, for friends and spouses of internees who had passed away elsewhere, and for family members, particularly sons in the military who had been killed in action. For the camp community, these services—rituals of mourning—were conducted with great deliberation and deliberateness, manifesting the internees' careful attention to custom, exercising their cultural literacy to the last detail. Some services were more elaborate than others, complete with handmade wreaths and ribbons announcing the donor(s) and scores, sometimes hundreds, of mourners.

A most unusual phenomenon in the DOJ/army internment camps was the large representation of men of the cloth—Buddhist priests, Shinto priests, Christian ministers—there because the authorities considered them "potentially dangerous." They attended these services as Japanese men, some officiating, some in attendance in the audience, participating in services across faiths, paying their respects to the deceased, all locked up together. Besides his barrack photo, my mother found her father in several of these large group photographs from other families, affirming his presence and participation in the internee community.

Three technically exceptional images, considering their survival over so many decades, depict the funerals of Nizo Nishizaki, Reverend Kinzaemon Odachi, and Hiroshi Tahara, all of Hawai'i Island. In the service for Nizo Nishizaki on 24 July 1943, his soldier son stands behind his father's casket, along with at least twenty-two Buddhist priests in full regalia and hundreds of other men in attendance. This photo became iconic in the 1990s in the SFIC Historical Marker Committee's efforts to establish a historical marker above the site of the original internment camp. As noted earlier, the issue of the marker was extremely contentious within the Santa Fe community, and the photo, published with an article by Thomas Chávez, may have played a role in humanizing the men imprisoned there.

Similar in scope and poignancy to the Nishizaki service is the funeral probably of Rev. Odachi, a Tenrikyo priest, who was on Transfer Boat 3 along with George Hoshida and my grandfather. Tenrikyo is a sect of Shinto, and the photo captures a number of Tenrikyo priests standing behind the casket, with hundreds of men and the internee-built theatrical stage at SFIC in the background. Mrs. Odachi and the couple's four young children had been removed from Hilo to the Jerome WRA camp in Arkansas, where they awaited reunification with Rev. Odachi, but according to Hoshida, while they waited, he became critically ill in Lordsburg in March 1943 (Hoshida and Hoshida 2015, 166). His wife was notified and was able to take their oldest and youngest children from Arkansas to New Mexico to visit him in the camp hospital for a few days (167, 175–176), but his middle daughter, June Odachi Shigemasa, who was seven at the time, told me that she never saw her father again (2007). He died on 21 October 1943, a few months after being moved to the Santa Fe Internment Camp; his ashes were sent to the family in Jerome (Hoshida and Hoshida 2015, 208–210).

FIG. 5.11. Buddhist funeral service for Nizo Nishizaki attended by his son Ogden (*center*), SFIC, 24 July 1943. *Left to right: row 1:* Rev. Ryuten Kashiwa (*2*), Rev. Kodo Fujitani (*5*), Rev. Kenjyo Ohara (*11*), Ichiji Kinoshita (*18*) (courtesy Kinoshita Family Collection).

FIG. 5.12. Tenrikyo funeral service, probably for Rev. Kinzaemon Odachi, SFIC, October 1943 (courtesy Kato Family Collection).

After the war, Rev. Odachi's wife carried the precious urn with his ashes back to Hilo, but June told me another story related to the infamous tidal wave of 1946 that took the life of Craig Hirashima's father: To the Odachi family's great distress, the tidal wave washed the urn away, and they thought it was lost forever. Miraculously, however, it appeared intact in someone's basement! The name on the urn was announced on the local radio station, allowing the family to reclaim it (Shigemasa 2007).

Hiroshi Tahara passed away on 31 August 1945 at the SFIC, soon after the war's end but several months before the main body of internees had been returned to Hawai'i. Described by Otokichi Ozaki as being "once renowned throughout Hawai'i," he "became seriously ill during his internment and was confined to bed" (2012, 33). Though attendance at his service was relatively modest, the photograph captures the regard that the internees and others had for this man, not only in its solemnity but in the eight wreaths displayed at the event. According to the ribbons attached to the wreaths, they were from different groups, among them Japanese language educators from Hawai'i, the Soto Buddhist congregation, Hilo City, hospital staff members, and friends from Pāpa'ikou, Hawai'i.[3]

Photos of funeral services such as these were taken in the SFIC *kinen ni* (in commemoration of the event), but for descendants like me they serve as powerful statements regarding the internees' control over the significant events of their lives and the respect extended to them by their captors, who allowed such gatherings according to the statutes of the Geneva Convention.

As for my grandfather, Rev. Watanabe continued his ministry from the beginning of his imprisonment, conducting services at the Kilauea Military Camp, where he was first detained in December 1941. He tells the interrogators at his hearing: "About 65 brothers come every afternoon and we study in the Bible. I offer prayer[s]" (OPMG 1942c, 10). If he was arrested as a leader in his community, he ironically maintained his role in full view of the authorities. Through his internment papers, I learned that he and other Christian ministers continued to conduct church services and prayer meetings throughout their incarceration. Rev. Ohara, one of the Buddhist priests whom I interviewed, made the comment that the Christians were "more organized" (2003). In letter after letter to my mother, Rev. Watanabe refers to current or future sermons and to biblical passages that he considered quoting or drawing from in his addresses, as if he were rehearsing his thoughts with her. In the 1943 directory of internees at Santa Fe, he is listed as the "chairman" of the Santa Fe Christian Church and took his turn in various services. His letters reflect how central this mission was to his identity, life, and sense of purpose.

My grandfather and his fellow Christians apparently also wrote play scripts, such as "An Evening in Bethlehem," presumably a play for the Christmas season. In other letters to my mother, he mentions that in Lordsburg in 1942, "we had a good Christmas exercise and had a play of prodigal son [who] came back to father," and then asks her from Santa Fe, "if you found out a good play for old folks please send it as soon as possible" (2 October 1943). In his next letter, on 15 November 1943, he writes in exasperation, "Sumi, really it is very hard a request to get Christmas play of old men. So we decided to play the same play which [we had] last year," likely "The Prodigal Son." In addition to Christian activities, many Issei participated in Buddhist festivities such as Hanamatsuri, honoring the birthday of the Buddha, as occurred at Camp McCoy.

Despite their various geographical paths and locations, the Hawai'i Issei and their fellow prisoners resisted complete domination by authorities and created distinct subcommunities around the "many activities" mentioned by Hirano to battle "barbed wire disease." They thus promoted not only the activity but, more important, the camaraderie of those with an old, or in some cases new, interest, thereby ensuring the internees' mutual survival. As these were among the most literate men of their home communities on O'ahu, Maui, Kaua'i, Hawai'i, and other islands, perhaps it is not surprising that much of their time would be occupied by artistic, intellectual, and religious activities, but their belief in their intellect and the literal power of words is even more clearly demonstrated by the literacy acts described in the following chapter.

CHAPTER 6

In Exile III
Literacy and Surviving Captivity

Ironically, a primary way that the Hawai'i internees survived their long captivity was their use of the very intellect, imagination, and literacy that had resulted in their imprisonment in the first place—that had made them leaders in their communities and therefore a seeming threat to "national security." Personal, private, intimate acts, such as the writing of letters, journals, notebooks, diaries, and poetry, principally benefited the individual and his family and friends; public acts, including the writing (and publishing) of newsletters, petitions, rosters, and sermons, were aimed at the collective welfare of the larger internee community. Further examples and more detailed analyses of personal and public expression from Hawai'i's Issei serve as compelling evidence of John Culley's claim regarding the internees' assertive role in shaping their experience, and their formidable awareness of language in its various forms.

Surviving Captivity: Personal Writing

Because of government censorship regulations, personal correspondence was generally limited in length to one page or one side of a postcard or sheet of government stationery and in content by government rules.[1] In 1942, while still at Sand Island, Kango Kawasaki wrote to his daughter, "We got back our pens & much easier to write now"; about "new rules" for outgoing mail, he told her, "2 letters, 1 p. each, 24 lines, per wk."[2] Kato describes in his journal how essential letters to and from home were to the prisoners—and the government restrictions on content:

> We spend free time writing diaries or letters to families. . . . We are allowed letters only to and from families and relatives and written only in English. Restrictions were numerous such as there should be no mention of names, or numbers of people, and definitely nothing about our prison conditions to the outside world. Any violation meant confiscation of the letter or censorship, or sometimes [being] returned to the sender to be re-written. . . . Letters, after having been received and read, cannot be

kept in our hands but must be submitted to them. No books or printed material was allowed and absolutely no Japanese word should be used in letters. They were especially strict about that. . . .

The opportunity to send letters to families twice a week is the most important thing to us all. To hear from our families twice weekly is the most exciting and certainly the brightest moment of our camp life. (n.d., 19, 22)

But letter writing, especially in the early days of internment, when suspicion was high and restrictions were many, was fraught with problems for many Issei because of language issues. Despite a mandate in the Geneva Convention of 1929 that clearly states, "With respect to contact with the outside world during their captivity, individuals must be allowed to send and receive letters and postcards in their native language" (Fiset 2001, 24), executing the law proved to be another matter. After receiving a precious letter from his family, Kato writes:

Last night my mind was filled with thoughts of my family. I could not sleep. Today I am anxious to write a reply. I sit prepared with paper and pen and wait for my friend . . . to write for me when he is free. I could easily express my thoughts in Japanese, but an important letter such as this to be written for me by someone else is frustrating and painful. I cannot ever forget this helplessness I feel. At my age I cannot even begin to think of mastering the English language. My friend is kind and he writes for me. He is thorough and asks for clarification. As I reply I tremble with emotion and fill up with tears. With mustered courage I tell him what I can, but that is not what I truly feel. How can I ever forget this feeling of inadequacy and frustration! For the rest of my life I shall remember this. . . .

Oh, the joys of hearing from my family! But the futile reply I send with lead-weighted heart is something that is impossible to put into words with my lips or even with the pen. (n.d., 23–24)

Conversely, from that "friend's" view, the bilingual George Hoshida writes from Lordsburg on 14 September 1942 of his task as writer/interpreter/translator of others' thoughts and words:

Have changed ink for my pen today. There's a little history behind it. The black ink which I had been using was purchased at Texas Sam Houston Internment Camp a couple of days after reaching there by Mr. Kagawa. He had given custody of the ink in my hands for me to help people correspond with their families. It has served us very well until yesterday. There is a bit left, perhaps enough for 2 or 3 fillings, at my desk in our barrack.

I have written a lot of letters with it for myself and others. Perhaps more for others because letters had to be written in English and practically all the people in the barrack couldn't write in English. I also had to read and interpret their letters from home. The letters to their families must have gladdened the hearts of many when they received the papers which the ink had turned into affectionate letters. These letters have traveled for thousands of miles, and if they were alive, what stories of joys, sorrows, and longings they could have revealed. A bottle of ink, just ten cents in money, but its work cannot be figured in money. . . . It has carried messages from hearts to hearts and created emotions which cannot be fathomed materially. (n.d., 327–328)

Hoshida's empathy for his fellow internees and his full appreciation of the power of the ink reflect not only the sensitivity of his perceptions but also the depth of his analysis.

Whether in translated, halting, or fluent English or in Japanese (here in English translation), as restrictions relaxed, internees' voices reflected their varying personalities, circumstances, and outlooks on life. Rev. Matsuura, the Soto Zen minister whom I interviewed (2003), was a young man with a young family and was a prolific letter writer. His postcard written in English to his wife from Camp Livingston reflects a need to reassure, spare his family of worry, and maintain hope—hence the references to familiar and heartwarming details as well as attempts at gentle humor:

Oct. 18, 1942

My darling wife Masue:

Today is very fine day. The right gentle wind is blowing through the pine forest. . . .

Yesterday, I made three lovely wooden slippers after I wrote a letter to you. Do you guess for what these are? Yes, there are my Christmas presents for our darling Phoebe Chii-chan and Yoshinao-chan, and . . . another is Hatsu-chan's father's gift for her.

Now-a-day, I can not help without writing to you even if it is a clumsy English letter so just like as a love letter of sweetheart! Ha-ha-ha!

Well, I'll write you again. Please give my deepest love to Phoebe and my most cordial wishes and best regards to Mrs. Kokuzo, Hamada, our parents and all.

> With much love, your husband
> Gyokuei Matsuura

Fig. 6.1. Rev. Gyokuei Matsuura (*row 2, far right*) and Buddhist ministers, SFIC (courtesy Matsuura Family Collection).

But letters were more or less censored. Because of slow mail service or letters being rejected or being returned by censors, Rev. Matsuura had to rewrite a letter in December that he had written a month earlier from Camp Livingston, a letter concerning his wife's health:

December 24, 1942

My dearest wife,

Now-a-day, our registered letters were [words excised] by the government. I'm sorry [long excised section]. I'm going to write you again the same letter of Nov. 28. [excised section] received your two letters of Oct 2 and 14. I was surprised to know that you were operated on Oct 3. I've never known about it until to-day because Mrs. Kokuzo's letter doesn't reach us yet. Anyway, I'm so glad to know about your operation through your own writing. I'm indeed so surprised that I've been trembl[ing] with your letter when I read down your every word, but my heart was calmed down little by little to find out that you were saved from the serious condition and recovering so fast. Really, I'm filled with tears when I thought how you felt lonesome without Phoebe and [me] when you laid down on the operation table.

Censorship, in addition to ill-timed mail, must have added to the anxiety of internees who, like Rev. Matsuura, had families in distress. As Fiset points out, "Not only were words, phrases, sentences, and even whole paragraphs excised from both incoming and outgoing letters, but also the mere presence of the censor inhibited letter writers, who practiced self-censorship to avoid the possibility that their correspondence would not be forwarded or that they would lose their letter-writing privileges altogether" (1997, 103).

In my mother Sumi's collection is a total of thirty-five letters from my grandfather, eight from Lordsburg (Barrack B4, 17 August–30 November 1942; and Barrack B13, 18 January–26 May 1943) and twenty-seven from Santa Fe (Barrack 64, 25 June 1943–8 March 1945; and Barrack 4, 5 April–20 July 1945). Rev. Watanabe managed to avoid the censors' principal red flags, as his topics tended to revolve around limited subjects, such as his concern for his family's health and well-being, as well as their correspondence with him; his Christian church duties, activities, and learning; and his hobbies and pastimes. Although he refers to writing letters to my grandmother and his two sons, he seemed to manage about one letter a month to my mother, most of them written in English, each acknowledging her letters and the "clipper stamps" that she had enclosed. On 16 August 1943, two months after arriving in Santa Fe, he describes his average day there: "Every morning before breakfast I have exercise with my barrack group and read Bible one chapter each time. I use my best effort for my sermon. Then read books and magazines for my work."

Perhaps most astonishing—and touching—to me, however, is that his letters from both Lordsburg (after December 1942) and Santa Fe reveal his involvement in my birth and my growth, an intimate relationship about which I had no knowledge. The first time I read these letters, I realized that he wasn't at all absent from my childhood, despite the geographical distance, his unwarranted incarceration, and my loss in not having had this grandfather present.[3] He approved of my Japanese middle name, Yukie, commenting in his halting English that "the sound is very nice as for a girl's name" (1 February 1943). After not receiving mail from my mother for several weeks in Lordsburg, he writes on 26 May, "I am worried about your health and baby Yukie and all your family members. Please write to me how you are getting along," his anxiousness being a natural response for someone who had lost his youngest child in 1922 and who was now isolated from his family. Through his comments on my baby pictures, I learned how engaged he was in my earliest years: "I do not hear Yukie's voice, but I get used to see her picture [on] my desk. Her innocent face attracts me from the bottom of my heart. Now in my old age I feel I could understand more why Jesus loved a small child" (26 May 1943).

A few months later, from Santa Fe, he begins referring to me by my English name: "Gail is very happy to grow nicely day by day. I have now received eleven of her pictures. They show a good process of her growth" (2 October 1943). (My father, who took many photos of his first child, also undoubtedly tried to compensate for his father-in-law's forced absence from his first granddaughter.) When I was about eighteen months old, he wrote in Japanese: "Gail holding the head of the wooden horse with her tiny hand and grasping some candy in her left hand . . . is a great picture. . . . She seems very healthy, and that is good" (12 May 1944, trans. Rev. Y. Fujitani). A few weeks later, he writes, "Your writing [about] Gail is very interesting because I can see how lovely she is growing day by day. I hope she will grow without any mishap" (27 June 1944), the last wish laden with his own loss. A year later, he comments in Japanese on two more snapshots: "Gail has really grown, hasn't she? Just like the photo of Sumi taken in Stockton, Gail looks exactly like Sumi when you were little. I'm happy to know that she will be going to kindergarten in September" (6 June 1945, trans. Rev. Y. Fujitani).

Kango Kawasaki's letters to his daughter, Sumie, a college student, are particularly animated, reflecting his native command of English (1942–1943). Upon his departure to the mainland, he writes to her on 23 May 1942:

> When Peace returns someday, I'll be seeing you and ma in good spirits. In the meanwhile, keep your head up, old girl, and continue smiling. That's my last wish before departure. Be strong & cheerful. I can "take it" and will not whimper, nor will you!
> "Adios!" then, to you & ma, Nero & Ichikawa families.
> Your ever loving Dad,
> Kango Kawasaki

Some letters in Kawasaki's collection appear to have been returned, rejected by the censor, but they provide us with an insight into disallowed information during particular periods in particular camps. In March 1943, Form 1603 is attached to a letter from Lordsburg written in English to Kawasaki's daughter at the University of Hawai'i, a slip with a checklist of four different reasons that verify his fellow internee Kato's description of mail regulations:

> This communication is returned to camp authorities because it reveals the details checked below:
> _____Identity of other internees.
> _____Number of internees.
> _____Transfer of internees.
> __X__Description of camp.

This 20 March 1943 letter was disallowed because Kawasaki provides a "description of camp" in answering Sumie's question about his daily life:

> How I spend my day? Here it is: I am mayor of Co. 5, (250 men from Alaska, Hawaii & U.S.). Also Lt. Gov. of (Compound) K 2; also English teacher, night school 2t per wk: [unreadable, covered with censor's note] self-Govt. in camp, electing barrack captains (8), & mayor (1) for each co. 3 or 4 cos. (Elect Gov. & Lt. Gov.) 3/20: Sunrise: 7:30, sunset 19:00, breakfast 7 (quite dark) lunch 12:00, supper 17:00. No blackout: Lights out: Sat. 23:00, other days 22:00. For 3/16 my schedule: 6: out of bed, 7: breakfast, 9–10: Mayors' meeting K2, 12: lunch, 12–12:30 Co. 5 Capts' meeting, 13:30: attend Funeral Co. 12, 17: supper, 19–20: night school, 20–22: Round table Conference K2 & K3. 22: to bed. (Of course, not as busy every day.)

This whole section is crossed out by the censor and appears in Kawasaki's collection; however, a few months later, in July, now from Santa Fe, similar information about his daily schedule was allowed, as was the following description of the camp in Santa Fe where they had been relocated: "We overlook the town—nice view @ night. No flowers, no trees within barbed fences. The surrounding hills are sparsely wooded by pines" (July 1943). Only the phrase "no trees within barbed" is circled, presumably by the censor. In another variation on censorship practices, a censor named Uyematsu writes a note, "Please return & cut out circle[d] item[s]," those items being a reference to the posting and receipt of letters from the Territory of Hawaii and about "there being no beer, nor wine, nor any soft drinks" in the canteen (July 1943).

As Sumie Kawasaki was an elementary education student at the University of Hawai'i, it was fitting that her father wrote her some thoughtful—uncensored—words from Santa Fe about her responsibilities as a teacher in the world:

> Dearest Sumi-chan: 12/20 Rec'd your good letter today & was glad to hear you're well & studying hard. Sad news that Kimi-chan became a war widow. War is Hell, indeed, & it is up to the teachers of the world to instill in the young minds of their charges that Love of mankind is the only solution for a peaceful world in the future: uproot racial prejudices, abolish religious intolerance, knock out inordinate national ambitions, cultivate "peace on earth and good-will towards men" of all races, color and creeds. What a mighty duty you, as one, have in the reconstruction of the New World! Put your Soul in the noblest work, dearest girl. (28 December 1943)

How apt this admonition continues to be.

Other forms of personal prose include journals, diaries, memoirs, and note-books, of which I have already provided numerous excerpts. Each piece of writing is a self-assertive act, recording a collective history, as well as an assertion of an individual ego and will.

Kato, as we have seen, records in his journal the details of his arrest and confinement and the agony of separation from his young family. Having the opportunity to write his journal in Japanese, he writes copiously. Such documents may be not only casual jottings but a deliberate record keeping of daily events, staving off the loss of personal memory or control, exerting will and words over time and tedium. Kato's journal concludes as he sets off from Angel Island on his journey of exile; the second half of his memoir consists of 167 letters that he wrote home to his family from 30 June 1942 to 7 September 1945, the uncensored versions translated sometime after his death in 1976 by his wife and daughter Haruko. Each one conveys his devotion to and concern for his family, his encouragement of his wife and children to keep up their coffee farm so that they can remain independent and self-sustaining—and hence safe in Kona—and a reliance on the value of *gaman.*

> May 12, 1945 (#153)
> It is now three years and three months of internment. . . . These days you are often in my dreams. . . . More than anything I wait for letters that say the family is well.
> The war situation is progressively changing. How much longer will it continue? . . . Day in and day out, year in and year out, I feel pressed down with a heavy weight. . . . We were born into this world during this difficult time and met this destiny. This is fate. It is something we have to live through. It takes much courage. . . . We must have courage, stamina, and endurance. Again and again, I pray for all of you to stay strong in mind and body. (n.d., 210–211)

Although he does not write a steady stream of haiku like some of his fellow inmates, Kato's poetry flows easily in and out of his prose, reflecting his complex feelings of the moment:

> August 8, 1945 (#163)
> This is yet another August. Longingly I think of the coffee beans, green berries with red showing here and there. You must be busy making preparations. School will be out in two weeks. I hope the children are enthusiastic about the coming harvest. Coffee is our livelihood and it is an

important industry for Kona. By all means, unite your efforts once again and gambatte kudasai (endure and do your best). . . . I am well as usual. . . .

At early dawn
I scoop my water,
I wonder what the cricket's saying,
He wants me to hear him.
Four years of this dragging trip,
As though in sleep my life's been wasted,
Beloved children beyond the sea,
I wonder if I am remembered.
(n.d., 220–221)

Perhaps one of the highest forms of Laffin's imaginative and intellectual strategies in the camps was a more formal practice of poetry writing. A number of Issei had belonged to poetry writing groups before the war, reflecting this highly refined form of cultural literacy, and they continued the practice during their imprisonment. In writing poetry, whether tanka (five-line Japanese poem), haiku (three-line Japanese poem), or other forms, internees—otherwise stoic men—created powerful expressions of emotion, records of their deepest individual experiences, which could not easily be erased. In the following tanka, Yasutaro Soga, using the pen name Keiho, raises the profound question of memory and remembrance—of the individual friend and, by extension, of the event, of the men who were imprisoned there, of lost years in thousands of lives:

When the war is over
And after we are gone
Who will visit
This lonely grave in the wild
Where my friend lies buried?
(1984, 64)

Rev. Odate, the Higashi Hongwanji minister from Kaua'i, "thought in haiku" when writing in his journal, according to his daughter Reiko (2002), capturing his thoughts and feelings in cryptic three-line images. From the Wailua Military Prison on Kaua'i, where he was first detained, he writes of extreme temperatures affecting his body and soul:

Thrown in prison camp
  Freezing morning weather
  Penetrates deep into my frame.
Warmth in my hands
  Abruptly blocked off by
  Old barbed wire fencing.*

But from the "New Mexico War Concentration Camp (1944)," most likely in Santa Fe, after three years of imprisonment in desert spaces, his images are more searing:

Blood, as well as bones
  Melting down*
  In the scorching sandstorm.
Those locked in the camp
  suffer from sand roughened skin
  drenched with blackening sweat.
Ear-piercing wind
  Sharp as a razor blade
  The moon is thinner than ever.
      —Odate (2000, 15–17, 19)[4]

As Soga explains in his preface to the collection *Kodama,* the Literary Society of Santa Fe brought together like-minded writers, including himself, Rev. Kashiwa, and Rev. Odate. That these Issei published their work and others' in collections such as *Kodama* is testimony to their long-term purpose, one transcending the boundaries of the SFIC's barbed wire.[5] Soga unequivocally states the purpose of the collection to be both cultural and political:

After the onset of World War II, from Alaska in the North to Hawaii in the South, Japanese men from all stations and walks of life were incarcerated in this camp in Santa Fe. Although we are from different backgrounds and situations, we are alike in that we have been forced to abandon our homes, leave our families, and experience the trauma and indignity of living in a prison camp. The Literary Society of Santa Fe, *Santa Fe Bungei Kyokai,* was born in this harsh environment and circumstances. We have bonded in a unique way—to express ourselves in poetry. We have created *kanshi, tanka, haiku, shinko-haiku,* and *senryu.* We decided to call for individual contributions of these types of poems and to publish this collection. The publication of this anthology, *Kodama,* is a demonstration to the world and future generations to come of the true Japanese spirit of *Yamato damashii,* the strong Japanese character of calm in the face of unbearably harsh adversity. It is our hope that this effort will help to establish a peaceful world for future generations. (Soga 1944, n.p., trans. Reiko O. Matsumoto)

Such highly literate men made every effort to maintain their cultural identities and forms principally and deliberately through language.

Kawasaki's scrapbook, cited in chapter 4, records the details of internment life, undoubtedly due to his leadership roles in various camps, his sense of order, and his belief in history. Many pages are carefully typed records affixed to the scrapbook page, accompanied by supporting notes. Even itineraries—such as one by Otani, a businessman; Fujii, a teacher; and my grandfather, a minister—are recordings of time taken in different locations, movement from place to place, information all the more important, considering how little control as prisoners these men had over that movement. Even though they could not know where they were going next, they certainly could keep track of where they had been and when.

In reference to keeping himself "out of [barbed wire] disease," Hirano refers in his notes to "participating in many activities at this camp" and provides a list, reflecting significant cultural variety as well as the talent and interest of the internees themselves:

> English Class—American Institution, Grammer [*sic*], Translation
>   Eng-Japanese, Business English, Personal letter writing
>
> Spanish class—Spanish Grammer [*sic*]
>   Spanish for beginners
>   Spanish for Advanced course
>
> Bookkeeping, Accounting, Accountant
>
> Horticulture, Poultry, Poleontology
>
> Japanese Penmanship
>
> Drawing Orient–Occident
>
> Yokyoku = (Recitation of classic drama)
>
> Gidayu (Operatic Song)
>
> Shakuhachi (Bamboo flute)
>
> Haiku (Short Poem) (1944, n.p.)

FIG. 6.2. Literary Society of Santa Fe members, SFIC. *Left to right: row 1:* Yasutaro Soga (*1*), Rev. Ryuten Kashiwa (*5*); *row 2:* Rev. Chikou Odate (*far right*) (courtesy Reiko O. Matsumoto).

In a letter to my mother, my grandfather also mentions the scope of offerings and their popularity: "In my place there are more than forty courses and sixty or seventy year-old fellows are attending faithfully . . . their favorite classes just as school children" (5 April 1945). He writes about taking music/piano lessons himself. Aka writes to his son Lee Ryoichi: "I will write a few lines about our English class for I think that you would like much to know it. The number of our classmate[s] is about 25 men which consists [of] so many kind[s] of professions: doctor, minister, merchant, *bonsan* (priest), principals and etc. Some of them are over 70 years and their average years is 56 years. Don't laugh [at] our classmate[s], Lee, they are studying hard every day" (DL, 58).

And no doubt as a part of his English practice, Hirano copied some words of practical advice, "The Secret to Longevity," accompanied by translations of some vocabulary into Japanese—all in perfect Palmer method penmanship:

1. First, avoid bad health condition.
   Keep your nutritional apparatus—digestion and elimination—in good working order; guard against endocrine gland upset and against all forms of infection.
2. Secondly, avoid the common mechanism of escape from life and reality. Don't go in for retrospection, dreaming endlessly of the

past, nostalgically yearning for what can never return. Also avoid rigidity, the clinging to the ideas and habits merely because you have had them for a long time[;] such practices carry you backward, mentally, to more primitive intellectual patterns.

3. Avoid a lack of mental exercise.

Don't let your mind get stultified and "rusty." Keep studying, advancing, delving into new fields and sectors of learning[;] you should continue learning new things, exploring new subjects of and practical knowledge to the very end! (1944, n.p.)

And there were the readers. Soga notes, "If you were reading or writing quietly, someone was sure to be reading aloud" (2008, 101). Kawasaki wrote to his daughter early on, asking her to send him "pronto" *Language in Action* and "another good, recent selection of Book of Mo. Club" (7 May 1942).[6] It was at Lordsburg that the internees requested a library; camp libraries eventually contained not only newspapers and magazines for the prisoners to keep up with the events of the outside world but volumes of books as well. Richard Melzer points out that at the SFIC, "Approximately 950 books were donated to the camp by the Japanese Red Cross. Most books were fiction or dealt with religious or philosophical themes" and "were carefully censored to avoid all literature that 'could tend to incite the internees against the [U.S.] Government and its policies'" (1994, 234, 219).

Surviving Captivity: Public Writing

What I have termed *public writing* encompasses literacy acts for the collective welfare of the internee community, informational and organizational documents such as the camp directory. All handwritten in Japanese, with stencils cut for mimeographing, these directories were great undertakings and represent the will of the internees to record information on each man: his name, *honseki* (origins in Japan), U.S. address, age, occupation, and the location of his family. Those elected barrack chiefs maintained rosters like one I found by Rev. Watanabe, who kept records of his barrack mates; because the information is the same as that in the directory, I surmise that these rosters were the basis for the camp directory. Such directories were sometimes decorated with a pen-and-ink floral sketch on the cover, which some internees chose to paint or decorate further, as in one by Aisuke Kuniyuki.

FIG. 6.3. Barrack 64 roster cover by Rev. Tamasaku Watanabe, SFIC, 1944 (Tamasaku Watanabe Collection).

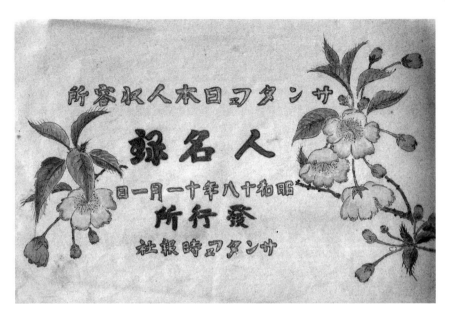

FIG. 6.4. Master roster cover, decorated using watercolors, by Aisuke Kuniyuki, SFIC, November 1943 (courtesy Kuniyuki Family Collection).

This collection of biographical data on the inmates, hundreds in a given year, reflects a formidable degree of organization, management, and control—and resistance. Because the directories were written in Japanese, they were clearly not for the benefit of the authorities but for the internees themselves, further reflected by the fact that they were found in the collections of different families. The significance of this undertaking was clearly not lost on the internees, as Kafu Koyama, the head of the Santa Fe Review Office, writes regarding the "Circumstances of Publishing This Directory" in November 1943: "When human beings join hands and move their feet, it is always because there is some purpose. However, we were an animal rare in this world that traveled without knowing our destination. That such as we were able to publish a directory at the Lordsburg internment camp in this same state of New Mexico and again were able to publish this directory at this detention station [Santa Fe] is believed by us personally to be a great accomplishment" (n.p.). This 1943 directory listed two Big Island men, Kango Kawasaki and Ichiji Adachi, as the incoming manager of general affairs and spokesman, and the clerk, respectively. The directory also reflects the self-government ensured by the Geneva Convention.

Similar in intent, though not in scope, was the "Kaiin Kyoyu Meibo" (Roster of the Members and Friends of the Santa Fe Christian Church), a twenty-page mimeographed directory in Japanese with the internees' names listed by barrack number (Santa Fe Kirisuto Kyokai 1943). In my grandfather's Barrack 64, nine men were either members or friends of the church, including Rev. Watanabe and Teiichiro Maehara. Melzer reports that "to help keep peace, camp officials separated internees in barracks based on their predominant political views regarding the war" (1994, 217); religion may also have played a role.

Another subtle form of Issei resistance to their captivity was the actual assertion of their human and civil rights regarding knowledge. Bilingual inmates used their literacy in English and Japanese to keep others informed about events of the day with regular news broadcasts. Hoshida's drawings depict specific bilingual men such as Kango Kawasaki and Toshio Sakaguchi, both from Hilo, who listened to the news, made notes from various broadcasts in English, and translated them into Japanese to broadcast to their camp mates. These were widely attended affairs, as one of Hoshida's sketches records.

They put daily news and announcements in writing as well. Soga, a principal Issei journalist in prewar Hawai'i, describes the importance of this publishing enterprise in Santa Fe and how it fit into the internee bureaucracy:

> A few days after I arrived at Santa Fe [in mid-June 1943], all the newspapermen gathered and decided to publish the *Santa Fe Times* as soon as possible. . . . Using a mimeograph machine that we had brought from Lordsburg, we began publishing from July 1. Our publishing office was independent at first, but became a part of the Japanese Internee Administrator's Office after the consolidation of various departments. Mr. Iwao Oyama managed the newspaper for a long time. After he was paroled, Mr. Toshio Sakaguchi served as manager until we left the camp.
>
> Although the department was small, we printed weeklies and other publications for the Buddhist and Christian groups in addition to our daily newspaper. The extent to which this old mimeograph machine contributed to the cultural enrichment of the entire internee population is immeasurable. The newspaper was reviewed by the censors every day prior to publication. News was limited to what was reported in the English language newspapers. (2008, 127–128)

The newspaper was primarily in Japanese but included names of camp administrators or short lessons in English. The *Lordsburg Times,* for example, sometimes included English wording that could be used by prisoners in writing letters home when English was required, as in the issue of 30 December 1942:

Even in here it is getting pretty cold nowadays. I got up early this morning and took a walk. A winter moon was seen shining in the sky. And the stars looked as if they were shivering with cold. Yes, it *is* cold now. We have ice— to say nothing of frost. But we are all in excellent health and we are keeping up our spirits. . . . This afternoon we planted a tree on each side of the entrance of our barrack. We feel good when we see the trees we planted. We are going to pound 'mochi' tomorrow. Some people are now pretty busy. They are going to entertain us on New Year's Day. ("English Lesson")

Sermons provide further examples of writing for a public purpose and of personal resistance to the indignity of internment. In Lordsburg and Santa Fe, Christian clergy established churches, wrote and delivered sermons, and produced their own publications, which were duplicated by Soga's publication department. In one letter to my mother, my grandfather mentions using the book of Daniel for one of his sermons. In the sermon itself, delivered on 24 October 1944, Rev. Watanabe describes Daniel as having been exiled to Babylon, comparing his predicament to the "similar circumstances as today's so-called internment," and uses Daniel as an example of one who lived a conscientious, moral, disciplined life, not succumbing to temptations, despite suffering in exile (1944b). Given their years in prison, Rev. Watanabe emphasizes the importance of leading a disciplined life and keeping up one's spirits. Rather than making literal references, he uses biblical analogies and characters, trying to instill courage in his fellow internees.

If they were not engaged in writing sermons, these men also wrote essays for the Santa Fe Christian Church newsletter, *Fuku-in,* as well as for a second publication, which my grandfather mentions in a letter to my mother: "As our church work we are used to publish[ing] a leaflet twice a month also weekly leaflet regularly. So I am interest[ed] to write [for] either" (28 August 1944). In *Fuku-in,* for example, he writes a short essay on anger and illness, giving his readers some practical advice: "Extreme anger will not only harm your digestive organs, but also endanger your health. . . . A person I know always goes to sleep whenever he's angry, but anger disables people. Anger, emotional imbalance, despair, and worry generally cause many disturbances to digestive and sex organs and cause illnesses" (1944a). Comparing the teachings of Jesus to the psychology and medicine of the time, he encourages his fellow internees to see its practicality, his own practicality being reflected in his attention to virility, of some common concern, perhaps, to the men of various ages in the camp.

At one point, Rev. Watanabe also records survival principles that were meaningful enough for him to copy down in English and translate into Japanese for his brethren:

I am really on the path

1. If I always look for the *best* in each person, situation, and thing.
2. If I forgive *everybody* without exception, no matter what he may have done, and if I then forgive *myself* whole-heartedly.
3. If I regard my job as *sacred* and do my day's work to the very best of my ability (whether I like it or not).
4. If I take every means to demonstrate a healthy body and harmonious surroundings for myself. . . . (n.d., Notes)

In the archival internment materials located thus far, petitions become key documents, for in using the petition, the Issei were employing a document and discourse categorically outlawed to them. Although the U.S. Supreme Court in *U.S. v. Cruikshank* (1876) had declared that the right of the people to petition is "an attribute of national citizenship," *Ozawa v. U.S.* had reaffirmed the Naturalization Act of 1790, excluding the Japanese from U.S. citizenship altogether based on their race (see chap. 2). Yet the desire and mechanism to petition prevailed, as self-, family-, or group advocacy.[7] In the context of public writing for the collective welfare, two examples of petitions may suffice—one requesting return to Hawaiʻi, signed by a large group of internees, and one by an individual for the sake of his family members.[8] A more than cursory reading allows us to observe the internees' understanding of the power of words and their confidence in their use of them in the face of a monolithic authority.

A Collective Petition: The Nearly Two Hundred

On 24 February 1944, nearly two hundred Issei from Hawaiʻi at the SFIC collectively asserted themselves in a document that I discovered in an obscure file in the National Archives (Shigenaga et al. 1944).[9] They address their petition separately to Lieutenant General Robert C. Richardson, military governor, Territory of Hawaii; Edward J. Ennis, director, Alien Enemy Control Unit, Washington, DC; I. M. Stainback, governor of Hawaii; and Joseph R. Farrington, delegate to Congress. Following conventions of petition writing, these Hawaiʻi Issei adopt a "deferential style" in English (Van Voss 2001, 2–3), achieving a customarily solicitous tone despite minor indications that they are not writing in their native language.

The internees' request is unified and straightforward: "We, the undersigned, hereby respectfully submit this petition, based upon the hereinafter mentioned grounds or circumstances, asking for an immediate transfer of all of us from Santa Fe Detention Camp to some similar internment camp or camps located and maintained under your command in Hawaii" (Shigenaga et al. 1944, 1). They assert their separate selves as one "we" and argue their case as a collective life and identity, turning the dehumanizing stereotypes and generalizations that had incarcerated them in the first place—for example, Lieutenant General John DeWitt's "a Jap is a Jap" comment (Kashima 2003, 133)—to their rhetorical advantage. They assume their agency as a group. Although they were from different regions in Japan, islands in Hawai'i, occupations, and faiths, they quite consciously construct their unified image, first citing common age and commonalities of experience to justify why they deserve to be heard: "More than half way past in our span of lives as permanently domiciled alien[s] in the enforced status of ineligibility to citizenship, we have inner satisfaction and self consolation of having performed all that [was] good [for] the communities we lived [in] and to the country which protected us" (Shigenaga et al. 1944, 1).

With an average age of fifty-five, these men were generally established, productive, and contributing members of their communities and adopted country. After all, it was precisely because they were community leaders and organizers that they were believed by authorities to be "potentially dangerous." Moreover, as resident aliens in the "enforced status of ineligibility to citizenship" (Shigenaga et al. 1944, 1) due to race, they ironically base their argument on their good citizenship. Mindful of their personal benefits and contributions in America, they argue that they are *in fact* good citizens, as evidenced by gainful employment, public service, and lawfulness. They also assume the stance of a petitioner who believes in the goodness of the authority who can be reasoned with, one good citizen to another:

> Despite our present predicaments, we are not forgetful of what we owed the territory of Hawaii in enabling us to live happily with our families and engage in gainful occupations and share in the benefits of public education [for] our children. We are proudly conscious also of our prompt and pleasant participations in and responses to practically all undertakings of public nature, sponsored by public spirited men and women for the welfare of their communities and nation. We committed no offense against our neighbors or public institutions. We only endeavored and strove to do all that any good citizens could or should do. (Shigenaga et al. 1944, 1–2)

Finally, they cite their immediate problem to be their physical, medical, and mental health in this exiled environment, by contrasting their lives in Hawai'i to their lives of duress in New Mexico:

> As we lived in Hawaii for scores of years, . . . it was difficult for us to be readily acclimatized in the mainland. It does not agree with us but

steadily reacts in impairment of our health. The majority of us here are aged, past the sixty mark and are hardly able to overcome the rigor of extreme climates, particularly at high elevation with rarefied atmosphere. No wonder, we were the first in succumbing to the influenza that recently threatened the entire camp population, and over ninety percent of those who have undergone the hospitalization were the Hawaii group. (Shigenaga et al. 1944, 2)

Matters of health can translate into matters of life and death. Rather than requesting release, however, they are reasonable men, making a more reasonable request: a return from exile while remaining incarcerated. Their argument is a humanitarian one:

Separated afar from [our] family folks, personal visits even in cases of serious illness are out of [the] question. But, if we are staying at any Hawaiian localities, our relatives or friends may conveniently succor to [our] aid or be able to comfort us. Even [if] death should occur the presence of his wife at his bedside could hardly be expected. In this particular instance we are less favored geographically than our fellow internees of the mainland. (2–3)

They were also "less favored geographically" than their fellow internees imprisoned at Honouliuli Internment Camp on Oʻahu; Saiki points out that "in many ways Honouliuli was preferable to Mainland Department of Justice camps" (1982, 162), precisely because of the proximity of the prisoners' families and friends and the fact that they were allowed to visit the internees after some time.

The petitioners' final point is a clear assertion of their adopted American identity and reiterates their attachment to Hawaiʻi in relation to the three alternatives provided by the government—"repatriation" to Japan, parole or release on the mainland, or "reunification" with their families on the mainland: "How singular were our affections towards Hawaii and how true were we to the destiny of the territory can be shown from the fact that almost none of our group did take the exchange vessel for the repatriants, simply because we all wanted to go back to Hawaii and stay there no matter what happens. We did not and still do not desire to be paroled or released here in the continent and invite our families" (Shigenaga et al. 1944, 3). Given their forced alien, now alien enemy, status, such a choice of identity was no small matter. Others from Hawaiʻi and the mainland had chosen repatriation to Japan, some had chosen reunification with their families in WRA camps or parole on the mainland, but these men remained stalwart in their choice to return to the islands; their preeminent desire was to return to their families and family life.

In their concluding paragraphs, they reassert their collective image and restate their unity of mind, acquired through common experience and consensus of opinion over years of incarceration:

> Our mental attitudes are as one—a normal result of natural process of no short duration by which the idea of home life and its surroundings became more precious to our hearts than anything else in the world.
>
> Wherefore, we, each of us, jointly pray for a way be opened through your good offices for us to be within your jurisdiction or, at least, a practicable plan be adopted with some measure to mitigate our adverse circumstances. (Shigenaga et al. 1944, 3)

The main signatory was Shigeo Shigenaga,[10] a Honolulu businessman, designated as being "in charge," although it is not clear that he authored the petition. According to W. F. Kelly, the assistant commissioner for alien control, INS, in a memo to Colonel Howard F. Bresee, OPMG, this document was disallowed by censors for issues of protocol—the internees were told to go through the Spanish Legation, the protecting power—and never reached the proper authorities (1944). Their use of the form, however, reflects a clear attempt to express their desires and argument in the discourse of their captors. Shigenaga, along with Rev. Watanabe, Rev. Fujitani, Kato, Kuniyuki, and nearly two hundred others, signed this petition, some affixing their names in flowing Palmer method penmanship.

An Individual Petition: For the Sake of My Children

With the misdirection of the February 1944 petition, my grandfather set about writing his individual petition more than a year later, on 9 May 1945, a copy of which I found in his World War II papers, the original in a file in the National Archives. It is three single-spaced typed pages, addressed to Major Stephen M. Farrand, Legal Branch, Prisoner of War Operation Division, OPMG, and requests that Rev. Watanabe's case be reconsidered and that he be allowed parole to Hawaiʻi: "I, the undersigned TAMASAKU WATANABE, ISN-HJ-1097-CI, being interned at Barrack 4, Alien Internment Camp, Santa Fe, New Mexico, hereby respectfully submit this petition to your good office, beseeching for rehearing or reviewing of my case for the purpose of reinstating of my present status and eventual parole to Hawaii, the permanent residence of mine. I beg to base my application on the following facts" (Watanabe 1945, 1). He writes in an appropriately deferential style, as did the writers of the collective petition, his language sometimes more exaggerated in its solicitous tone, though more awkward in syntax and diction, than the previous petition due to his nonnative use of English. During his hearing in February 1942, described earlier, he had chosen to trust his ability in English, speaking without a translator, and presumably composed this document independently as well.

Faced with the same compromised status as he and his fellow internees had encountered the previous year, Rev. Watanabe uses the "following facts," which amount to basic personal information, to establish his personal identity and credibility: his name, birth date, age (sixty-two and five months), address in Hawaiʻi, immigration to the United States, visits to Japan, choice of profession, and identification of family members. In his narration of the events, however, he is careful to create his image on his own terms, to emphasize his purposes so that they will not be misunderstood: He had immigrated to the United States to study the Christian ministry; traveled to Japan to marry my grandmother and to visit relatives and his parents' graves; and entered the ministry to serve as an evangelist among the Japanese, "participating [in] evangelical works of Christianity in this camp, having morning and evening services every Sunday and regular prayer meeting[s] in every Wednesday evening" (1945, 1). Whereas the collective petition had alluded to scripture, Rev. Watanabe here insists that as a devout Christian he belongs to the same citizenry as his captors, a fact he clearly wishes to drive home when he makes reference to *his* parsonage in relating the facts.

The "facts" also include details of Rev. Watanabe's arrest, hearing, and captivity from the outset to the time of writing. This itinerary reflects his impulse to keep records of his movements and whereabouts, over which he otherwise had no control; it also gives authorities the indirect message that he maintained some degree of control over the information.

Like the signers of the collective petition, my grandfather also references the citizenship he was denied, a status that could not be denied to his American-born children. Thus, in describing his family, he is careful to identify his three children as being "all American citizens, all married to American citizens of Japanese parentage," and adults in professional, public service occupations:

[My] oldest son is 31 years old serving . . . as a Deputy Attorney General for the Territory of Hawaii, 2nd son is 27 years old, serving in teaching staff of one of the Public Schools and the daughter is 29 years old, married to a public school teacher and she, herself, is serving in teaching English at University of Hawaii. They were educated in American schools only, never been out side of the United States of America and they know only American way of life. They are hundred percent American citizens, confirming American citizenship only by expatriating from Japan each respectively. (1945, 2)

Although all children born in the United States, regardless of their parents' nationality, were automatically American citizens, Japanese law also gave them Japanese nationality, and dual citizens had to be expatriated to claim a singular American citizenship. Furthermore, because some U.S. officials, including Roosevelt and Patton, painted all persons of Japanese ancestry with the same broad alien / alien enemy brush, Rev. Watanabe's meticulousness is certainly warranted. In describing his children, he describes himself: In that they are wholly good Americans, even one being an English teacher, he is a father who raised them "right."

Accordingly, my grandfather creates a second section that he labels "Loyalty," which is based on his conception of good citizenship and under which he lists thirteen supporting points, including his continuous residence in the United States, paying taxes, lawfulness, being law-abiding and peaceful, not being disloyal in act or word, his commitment to his Christian ministry as an evangelist among the Japanese, his contributions to the American Red Cross and other civic organizations, his preaching loyalty to the United States as a part of the Christian creed, and his belief that "every one born in the continent of the United States and in her Territory of Hawaii and hence American citizen owes unqualified loyalty to the United States of America regardless of his ancestry" (1945, 2). On these personal acts of loyalty and good citizenship—a self-defined image—he bases his case for favorable consideration by U.S. government officials. And given his internment, he also includes several related points about compliance and cooperation, his idea of being a "good citizen":

10. During my internment of over three years I have been obedient to the rules and regulations whatever we, internees should comply with. I respected the authorities and cooperated with them and never made complaint against the authorities or the United States of America for my [self-interest].

11. I have no ill-feeling toward the authorities and the United States of America notwithstanding that I am now interned in this internment camp and [have] been detained over three years, because the United States had [the] right to apprehend all the nationals of [an] enemy country.

12. Although I am foreign born and not eligible to be a naturalized citizen of this country, [I] am an American citizen by spirit since

> I have lived nearly two third[s] of my life in this country, having
> three children of American citizen[ship] whom I have to depend
> upon at my old age because I have no property of any nature in
> Japan, which would be the resources of my life in Japan. All the
> money I earned by salary in this country [was] expended for edu-
> cation of my children in higher learnings in universities and
> could not spare a cent for my selfish purpose or sending any
> amount out side of this country. These facts show that the money
> I spent was for the welfare and betterment of the community as
> well as for the country. (1945, 2–3)

These claims reflect increasing levels of commitment to his adopted country, despite his "not [being] eligible to be a naturalized citizen." As a pastor, Rev. Watanabe did, in fact, expend what would have been a minimal salary to provide for the higher education of his children at private and public institutions (his eldest son attended Stanford University Law School, his younger son and daughter graduated from the University of Hawai'i in Honolulu), and each of them was engaged in public service.

In a section titled "Remarks," Rev. Watanabe makes a claim consistent with that of the group more than a year earlier: that unlike those who chose repatriation to Japan, he rejected it, reflecting his determination to return to Hawai'i "no matter how long that will take to become reality." He also reveals that his primary motivation in submitting this petition is less for himself and more for the sake of his children:

> My purpose of submitting this petition for rehearing or reviewing of my
> case is not for the selfish purpose, but to clarify my innocen[ce] for the
> welfare of my children. My present status seems to my children great
> agony which is my unendurable anguish. As for me alone, it is not much
> concern whether I be paroled or not and if it is necessary for the United
> States Government to keep me here in this camp, then I will be here even
> [for the] duration of the war and willingly will cooperate with the author-
> ities here in this camp, since I believe [it is] my duty regardless of my sta-
> tus as a civilian alien enemy, to cooperate with them to respect and obey
> all the laws and regulations in force. (1945, 3)

Whether he felt that such an admission would strengthen his case or not, for it would seem to almost undermine it, the sincerity of his statement might be understood in light of his strong commitment to his calling, ministering to those in need; he was, after all, doing his job among those prisoners gravely in need, especially by May 1945.

In his concluding remarks, Rev. Watanabe reflects a conscious use of his "life history and record in the U.S.A. [to] show that I have been a peaceful and loyal resident and hope that the military authorities will find that I am entitled to be released to my home in Hawaii and live peaceful life there as before [for] the rest of my life" (1945, 3). Unlike the group petition, his request did receive a response from the "established authority," for Maj. Farrand acknowledged receipt of his letter, and it went through the chain of command. In a letter dated 23 June 1945, Robert B. Griffith, Office of Internal Security, informed my grandfather that his case had been reviewed, that he had been "recommended for parole on the Mainland and that your return to the Territory of Hawaii [will] be favorably considered" (1945b). However, he was not returned to Hawai'i until November 1945, months after the war's end, along with hundreds of other fellow internees. His case—and his rhetorical strategy—was successful, even if the desired result was finally obtained not by his petition but by standard practice at the end of the war.

A final example of public writing, "Song of Internment" consists of twelve verses by one of Kato's closest friends, Hikoju Otsuka, also of Kona, and captures the Hawai'i internees' story in all its poignancy.[11] Excerpted here in part from Kato's memoir, it documents the experience of Otsuka and hundreds of Hawai'i prisoners:

1. Thousands of miles from Hawaii am I
In this far off USA
Exiled in New Mexico's Santa Fe
In a camp atop a city
Isolated from all else.

2. Over three long years since the war began
As an enemy I am looked upon
Pitifully, sorrowfully,
No crime or guilt
But punished harshly just the same.

3. First to Honolulu's Sand Island
To an internee camp make-shifted there
Then to Mainland USA
Misery and hardship day after day
Have become my way of life. . . .

11. Ah, Hawaii, my home sweet home

My beautiful land of paradise
Where dwell my beloved wife and children,
Without a man, how will you manage?
Fatherless children, how do you fare?

12. Days are long and empty and hard,
I write home details big and small
Of lonely heart and anxieties
I think of you longingly,
Unconsciously I'm flooded by tears.
                    —Hikoju Otsuka (n.d.)

So it was that, as three years spilled into a fourth, the Hawai'i Issei in unwarranted captivity occupied their time, which must have seemed interminable; occupied their minds and spirits, which allowed them some sense of liberation from the literal confines of the barbed wire; occupied their wills, their sense of control and purpose, as they advocated for their rights as human beings facing "unbearably harsh adversity" (Soga 1944). As exiles, in contrast to those interned in island camps such as Honouliuli, they were deprived not only of their freedom but of the comfort of the familiar—weather, foliage, and family, most acutely. Many were fortified by their cultural practices and philosophies, which helped them survive their captivity. And the war also brought surprises.

CHAPTER 7

Compounded Ironies I
"Alien Enemy" Fathers, American Patriot Sons

Sailing on separate decks—
The son,
A U.S. soldier;
His father,
A prisoner of war.
—Muin Ozaki (1984, 29)

The story of the father and his son in this poem is often overlooked in the wake of heroic stories of the Nisei soldiers in World War II's European and Pacific theaters. But my grandfather and other internees, who lived with this father and others like him, knew of their pride, their apprehensions, and their anguish in having sons in the U.S. military on both battlefronts. They bore witness to this irony. They were members of home or barracks communities, sometimes both, friends of the fathers, sometimes the sons. At least three of my grandfather's barrack mates had sons in military service: Teiichiro Maehara, a friend from Puʻunēnē, Maui, had two sons, First Lieutenant Saburo Maehara, 100th Infantry Battalion, 442nd Regimental Combat Team (RCT),[1] and Second Lieutenant Edward Goro Maehara, also 442nd RCT; Genichi Nagami, of Hilo, Hawaiʻi, also had two sons, Sergeant Hiroshi Nagami and Private Toshio Nagami, Company F, Second Battalion, 442nd RCT; and Ryozo Izutsu, from Kauaʻi, had one son, Private First Class Tadami Izutsu, also 442nd RCT. There were, of course, scores more—a total of 210 sons of 161 interned fathers from Hawaiʻi alone.

During my months at the National Archives digging through endless nondescript gray file boxes, I came across a document that was as disturbing to me as it was startling: a list titled "Japanese Civilian Internees from Hawaii with Sons in the Armed Forces of the United States—Consolidated and Revised List, 20 June 1945,"[2] in which the government recorded the irony—and the injustice—in black and white (OPMG / U.S. Department of Justice 1945). I was stunned, saddened, and angered all at the same time. This is an eleven-page list of names of internees with sons serving in the U.S. military. Some sons were drafted; many volunteered despite, perhaps because of, the intense racial politics of the time. In numerous families, as with Maehara and Nagami, there were two sons; in more than a few cases, as with Matsujiro Otani, there were three and four sons in military service by June 1945, when the list was revised.

What prompted this list in the first place? Who noticed this irony? I found correspondence between U.S. military and Justice Department administrators that sheds partial light on these questions: Apparently, Robert S. Miyata, a private in Company G, 442nd RCT, and probably a volunteer from Hawai'i, wrote a letter on 26 September 1943 to the Alien Enemy Control Unit (AECU), Department of Justice, headed at the time by Edward J. Ennis. Although that letter is unavailable, references made in answer to it by Lieutenant Colonel A. M. Tollefson of the Prisoner of War Division, Office of the Provost Marshal General (OPMG), indicate it had to do with the internment of his father, Kyoichi, in Missoula, Montana (Tollefson 1943a). This letter—and possibly others—led AECU director Ennis to write a letter on 1 October 1943 to the provost marshal general regarding "the reconsideration of cases of Japanese internees from Alaska and Hawaii whose sons are members of the Armed Forces of the United States"; he possibly also requested a list of internees at Fort Missoula (Tollefson 1943b). From this list of twenty-six Issei from Missoula, there are internee names from this study: Ryosei Aka, Katsuichi Miho, and Jinshichi Tokairin. In his reply, Tollefson similarly requested that the AECU or INS prepare a list of Hawai'i and Alaska Japanese imprisoned in Santa Fe, New Mexico, whose sons were in the military.

This correspondence provides insight into the collaborative relationship between the Justice and War Departments, mentioned in the introduction, as well as the curious values motivating their decisions. Tollefson concludes his 18 October letter to Ennis by presenting the view of the OPMG:

> This office has forwarded copies of your letter and the list to the Commanding General, U.S. Army Forces in the Central Pacific Area for his consideration and recommendation in this matter with a statement that *this office feels that consideration should be given to cases where the sons of the internees are serving the United States as members of the Armed Forces.* Concurrently, the War Department will check the records of the sons, as *the conduct of the sons in the Army, may have some bearing upon the ultimate disposition of the fathers.* (1943b, emphasis mine)

Also on 18 October, Tollefson had not only invited the commanding general's recommendation but also requested his recommendations "for or against parole . . . in those cases upon which you have not already passed. The War Relocation Authority has informally informed this office that it will accept into its Projects internees from the Territory of Hawaii . . . , particularly where sons of the internees involved are serving in the United States Armed Forces" (1943c).

To the government's credit, the moral irony of the situation apparently did not go unnoticed, and some action had been taken within a month of Private Miyata's letter. Yet what calculus could have applied in the "conduct of the sons"? This was a strange measure of worth of the fathers and sons, in any case.

Unlikely Visits

From the internees' viewpoint, the measure clearly differed from that of the government. The February 1944 petition, discussed in the previous chapter, captures the collective grief of fathers and husbands separated from families and home— the plight not only of the prisoner but also of the exile. The nearly two hundred men who signed that document were not petitioning so much for their release as for their return to Hawai'i, to be closer to their families in times of illness and strife—and what greater strife might there be than the loss of a child?

As I interviewed some of the internee sons who had served in the military, many by then in their eighties, I began to realize another irony in Muin Ozaki's poem: It was precisely because those young men, all American-born and in their late teens or early twenties, had been shipped from Hawai'i to the mainland for their military training that some were also able to visit their immigrant fathers, who had been outlawed from Hawai'i to the mainland internment camps—a financial improbability under other circumstances. Even those who may have had distant or strained relationships with their fathers before the war made the effort, elevating the sons' and fathers' sacrifices, reflecting their respect for one another, and illustrating the power of *oya/koko* (filial piety) over difficult relationships. Some visited their fathers in Camp Livingston, Louisiana, and Fort Missoula, Montana.

MAKING THE EFFORT: THE TOKAIRINS

Hideo Tokairin was drafted in June 1941 into a unit that consisted of the 298th and 299th Regiments and eventually became the initially controversial and orphaned 100th Infantry Battalion.[3] In June 1942, his unit was secretly shipped out to the mainland to train at Camp McCoy, Wisconsin. His father, Jinshichi, had been arrested in December 1941 and exiled from Hawai'i on Transfer Boat 1 in February 1942 by way of Camp McCoy, so the father and son had unknowingly crossed paths at McCoy, passing through the camp within months of each other.

Although he was not particularly close to his father, Hideo told me in an interview that he felt sorry for him for being unjustly imprisoned—*kawaiso* (sad, pitiful)—and in early May 1943, he made the trip by train from Wisconsin to Camp Livingston, Louisiana, to visit him (2004). Overhearing someone using a racial slur, recalled Hideo, provoked his complaint to the captain about the soldier's attitude. In a letter to his wife on 8 May 1943, the elder Tokairin expresses his joy over his son's visit: "Yesterday, Hideo unexpectedly visited me but stayed for only three hours. He received a short break during maneuvers. . . . After the maneuvers, he will get about 10 days of leave and will visit me again at that time. He was very happy when I gave him some of the *umeboshi* and *shiso no tsukemono* [both Japanese pickles] you had sent. Hideo seemed to be in good health. He wore three medals on his chest and looked great as a soldier." A treasured family photo shows the two men standing side by side with pine trees in the background. On 1 June 1943, Hideo visited his father again, this time from Camp Shelby, Mississippi, where the 100th Battalion had been transferred for further combat training. This time, Pfc. Tokairin dissuaded his father from thoughts of repatriation to Japan. Soon he shipped out to North Africa and to Salerno, Italy, where he would earn a Bronze Star and Purple Heart during the Italian campaign.

Two Contrasting Visits: The Mihos

Although many Hawai'i-born Japanese, all, of course, American citizens, sought to enlist in the U.S. military after Pearl Harbor was attacked, they were labeled 4-C, "enemy aliens" (the term applied to their immigrant fathers), by executive order and were ineligible for military service. It wasn't until 1 February 1943 that President Roosevelt was persuaded to authorize the formation of the segregated Japanese American 442nd Regimental Combat Team,[4] so that Nikkei men and women were finally allowed to respond to the nation's call to arms. In Hawai'i, this resulted in ten thousand volunteers, although only fifteen hundred had been anticipated by the army. The Miho brothers, Katsuaki and Katsugo, soon volunteered for service in the new unit and, with their predecessors in the 100th Battalion, including Hideo Tokairin and Edward Ikuma, were in basic training at Camp Shelby.

Upon learning that their father, Katsuichi, a Maui hotel owner, was imprisoned at Camp Livingston in a neighboring state, the brothers paid him a visit in August 1943, making the two-and-a-half-hour bus ride to Hattiesburg, Mississippi, where they met four other GIs who also had fathers imprisoned at Camp Livingston. It was nearly midnight, so they shared a taxi to the army camp, arriving at 5:00 a.m. In talking with me, Katsugo described a "Quonset hut POW camp" where they had to speak in English and were allowed only an hour and a half visit (2003). It was the first time the twenty-three-year-old had seen his father since September 1941, so the elder Miho was naturally interested in how his youngest son was getting along. In this reunion, they spoke of pleasant things such as picnics, hiking, and the son's activities.

Sometime after that, Katsuaki was killed in a stateside truck accident and Katsugo carried his brother's urn over several states to their father, who by that time had been moved from Livingston to Fort Missoula, Montana. But at Missoula, when Katsugo turned over his brother's ashes to his father, he was not allowed to enter the compound for the services held for Katsuaki the next day. A bitter memory.

Once overseas in Europe with the 442nd RCT, Katsugo received regular letters from his father in Japanese and, in turn, wrote V-mail messages to him in Santa Fe after his father was transferred to the SFIC from Fort Missoula. In one, the son describes his awe at being in Rome (which the 442nd was not allowed to liberate, possibly on account of the army's racial politics); in another, he reflects the reverse difficulty from that expressed by Kato (in chap. 6) with regard to the Japanese language:

> Dear Dad:
> It is good to hear from you regularly but sometimes your letters are just a bit hard for me to understand. You use such big words. Remember I was definitely not an honor student in Japanese and being so far away from home sometimes I have to think twice about the kind of words you use. Please make it a bit easier for me.
> I have everything I want out here. . . .
> Am healthy in mind and spirit.
>
> Your loving son,
> Katsugo (Miho 1944)

Because many internees were incarcerated for longer periods at New Mexico's Santa Fe Detention Station / Internment Camp than anywhere else, some sons made their way to the high desert from army camps such as Camp Shelby, and the language training school for the Military Intelligence Service (MIS) at Fort Snelling, Minnesota.[5]

"A Perfect Visit": The Otanis

Akira Otani, the oldest of Matsujiro Otani's four military sons, visited his father in Santa Fe in November 1943, when he was twenty-two. The elder Otani had been a successful businessman in Honolulu when the Pacific War broke out, and Akira recalled clearly in his eighties how his father, suffering from a serious heart condition, was roughly arrested at their Mānoa home on 7 December 1941 (A. Otani 2003). Having been a member of the Reserve Officers' Training Corps (ROTC) before the war as a University of Hawai'i student, Akira became a member of the Hawaii Territorial Guard (HTG) when it was formed from ROTC units only hours after the Pearl Harbor attack. When the HTG was disbanded on 21 January 1942, in a climate of intense anti-Japanese racial politics,[6] he joined the Varsity Victory Volunteers (VVV), an army labor unit, and finally volunteered for the 442nd RCT immediately after the unit's formation. He was a staff sergeant stationed at Camp Shelby at the time of his visit to his father in 1943, a lieutenant by mid-1945.

Traveling with his cousin, also in the 442nd, by train from Hattiesburg to Santa Fe, Akira initially encountered what he described in 2007 as a prisonlike setting: His father was seated across the table from him and his cousin, with an armed guard looming over them throughout their visit. This distressing arrangement was later relaxed, probably after he brought it to the attention of the authorities (A. Otani 2007). Akira also recalled that his father gave him his ring, made from a silver dollar, as a memento of their visit, and that he, in turn, bought a Native American–made turquoise ring in the town of Santa Fe to give to his father as a keepsake (A. Otani 2003).

On two occasions, father and son were allowed to step outside to be photographed with the juniper-dotted hillside in the background. In one shot, the Japanese father, formal, unsmiling, and dapper in a leather jacket, stood beside his American soldier son, ruggedly energetic in his army uniform. In another, with the same hillside background, both men are bundled up in coats and gloves.

On his way back to Camp Shelby, Akira wrote to his older sister in Honolulu reflecting his youthful enthusiasm and their affection for their father:

> November 14, 1943
> Dear Sis,
>   Am in Houston, Texas, on my way home after a perfect visit to Father at Santa Fe. Father was really overjoyed to see us, and it was the same with us too. Every day of the 8 days that we stayed in Santa Fe, we visited him, always at the same time, always for two hours. Every day we would bring . . . things that he would ask us to bring . . . or, if he did not ask us, we would bring him some kind of fruit for him to eat and enjoy. He in turn would buy some things for us at the canteen, and we would have a swell time at "Visitor's Hall" eating and swapping stories. . . . The last day

of [our] visit, we had a farewell party, just as he requested. For eats, we had fried chicken and some ham and hamburger sandwiches, plus a few bottles of coke. We enjoyed it immensely. (A. Otani 1943)

Because their father had a heart condition that caused the family great concern, Akira also reassured his sister "and the rest at home" that "he's in the best of health, having recuperated almost completely from his illness."

"How Come . . . ?": The Izutsus

Like Akira Otani, Tadami Izutsu also volunteered for the 442nd RCT in 1943, "much to the dismay of my mother who was very upset for Father had been recently interned." He was eighteen. Shipped from a sugar plantation camp in Makaweli, Kaua'i, to Camp Shelby for his basic training, he writes in a family memoir: "I clung tightly to the good luck charm, which Mother had [had] blessed at her Buddhist temple to keep me protected at all times. I carried this priceless charm with me from Makaweli to Mississippi . . . , during 18 months of front line combat, and hospitalization for my war injuries" (Izutsu n.d., 2).

Continuing in his memoir, Tadami briefly relates his visits to his interned father, Ryozo Izutsu, who had been a storekeeper in Makaweli before being arrested. Imprisoned in Kalaheo Detention Camp in July 1942 and transferred from Kaua'i to Sand Island in Honolulu in August, his father was shipped into exile on 16 September 1942, on the sixth transfer boat to Angel Island / Fort McDowell in California. He was then sent to the Lordsburg and Santa Fe Internment Camps in New Mexico, where he shared the same barrack with my grandfather in Santa Fe. "While stationed at Camp Shelby," Tadami writes, "I visited Father twice at the internment camp in Santa Fe. . . . My friend, David Miura, also visited his father there" (Izutsu n.d., 2).

On their first furlough, the taxi driver transporting them to the prison camp asked them, "How come you have somebody in here when you're in that uniform?" The contradiction was apparent even to an outsider. In an interview with Ted Tsukiyama, historian for the 442nd RCT and MIS Veterans Clubs, Tadami described his first meeting with his father: "It was a very intense emotional moment when I hugged my father. I was relieved that he was in good health and appeared to be in good spirits. . . . I knew he missed the family, and I told him not to worry" (Izutsu 1997, 13–14). In his memoir, the son writes,

Something stirred deep within me when I saw my beloved father helplessly imprisoned but never complaining about the injustices of war. After my second visit to Father, I . . . with an 18-year-old's determination[,] wrote a letter to the then commanding officer of the U.S. Armed Forces, General Marshall, to consider releasing my father . . . from his internment[,] for I was now actively serving the United States of America, proof of my devotion and willingness to die for my country. I later surmized [*sic*] that my letter was intercepted and never reached its destination[,] for all of our letters and parcels were subject to censorship. However, in my heart, there was some consolation that I had done everything possible to help my father. (n.d., 2)

"A Wire Cage": The Ohamas

In November 1943, at around the same time that Akira Otani was visiting his father in Santa Fe, Katsumi Ohama, a University of Hawaiʻi premed student, reported to Schofield Barracks on Oʻahu. He was first sent to Little Rock, Arkansas, for infantry training, but was transferred in midwinter to MIS training at Fort Snelling in Minneapolis, Minnesota. There, he wrote in an email to me, "Because I was already proficient in the Japanese language, I was placed in the advanced Japanese military intelligence classes." Whereas his father, Futoshi Ohama, a Japanese language school principal, introduced earlier, had been arrested and incarcerated *because* he was a Japanese language school principal, his son was now an asset to the U.S. military precisely because of his Japanese language skills. "Within three months," he continued, "I was ordered to go to the Pacific War. Before departure, I requested to see my father at the Santa Fe Internment Camp. My request was granted" (Ohama 2006). However, getting to Santa Fe was challenging; it took two days by train, with several transfers across different states. From the Santa Fe train station, there were no buses to the internment camp, so after checking into a hotel, he, like Tadami Izutsu, hired a taxi to take him to the camp on the outskirts of the city.

As a technical sergeant in the Army Intelligence Section / MIS, Katsumi wore a U.S. Army uniform and already had been assigned to General Douglas McArthur's Army General Headquarters in the Pacific. Yet, he recalled, he was "not allowed to enter the camp": "Like in a prison, I was escorted into a waiting room with a wire enclosure separating myself from where my father arrived with a guard who stood by closely all the while during our tearful meeting. Because of the wire enclosure separating us I was not able to hold his hands. Only one hour was allotted for the meeting. I was very sad to see my father so skinny compared to the day he was whisked away by the FBI in 1941" (Ohama 2001). After his return to Fort Snelling, Katsumi "was assigned to lead 120 newly graduated all Japanese Americans to go to somewhere in the Pacific War. We shipped out of San Francisco in a convoy in summer of 1944" (Ohama 2006).

Two Camps: The Fujitanis

In June that same summer, Private Yoshiaki Fujitani was also stationed at Fort Snelling for further military intelligence training after the Military Intelligence Service Language School (MISLS) at Camp Savage, Minnesota, was moved there. Like Akira Otani, he had become a member of the HTG as a University of Hawai'i ROTC student after the outbreak of the Pacific War, as well as the VVV, but had quit the VVV in disillusionment and anger when his father was arrested and interned. Eventually responding to recruitment efforts, he volunteered to serve in the MIS at age twenty and ended up in Minnesota. On his first furlough, he decided to visit his father, Rev. Fujitani, a Buddhist minister introduced earlier, who had been on Transfer Boat 3 along with my grandfather and in Santa Fe since June 1943.

The son found his father behind a high barbed wire fence, in a "stockade-like place" (Y. Fujitani n.d.). "It was an incongruous scene," he writes in *Japanese Eyes... American Heart*. "A son in the U.S. Army meets his father who is suspected by the government of being a 'potentially dangerous enemy'": "I presented myself at the internment camp office, asking to see my father. After what seemed a long wait, Father was permitted to leave the barbed-wired and heavily guarded compound. He was dressed in a tan suit, sporting a goatee. He was in good health and spirits. It touched me to think that he felt he had to be dressed in a formal way to greet his son who was serving in the U.S. Army" (1998, 98). They had a quiet visit. In an email to me, Rev. Fujitani, the son, who had advanced from private to master sergeant during the war and is now a retired Buddhist bishop, writes, "The meeting with Dad in Santa Fe is very vague in my memory. All I remember is that we compared our lives in camp, me in the army, and him in detention camp. We were having the same kind of food, like powdered eggs and luncheon meat. We both complained about the breakfast food.... I think the rest of the time was spent talking about the family" (2003).

At one point, the father and son stood and had their picture taken with the juniper-bespeckled hillside behind the camp in the background—the father standing erect in his three-piece tan suit, the son in army dress uniform with his cap slightly askew. In a filial act of kindness, Yoshiaki had his father stand on an elevated mound so that he appeared the taller of the two—for posterity. Decades later, the son wrote of the photograph:

> To the casual viewer it must be an uninteresting photo of two rather grim gentlemen, but for me it has a very special meaning, since it is a souvenir photo of my dad and myself taken right outside the barbed wire fence of the camp in Santa Fe.

That picture serves as a reminder of an intensely emotional moment in my life, when I traveled hundreds of miles from Minnesota to meet my father after a separation of two years.

About a year before that picture was taken I had written a letter to my father from Hawaii expressing hope that since we were not very close and unable to sit down and have a good heart to heart talk in the past, the next time we meet we ought to do that—over a bottle of beer or two—which, obviously was just a nineteen-year-old son talking big to the father he missed.

When the meeting finally did occur, all the bravado and confidence deserted me, and all I could muster was, "Dad, how are you?" There was nothing else that could be said at that time. That moment is captured in the photograph. . . . It doesn't show in our [faces], but I know that we were happy to see each other, and I'm sure Dad felt very proud standing next to his American soldier son in his buck private's uniform. (Y. Fujitani 1980)

FIG. 7.1. Rev. Kodo Fujitani (*left*) and son Yoshiaki, SFIC, June 1944 (courtesy Fujitani Family Collection).

A Request from a Sick Father: The Ishidas

Several months later, on 6 November 1944, internee Kyujiro Ishida, a patient at the SFIC Hospital, wrote a letter to a hospital administrator, requesting her assistance in "help[ing] to bring my son here to see me" (1944b). As I related in chapter 4, Ishida had suffered a stroke on 20 October 1942, while imprisoned at Camp Livingston. He had been paralyzed and hospitalized since then in the camp hospitals in Livingston and Santa Fe. He had previously written to his son Hisao, a private in the Sixth Regiment at Fort McClellan, Alabama. In his letter, the father assures his son of the well-being of his mother and the rest of their family. He also describes the grueling itinerary that he and other internees on Transfer Boat 1 were subjected to, his own medical condition, and the treatment he received in the internment medical facilities, offering a rare insight:

> My dear Son,
>   I am glad you had received my letter. The climate here is ideal, not so cold during the winter and not so hot during summer. Unfortunately, however, I am stil[l] in the hospital where the hospital folks and my friends are exceedingly kind to me and I am grateful to them. You never can expect any better treatment anywhere else. Truly it has been quite long time since I left home. It is nearly three years. I remember I arrived at San Francisco in March, 1942. From there, I was removed to Camp McCoy, Wis. and then to Camp Forrest, Ten. In about a month, I was removed to Camp Livingston, La. While there, in October, 1942, I became sick and was removed to the hospital and ever since, I am confined in the camp hospital. On June 7th, 1943, I was removed to Santa Fe Detention Station Hospital where I am now. . . . On warm, sunny days, they kindly place me in a wheel-chair and leave me in the sun on the hospital porch. You see they are very nice and I enjoy the sun-bath very much.

Finally, he asks in firm yet polite and solicitous language that his son visit him:

> I was wondering for sometime . . . if there won't be any chance for you to come here to visit me. You know, sometime[s], I get quite home sick wanting to see you and other home-folks. Quite a few soldier boys from Hawaii had visited their father[s] who are here.
>   I was given impression that the army would consider granting furlough to a soldier to visit his sick father. If such was the case, I would like to have you visit me as early as possible. Of course you remember your

duty as a soldier come[s] first and I will never want to cause you or your commander any inconvenience in your training. (K. Ishida 1944a)

The SFIC commander, Ivan Williams, apparently did not see the need for such a visit and, on 22 November 1944, left a telephone message for the Midwestern Area Red Cross that the "DOCTOR STATES SONS PRESENCE NOT NECESSARY AS SUBJECTS CONDITION NOT CRITICAL." However, Hisao, who had been transferred to the MISLS at Fort Snelling—joining Katsumi Ohama and Yoshiaki Fujitani—persisted in following his father's request in January 1945, writing to Williams:

May I have your permission to visit my father, Kyujiro Ishida, during my furlough beginning the 17 to the 24th of February.

He has been sick for about two years at the hospital there, and requested me to see him several times since I came to the mainland. But I was unable to secure furlough till now as we are having a school break.

I would appreciate it very much if you would be kind enough to send me the permit to the above address at your earliest convenience, for my entire activity during this furlough will depend upon this permit. (H. Ishida 1945a)

This time, Williams granted permission promptly, and Hisao visited his father on 20 and 21 February 1945. He visited a second time, from 21 to 23 May 1945—he was then at the rank of T/5 (Technician Fifth Grade)—and registered at the Hotel Montezuma in Santa Fe. A letter written several months later from Fort Snelling after the war's end, indicates that Hisao was actually allowed to stay with his father in the hospital.

August 17, 1945
Dear Sir
Thank you very much for everything you have done for my dad and my stay [making it] possible [for me] to meet and stay with him in the hospital. I am very sorry I wasn't able to thank you earlier since we were in a rush for packing and processing before shipping [out].

Rejoice that peace has come to the world again. I believe everyone in the camp [is] glad. But we of the intelligence [service] [have a] much more vital job than even before of translating and interrogating.

Closing, I, on behalf of my dad, mom and my brother, wish to express our sincere thanks to you. I wish you best of luck and God bless you.
Sincerely,
Hisao Ishida (H. Ishida 1945b)

FIG. 7.2. Kyujiro Ishida (*center*), son Hisao (*in uniform*), and friends, including Rev. Fujitani (*last row, right*), SFIC Hospital, 1945 (courtesy Ishida Family Collection).

Williams forwarded this letter to W. F. Kelly, assistant commissioner for alien control, with a memo dated 23 August 1945:

> There is attached hereto, copy of letter received from PFC Hisao ISHIDA, Fort Snelling, Minn., which has reference to his visit to this Station.
>
> PFC ISHIDA came here to visit his father, Kyujiro ISHIDA, who has been seriously ill for quite some time and who has now been approved for return to Hawaii.
>
> It has been the policy of this Station to extend all courtesies possible to these Japanese American boys who are serving in our Armed Forces and who visit their fathers at this camp. (Williams 1945b)

Perhaps Williams, too, came to see the contradiction and irony of this situation, its magnified poignancy and injustice: that American sons were serving in the military while their Japanese fathers were locked up behind barbed wire.

Ultimate Sacrifices

As you light a candle
A thin thread of smoke
Rises ever so faintly
Between your aged hands.
—Sojin Takei (1984, 60)

In a small pocket notepad spanning the period 1944–1945, when he was elected as chief of his barrack and kept track of not only his own activities but also daily events and news of his barrack mates, my grandfather noted on 4 August 1944, "Kihachiro Hotta (21) killed in action July 10" (13a), and "the third son of Genichi Nagami is killed in action. The second son sustains serious injury" (13b). In such recordings, he was not one to embellish, but from the government list mentioned earlier, I learned that Kiyoji Hotta was the father of Kihachiro, killed in Italy that day in July, leaving a brother, Kiyoshi; that Genichi Nagami lost his son Hiroshi in Italy two days later, on 12 July 1944, leaving his second son, Toshio, badly wounded; and that my grandfather's friend Teiichiro Maehara's son Saburo was also killed in action a month before the end of the war in Europe, leaving a younger brother, Edward Goro.

In fact, of the 210 Hawai'i internee sons in military service listed by the government, seven had been killed in action (KIA) as of 20 June 1945. Making this observation, realizing how the loss of the imprisoned fathers compounded the harsh irony of their imprisonment, I felt moved to learn and in some way to relate these stories in commemoration of the sacrifices of both the fathers and the sons.[7] Following is a list of the sons, their parents, and their military units in chronological order of their deaths:

PRIVATE FIRST CLASS ARTHUR AKIRA MORIHARA (10 April 1914–23 October 1943), son of Usaku and Umeyo Morihara; from 298th Infantry Regiment (IR) to 100th Battalion, Company A.[8]

TECHNICAL SERGEANT YUKITAKA "TERRY" MIZUTARI (3 May 1920–23 June 1944), son of Yasuyuki and Sueme Mizutari; 100th Battalion/MIS.

STAFF SERGEANT TOSHIO MURAKAMI (1 July 1920–9 July 1944), son of Shigeru and Motoye Murakami; from 299th IR to 100th Battalion, Company A.

PRIVATE FIRST CLASS KIHACHIRO HOTTA (7 May 1923–10 July 1944), son of Kiyoji and Tatsu Hotta; 442nd RCT, 100th Battalion, Company C.

SERGEANT HIROSHI NAGAMI (7 June 1923–12 July 1944), son of Genichi and Kuniyo Nagami; 442nd RCT, Second Battalion, Company F.

PRIVATE FIRST CLASS IWAO "BLONDIE" TAKEMOTO (24 April 1922–28 October 1944), son of Hikoju and Fusano Takemoto; 442nd RCT, Third Battalion, Company K.

FIRST LIEUTENANT SABURO MAEHARA (5 April 1915–5 April 1945), son of Teiichiro and Yoshi Maehara; 442nd RCT, 100th Battalion, Company C.

What the imprisoned fathers may not have known—certainly not then, maybe not at all—was when and where their sons died; somehow the losses of the fathers and the injustice of their imprisonment seemed to me most acute in those moments. Despite inconsistencies in the amounts of information that I was able to find on the sons and fathers, I provide here a brief personal and historical context for the sons' sacrifices, with thanks to Andrew Ono for much of the research on the combat narrative in this section and to the late Colonel Bert N. Nishimura for verifying specific information.

Born in Kealakekua, Hawaiʻi Island, Arthur Akira Morihara was educated on the Big Island, then worked for E. E. Black, Ltd., in Honolulu. He probably was drafted and entered military service sometime in 1941, before 7 December 1941 and the subsequent 4-C designation in 1942. After basic training at Schofield Barracks on Oʻahu while in the 298th Infantry Regiment, Morihara was sent to Camp McCoy and then Camp Shelby for advanced combat training, along with Hideo Tokairin and Edward Ikuma, where he was transferred to Company A of the 100th Infantry Battalion.

Pfc. Morihara served overseas in Algeria and Italy and "was killed in action . . . during the Salerno to Cassino Campaign on October 23, 1943" (Shoho 2007). According to war correspondent Lyn Crost, this "involved some of the most difficult fighting of the war" (1994, 75). Morihara's A Company was a part of the "fight to capture the small towns of Alife and . . . San Angelo d'Alife," where they were "stopped by enemy tanks" (82). The battle cost the 100th twenty-one lives with sixty-six wounded. Pfc. Morihara's death in his unit's hard-fought journey leading up to the 100th's major battle at Cassino constituted the first loss among the seven sons and an early sacrifice, only weeks after the 100th had started combat in September of that year in the south of Italy.

Yukitaka Mizutari, fondly known as "Taka-chan" by his family and "Terry" by many others, was the second Hawaiʻi internee son killed in action and the only one killed in the Pacific. Born in Honolulu to a large family that eventually settled in Kaūmana, Hawaiʻi Island, he became the *chonan* (eldest son) and, according to his sister Masako Yoshioka, was "raised in a very strict tradition like [their] father," Yasuyuki, who came from a samurai family. The elder Mizutari, as principal of the Kaumana Japanese Language School, also taught the martial art of kendo to his own and other children, so that Yukitaka grew proficient in both Japanese and kendo from an early age. Two of his sisters remember him fondly as being sensitive, kind, and "good in art and music"—painting and playing harmonica, ukulele, and guitar, as well as being a lover of American sports such as football, baseball, and basketball. He attended business school and worked as a clerk at C. Brewer & Company in Hilo before he was inducted into the U.S. Army in the second draft in November 1941.[9]

But it was his proficiency in the Japanese language that led Yukitaka to be selected from the 100th Battalion for duty in the MIS in November 1942. Colonel Harry Fukuhara, U.S. Army (Retired), then a private, was Mizutari's classmate at the MISLS at Camp Savage, and a close friend. In an interview with me, he recalled that Yukitaka never went to Japan but was very fluent in Japanese because of his father's training (Fukuhara 2008).

T. Sgt. Mizutari was appointed one of ten language team leaders and assigned to overseas duty in Australia and New Guinea in April 1943 (Nagasako n.d., 1). He and his team, including Fukuhara and Staff Sergeant Howard Ogawa, landed in New Britain in December 1943. In a 1944 article entitled "The Death of a Hero," Ogawa recalls the New Britain invasion—how their landing craft mechanized "steamed across the rough Coral Sea" and they "sighted the coast of New Britain in the far-off dark horizon." Suddenly, enemy planes appeared and attacked them, as they took cover, "trying to cram our whole bodies under steel helmets." The "first man to get off the craft was Sgt. Mizutari. Off he went into the jungle moving cautiously forward across the narrow beach, probing the tangled foliage for snipers and machine guns hidden behind cocolog bunkers."

After "there was no longer much to worry about air raids," Ogawa continues, "we both would lie awake late at night, talking about the folks back home. He would describe . . . how he struggled and worked his way through school to get an education, so he would be able to amount to something in this country of ours. . . . He sent home every penny he had, except for what he needed.[10] He was very 'oya koko' [filial] to his mother and father, and very kind to his brothers and sisters" (Ogawa 1944). For two of those months, Fukuhara and Mizutari shared the same foxhole every night and were "like brothers," Col. Fukuhara told me; Terry was "a good soldier, a good leader, and a good writer" (Fukuhara 2008).

On 23 June 1944, T. Sgt. Mizutari was killed by a Japanese sniper while defending the Sixth Infantry Division command post against a night attack. It is another grave irony that perhaps the most culturally Japanese of the seven was killed by a Japanese bullet. According to war correspondent Crost, "It was during the Battle of Lone Tree Hill at Maffin Bay in [May–June] 1944 that T. Sgt. Yukitaka 'Terry' Mizutari was killed when the enemy came through the jungle to infiltrate American positions near the shoreline" (1994, 42). Kiyoshi Fujimura describes how he and Terry took cover behind a tree trunk, and how Terry got shot and "died in my arms" (1988, 96).

Crost continues: "A longtime dedicated leader of a MIS language team, Terry had won the affection of both his Nisei comrades and his white officers" (1994, 42). Colonel Sidney F. Mashbir, chief of the Allied Translator and Interpreter Section of General MacArthur's Headquarters, wrote of his death, "The loss of Technical Sergeant Mizutari is considered with the deepest regret since this soldier was a soldier in every sense of the word and while serving with various language units in the field as well as at the Allied Translator and Interpreter Section, his contribution in fidelity and devotion to duty was outstanding. His record serves to exemplify the great work of the Nisei for the country to which cause he has given his life" (U.S. Army n.d.).

More poignant than this official word is the narrative of Yukitaka's sister Fusako Nishikawa, who termed this loss "a double dilemma in death": "It was an ambush. He was reloading his rifle when a bullet hit him directly in the heart. If he had died in the European front, Dad, who was interned in Santa Fe, New Mexico, as an enemy alien, would not be as jarred over the grief of losing his son. Dad's countrymen had killed Yukitaka, and I feel that Daddy must have cried, alone, in the detention camp without family to share the unbearable grief" (2002, 3). Yukitaka was awarded numerous medals, including the Silver Star, the nation's third-highest combat medal for gallantry in action, and the Distinguished Unit Badge.

On the other side of the world, the five remaining sons met their deaths in campaigns in Italy and France. Toshio Murakami was born in Wailuku, Maui, and educated in the local public schools, before serving as a defense worker at Territorial Airport Contractors on Maui. His sister Hazel, who was five years younger, idolized him and remembers that he called her "sweetheart" (Nitta 2017). Like Morihara and Mizutari, Toshio was probably drafted into military service before 7 December 1941, as he was inducted into the army at Wailuku, Maui, on 23 February 1942, after the ban against Nisei enlistment had gone into effect. He was twenty-two. His father, Shigeru, owned a local billiard parlor and served as the secretary-treasurer of Wailuku Hongwanji, a Pure Land Buddhist temple, before being arrested, imprisoned at Haʻikū, and sent to Sand Island Internment Camp (Nitta 2017) and into mainland internment months later, on 10 October 1942, on the seventh transfer boat. He ended up with my grandfather and hundreds of other Hawaiʻi Issei in Lordsburg, New Mexico. According to Shoho, Toshio "trained at Schofield Barracks, Oahu, with the 299th Infantry Regiment" and was later "assigned to Company A, 100th Infantry Battalion, for advance combat training" at Camp McCoy and Camp Shelby like Pfc. Morihara. His sister shared the poignant fact that Toshio had visited his father before being shipped overseas, so, I believe, in Santa Fe, meaning that Shigeru was the last family member to see him alive. After completing combat training in the States, Toshio "was dispatched overseas to Algeria, Africa, and subsequently participated in the landing at Salerno, Italy, and the Italian Campaign" (Shoho 2007).

Kihachiro Hotta, one of the sons mentioned by my grandfather in his notebook, was probably among the 442nd RCT volunteers. Like Murakami, who preceded him, he was from Wailuku and was described by his younger brother Shoma as tall and husky and recruited to play football at Lahainaluna High School, a boarding school (Hotta 2017). A boyhood friend remembers Kihachiro as "a true gentleman" (Hamasaki n.d.). His father, Kiyoji, had fought as a corporal in the Russo-Japanese War in 1904–1905 before leaving for the islands, when the family farm went to his eldest brother. He began peddling various goods at the Japanese camps on Maui and later in Wailuku opened a store that sold fine items such as felt hats and silk stockings (Hotta 2017). He was arrested on 2 April 1942. According to Shoho, before entering the service, Kihachiro worked as a clerk in the family's Hotta Store, which my mother remembered from her childhood in Wailuku. He was inducted into the U.S. Army in March 1943, at Schofield Barracks. Serving with the 100th Battalion's C Company, Kihachiro trained at Camp Shelby and stopped in Santa Fe to visit his father before being shipped overseas with the 442nd RCT replacements.

Of Hiroshi Nagami, my grandfather notes that he was the third son of Genichi Nagami, his barrack mate and a small business owner, originally from Tottori Prefecture. The elder Nagami, another son, Teruo, told me, had worked at the Pepeekeo Sugar Mill on Hawaiʻi Island before becoming a manager of a soda works factory in Hilo and actively serving his local Buddhist temple (Nagami 2009). His son Hiroshi was born in Pepeʻekeo, received his public school education at Kapiolani School and Hilo High School, then enrolled at Honolulu Business College before entering military service. In March 1943, he was inducted into the army, also undoubtedly as a volunteer, training at Camp Shelby, together with Morihara, Murakami, and Hotta, and serving with the 442nd RCT, Second Battalion, Company F, alongside his brother Toshio, on the U.S. mainland and in Italy.

The only native of Kaua'i among the seven sons, Iwao "Blondie" Takemoto was born in Kapa'a and attended Kapaa High and Elementary School, Kaua'i High School, and Kalaheo Vocational School. He had been employed as a welder for the army prior to his military service. Inducted on 24 March 1943 at Schofield Barracks, he trained at Camp Shelby with Hotta and Nagami in the 442nd RCT, but unlike them, he was a member of Fourth Platoon, Company K, Third Battalion, and served in Italy and France.

The last of the Hawai'i internee sons killed in action was actually the first among them to serve in the military. Saburo Maehara was born in Pu'unēnē, Maui, the third son of Teiichiro Maehara, a Japanese language school principal introduced earlier. He attended public schools on Maui as well as the University of Hawai'i on O'ahu. Having participated in the university's army ROTC program, he received his second lieutenant's commission in June 1936, upon graduation. Saburo then became a public school teacher, an agricultural instructor at Baldwin High School, his alma mater, and on 16 May 1941, he married Louise Sasai. They had a daughter, Susan.

In a 2008 interview, his brother-in-law Samuel Sasai told me that Saburo was a "very caring teacher, interested in his students being successful" (2008). Like Yukitaka Mizutari's, his younger siblings looked up to him and considered him a leader. Among his fellow soldiers, too, he was well liked; Ed Ikuma, the first veteran whom I interviewed in the early days of this project, was a sergeant in the 100th Battalion, and when I spoke to him again in 2015, he clearly remembered Lt. Maehara as "a kind person—everyone liked him; he was one who didn't brag even though he was an officer" (Ikuma 2015). According to Sasai, who also served with the 442nd RCT, Saburo looked out for him at the battlefront. Lt. Maehara's not being called to active duty until March 1943, after the activation of the Japanese American unit, placed him with the 100th/442nd RCT.[11] Although he was a second lieutenant, it had been more than six years since he had been commissioned, and he would have lacked experience. Upon the 442nd arriving for training in Camp Shelby, he was sent to Fort Benning, Georgia, for officers' training.

Valor, after all, is paid for with casualties. The men of the 100th had left their brethren of the 442nd in August, still training at Camp Shelby. From its initiation into combat in Algeria and then southern Italy in September 1943 to the devastating battle at Monte Cassino in January 1944, the 100th paid heavily for its service, with losses such as Pfc. Morihara—an early deposit for its celebrated valor. The ranks of the over-strength five infantry companies of the 100th Battalion (normal battalions had three infantry companies) had been so depleted by the time it was withdrawn from Cassino that the First Battalion of the 442nd, still in training at Camp Shelby, had to be rushed to the 100th as replacements at Anzio.

Lt. Maehara must have been sent into combat with the First Battalion replacements along with Pfc. Hotta. Having started at Anzio, then, he must have witnessed the 442nd's arrival in June 1944 "when the two came together and the 100th formally became part of the 442nd" on June 15 (CWRIC 1997, 257). Despite being absorbed into the 442nd RCT as its First Battalion, however, the 100th was, by presidential dispensation, allowed to retain its designation "100th Battalion" for demonstrated valor, a designation originally foisted on them because they were an orphaned unit, welcomed only by Lieutenant General Mark Clark of the Fifth Army (Crost 1994, 69).

At the 442nd's initial battle at Suvereto/Belvedere, Colonel Charles Pence put his as yet untested Second and Third Battalions in the lead positions. Both had problems, typical of initiation into combat, while the 100th confirmed its experience by skillfully maneuvering behind the Germans at Belvedere; the unit earned a Presidential Unit Citation for what Crost calls "its brilliant performance" (1994, 149), then overcame many German troops that were retreating from the Third Battalion at Suvereto. Lt. Maehara and Pfc. Hotta, both in Company C, and Sgt. Murakami, in Company A of the 100th, would have been there at Belvedere. Sgt. Nagami of the Second Battalion would have been alongside, in that battalion's initiation east of Suvereto, and Pfc. Takemoto's Third Battalion would have been struggling to drive the enemy into the 100th's path and artillery, attacking frontally at Suvereto.

As the Thirty-Fourth Division drove the Germans north, the 442nd would have arrived to cross the Cecina River. It is north of that river that the Germans made a stand to delay the Allied advance until their defenses along the Arno River were completed. And it is in this swath of land that the deaths of three of the seven—S. Sgt. Murakami, Pfc. Hotta, and Sgt. Nagami—occurred in a seemingly compressed time frame during the Rome-Arno Campaign from 9 to 12 July 1944: Toshio Murakami killed in action near Castellina Marittima, Italy, on 9 July 1944; Kihachiro Hotta near Pomoja and Leghorn/Livorno the next day; and Hiroshi Nagami near Follonica, two days later, on 12 July. According to *In Freedom's Cause* (Lee 1949), Sgt. Nagami was awarded the Distinguished Service Cross, the nation's second-highest combat medal, for "extreme gallantry and risk of life in combat."[12]

Pfc. Takemoto's death occurred after the 100th/442nd was secretly transferred from Italy to France in September 1944,[13] and his K Company, Third Battalion, was engaged in the now famed Rescue of the Lost Battalion, the Texas unit trapped in the Vosges Mountains. It was somewhere near Bruyères, France, that he was wounded and lost his life on 28 October 1944. In a 1997 interview, Tadami Izutsu, who visited his father in Santa Fe as I related, recalls getting a glimpse of his boyhood friend after he was killed: "Blondie and I played football on opposite high school teams on Kauai. He was a husky, well built, healthy person, but it takes only a small piece of shrapnel the size of ½ of one's thumb to take a life. May the good lord be with him always" (24). The very next day, 29 October, the Third and 100th Battalions fought the bloodiest battle of that effort at La Croisette junction, charging against enemy automatic fire and hand grenades to rescue the entrapped Texans. Pfc. Takemoto was among the extraordinary number of more than 2,000 Nisei troops killed or wounded in that conflict to save 280 men.[14]

First Lt. Maehara was the oldest of the seven sons of Hawai'i internees when he died on his thirtieth birthday, 5 April 1945, in Italy during the Po Valley Campaign. That day was the beginning of the 100th/442nd's final campaign—from 5 April to 8 May 1945. The breach of the Gothic Line, which occurred the following day, 6 April, was the most physically dramatic of the 100th/442nd's battles. Troops had to climb the formidable cliff fronting Mount Folgorito and Mount Carchio. They did it at night, in full gear and carrying extra ammunition. They did it having been instructed not to utter a sound if they should lose their footing and fall. And a few did fall—without uttering a sound. Early the next morning, they surprised eight sleeping Germans and took them prisoner. By shortly after noon, L Company had captured the German observation post at the summit of Mount Folgorito, erasing the artillery threat in that area. It was strategic in bringing the war to a close.

As with many battles, however, success is achieved by the sacrifice of the diversionary units distracting the enemy's attention from the main effort. That was the role of the 100th Battalion. From early on 5 April, the 100th had started its climbing attack of the hills toward Mount Folgorito. The Germans were focused on the 100th and in that fighting 1st Lt. Maehara lost his life; family records cite Georgia Hill as the location (Maehara 1997).[15] Chaplain Israel Yost, who knew him as "a fine man all around," writes that "he was killed instantly" (2006, 242). If he had lived just one more month, he would have returned home to his young family. Sam Sasai, Maehara's brother-in-law, told me that he was taking a break on the front line one day when, by chance, he talked to a passing GI, who gave him the distressing news about Saburo's death (2016). Lt. Maehara's government awarded him the Distinguished Unit Badge. All seven young men were awarded the Purple Heart, the American and European–African–Middle Eastern Campaign Medals, and the World War II Victory Medal, among others.

Fig. 7.3. Internee son Lt. Saburo Maehara
with his wife, Louise, and daughter, Susan,
ca. 1943 (courtesy Samuel Sasai).

So, 1st Lt. Maehara's death was a sacrifice—part of the sacrifice to allow the surprise breach of the Gothic Line. But the deaths of all of the men of the 100th/442nd/MIS were sacrifices—for their families and loved ones, for all American Japanese who would follow them, for their country. And for Akira Morihara, Yukitaka Mizutari, Toshio Murakami, Kihachiro Hotta, Hiroshi Nagami, Iwao Takemoto, and Saburo Maehara, their fathers received news of their deaths, themselves prisoners in a camp in Santa Fe, New Mexico, or elsewhere.

Shared Sorrow

Morihara, Mizutari, Murakami, Hotta, Nagami, Takemoto, Maehara—these young men were the sons not only of their fathers but also of communities of men in camp society—their fathers' friends, men from their hometowns; they had communities of fathers. Among photos that I have seen, although many taken *kinen ni* (as a remembrance) are of fathers and their sons, such as the Fujitanis, many other photos of the sons' visits show the soldier son in uniform surrounded by men of the Kohala-Kona community or Kaua'i men or the hospital staff who cared for an internee father. One rare, rather startling photo shows nine unidentified Nisei

FIG. 7.4. Isoo Kato (*back, far right*) with friend Hikoju Otsuka (*front, center*) and son (*in uniform*), Ichiji Adachi (*front, second from left*), and Kona-Kohala friends, SFIC (courtesy Kato Family Collection).

soldiers, sitting in a row in dress uniforms, their buttons aligned, with a large group of internees standing in the snow behind them. The snow-covered brush on the hillside behind them suggests that this was Santa Fe's winter.

And when a son died, this was a community loss, a shared sorrow. When Katsuichi Miho's son Katsuaki, a corporal in the 442nd RCT, died in a stateside truck accident early in the war, his younger son Katsugo delivered his brother's ashes to his father interned at Fort Missoula, as I related earlier. Jinshichi Tokairin, a fellow internee, whose son was in the 100th and who had accompanied Miho and others on the long journey from Camp Livingston to Fort Missoula, recorded several memorial poems written by barrack mates in sympathy for their friend's loss:

1 It was like the chrysanthemum flowers, fruits of years of effort,
   Which withered before blooming due to an untimely night frost.
2 Trying to find words to console you, miserable and lonely, having
       lost a loved one,
   I felt heartbreaking grief, too.
3 Although everyone understands that it is the journey all have to
       take someday,

The parents must have felt mortified when the child took it earlier
than they did.[16]

In his memoir, journalist Yasutaro Soga records the Buddhist memorial service in Santa Fe for Pfc. Morihara of the 100th Battalion, the first soldier son of a
Hawai'i internee to be killed in action, in October 1943: "On December 9 [1943]
it snowed heavily all day. The roads were slippery and dangerous. It was the forty-
ninth day after the death in Italy of Mr. Akira Morihara, the third son of Mr.
Usaku Morihara, a shop owner from Kona. A memorial service was held at the
Lower Town [Shitamachi] mess hall in the afternoon, and many internees
attended. This was the first service in the camp for a fallen Japanese American
soldier" (2008, 144–145). Having experienced heavy snow and cold in Santa Fe, I
could imagine the chilling solemnity of the memorial service for their friend's
fallen son. On 10 December 1943, Isoo Kato, who was from Kona, like the Mori-
haras, wrote a more personal letter home about Akira Morihara's death:

> Last month [November] on the 29th I wrote to Haruko. We had notifica-
> tion that Isao's younger brother Akira had died. We held services and I
> have been busy. . . . Today is Akira's 48th memorial day. Kona [friends]
> held a memorial service for him. From early morning it has snowed heav-
> ily, so we had a very cold, quiet, and a solemn service. Isao's papa who had
> drained his strength and spirit now seems to have settled some. We do
> what we can to console him, but nothing we can say or do is that uplift-
> ing. It is so very pitiful. How can one understand the loss of a son in battle
> and the father imprisoned. (n.d., 139–140)

Also pitiful was the absence of Buddhist chaplains at the battlefront to minister to the wounded and dying soldiers of Buddhist faith, given American racial
politics and the fact that most Buddhist ministers had been locked up. The slight
discrepancy in dates between the Soga and Kato accounts raises the question of
historical accuracy in memoir and letter writing but, in this case, favors the
immediacy of the letter, especially one written by a fellow member of the Kona
community. George Hoshida, also of the Big Island, verifies the first service referenced by Kato in a sketch dated 28 November 1943, 7:30 p.m., clearly the initial
response to the news and attended by many. Apparently, Soga was aware only of
the second, more formal Buddhist service.

In the same vein, Soga mentions another service, this one for non-internee
sons: "On the night of the thirteenth [of December 1943], internees from Maui
held a memorial service for eight Japanese American soldiers from Maui . . .
who had been killed in Italy. The Reverends Ryugen Matsuda and Tamasaku

Watanabe delivered sermons and Mr. Tokiji Takei said a few words on behalf of the families. It was later reported that, of Japanese American soldiers from Maui, 8 had been killed and 180 injured" (2008, 145). In December 1943, these Nisei soldiers killed and wounded in action must have referred primarily to members of the 100th Battalion, who, like Arthur Morihara, were among the first Japanese American troops deployed to Europe. So my grandfather was not at all a stranger to this loss but must have felt it deeply, especially given that he spoke at this service. Having had a long ministry on Maui from 1922 to 1935, he may have known some of the young men.

In a much later letter, dated 1 July 1944, Kato writes home again about the sons in military service: "Noboru's and Akira's parents must have heavy hearts. One by one, our dear young men go off to war, get wounded, end up in a hospital, and wait for death. It all seems so wasteful and worthless" (n.d., 175). Again, on 24 July 1944, he writes to his family about the loss of internees' sons serving in the military: "Recently we had a memorial service for the internees who passed away here and also for our fallen sons in the war. It was a beautiful service. Bon dancing and sumo followed. One after another, there is the death notification of an internee son who has gone off to war. I read in the newspaper that the Kona AJA's are marching off one by one to join the war effort. It makes me very sad" (177).

This July service may well have included Yukitaka Mizutari, who was killed in the Pacific in June that year, as well as Toshio Murakami, Kihachiro Hotta, and Hiroshi Nagami, killed earlier in July. Sometime after the war, Otokichi Ozaki recalled the irony of the father's and son's fates—a clear reference to the Mizutaris, though he does not mention the less-known Military Intelligence Service when referring to military units: "Many Nikkei sons volunteered for military service and distinguished themselves in the war as members of the 100th Battalion and the 442nd Regiment. In one particular case, a father was living behind barbed wire when his son, who was fighting in New Guinea, was killed in action. The young man's memorial service took place in the internment camp with an American flag lowered to half-mast" (2012, 73).

Several weeks after the July service mentioned by Kato, my grandfather reports in his pocket notebook that on 17 August 1944, Reverend Kakichi Okamoto, a fellow Christian minister whose son was in the army, held a meeting for "families with sons in the military," and seventy of them showed up, only thirty-one of them being actual family members (1944–1945, 13b). This reflects not only the interest in the military sons among the internees but also the support they were willing to give their comrades.

Months later, Soga reports all too briefly that Lt. Saburo Maehara, "a son of Mr. Teiichiro Maehara of Puunene was killed at the Italian front" and that "on April 25, 1945, a memorial service was held at the Lower Town mess hall with Rev. [Benjamin Shuntaro] Ikezawa officiating" (2008, 186). Saburo, a son, husband, and father, was killed on 5 April, shortly before the end of the war in Europe.

While the loss and suffering of the interned fathers must not be diminished, another irony reflects both personal and traditional Japanese cultural values. I found some letters of fathers with military-age sons or sons already serving in the military to be revealing regarding loyalty and duty. In a letter to his younger son, Lee Ryoichi, on 20 July 1942, Ryosei Aka writes: "I am thinking that you are still a boy. But you became a man already and [have] gone to register for [the] draft. It is a pleasure to know that you are glad to be drafted to fight for . . . Democracy. I am glad that you are in manhood. Do your duty honestly and faithfully to [succeed] [in] your life, wherever you are" (DL, 21).[17] In a 31 May 1943 letter, Aka writes to his son Roy after the recruitment of Nisei troops began in February and possibly soon after Roy had enlisted: "Thank you for your letter. I received it a few days ago. I read it over and over and it made me very happy to know that you are serving your country in good health. Yes, Roy, I am proud that I have honest and faithful sons who are doing best of their duty to [ful]fill one's purpose in these days of trial" (DL, 73). By mid-1945, two of Aka's older sons, Raymond and Roy, were serving in the MIS.

Another father concluded several letters written to his soldier son in Europe with a phrase, possibly learned in an English class or translated by a friend from Japanese into English: "I wish you to perform your duty at the battle field, as a good American's fighting man and return safely to your native land after the war" (Anonymous). Considering that these fathers had been held captive by the U.S. government mainly on the basis of their Japanese nationality, one might wonder what prompted such encouragement of loyalty and duty to the country that had incarcerated them. According to Yukiko Kimura, in her book on the Issei in Hawai'i, "Issei accepted from the beginning the role of their children as American citizens. This sentiment was strongly expressed by the letters of the internees, instructing their wives to conduct themselves solely as the mothers of American citizens or instructing their sons not to let their father's internment interfere with their duty to their native land and to conduct themselves as loyal Americans" (1988, 226).

I suspect that the sons and especially the fathers were familiar with the classical adage cited by Ted T. Tsukiyama, historian for the World War II Nisei veterans: "*Chu naran to hosseba ko naran; ko naran to hosseba chu naran!*" (If I am loyal, I cannot be filial; if I am filial, I cannot be loyal!)[18] According to Tsukiyama, "All Japanese understood that when faced with conflicting loyalties, a man's loyalty must go to the higher authority . . . the . . . reason why we Nisei volunteered, served, and fought for America in World War II" (Tsukiyama 2013, 3).[19] Many incarcerated fathers understood, and apparently many encouraged, that view.

CHAPTER 8

Compounded Ironies II
Advocacy in Death and Life

In his letter home on 19 April 1945, Isoo Kato had reflected sympathetically on the strain encountered by fathers with sons in the military, in this case, probably Hikoju Otsuka: "My [friend] has gotten thin. It is not easy to be a father of fighting soldiers. He is very worried. . . . He and I are not in the same boat as he has two sons in uniform" (n.d., 209). By that date, my grandfather's barrack mates Kiyoji Hotta, Genichi Nagami, and Teiichiro Maehara had lost their sons in Italy, and Ryozo Izutsu's son had been wounded in action. They also were not "in the same boat" as my grandfather and others with different family circumstances; they knew the apprehension and agony of Kato's friend only too well.

Despite what must have been a constant fear of loss felt by the fathers of soldier sons, however, some sons and some fathers, as well as their families, recognized that it was strategic to employ the son's—or sons'—military service in advocating for the father's release. From family and government archival documents, I learned that, together with Private Miyata, who seems to have drawn the DOJ / War Department's attention to Hawai'i civilian internees with sons in the military, other sons and daughters also played a significant role advocating for their fathers' release, in addition to the efforts of the internees themselves.

Internee Families: Advocacy—in Death and Life

As I searched through hundreds of pages of weathered documents in the National Archives, one of the best collective examples of advocacy that I discovered is the petitions sent by soldiers of the 100th Infantry Battalion to the Provost Marshal General's Office. On 14 March 1944, prompted by these petitions, the assistant provost marshal general, Brigadier General B. M. Bryan, wrote a memo, "Reinvestigation of Detention of Civilian Internees Related to Members of the 100th Infantry Battalion," to the commanding general of the Thirty-Fourth Infantry Division, to which the 100th/442nd RCT was attached. In it, he refers to "a number of petitions" requesting the reinvestigation of the imprisonment of "fathers and other relatives of members of the 100th Infantry Battalion" and lists the thirteen internees and the "petitioning soldiers and relatives" in an enclosure (1944b, 1).

Bryan also cites the Tollefson memo of 18 October 1943, mentioned in chapter 7, that suggested to the commanding general, U.S. Army Forces in the Central Pacific Area (and military governor, Territory of Hawaii, because the islands were under martial law), a reconsideration of the cases of internee fathers with military sons. In turn, the commanding general replied that "he favorably considered such policy and suggested that the Provost Marshal General's Office consider all cases within that category" in light of the following five options:

    a. relocation in a War Relocation Project;
    b. resettlement in a family internment camp;
    c. parole on the Mainland;
    d. outright release; or
    e. continued internment if necessary. (1)

These instructions reiterated that "in no case [would] the internee be permitted to return to the Territory of Hawaii prior to the termination of the War" (Tollefson 1943c, 1).[1] In keeping with bureaucratic procedure, Bryan acknowledged having received lists of civilian internees with military sons from the Justice Department, together with the internees' desires regarding the five options, and included those desires in the enclosure with an outline of further procedures to be followed.

I noted that by the date of the March 1944 memo, the 100th Battalion had been fighting for more than six months in Europe (since September 1943), where they demonstrated great valor and incurred great losses in battles from Salerno to Cassino. Among the petitioners was "Private First Class Arthur A. Morihara, *deceased*, . . . Company A, 100th Infantry Battalion Sep." (Bryan 1944b, 3, emphasis mine), who had begun the petitioning process on his father's behalf well before he was killed in action in one of the battles leading up to Cassino. His father, Usaku, had chosen to be "paroled to Topaz Relocation Center, Utah," according to the memo, and his file had to go through the elaborate bureaucratic approval process before his desire could be fulfilled.

Another petitioner was Private First Class Kihachiro J. Hotta of Company C, who was killed in action several months after Pfc. Morihara and the Bryan memo, during the Rome-Arno Campaign. His father, Kiyoji Hotta, had "expressed desire to be paroled to Jerome Relocation Center, Arkansas" and had to go through the same red tape as Morihara (Bryan 1944b, 4). Private First Class Hideo Tokairin, Company B, who was wounded in Italy, petitioned for his father's release, with the elder Tokairin, like Hotta, expressing his desire to be paroled to Jerome. Although the sons' letters were not included in the file, their collective effort obviously made a significant impact on the authorities.

A few weeks later, on 3 April 1944, Bryan wrote another memo to the commanding general of the Central Pacific Area with the broader subject of "Japanese Civilian Internees from the Territory with Sons in the Armed Forces of the United States," updating him on the reconsideration of those Hawai'i internee cases and itemizing the resulting actions taken to that end. Although the memo is written in characteristic bureaucratic passive voice, we can assume that the OPMG / War Department requested that the DOJ interview the "internees in this category . . . to determine their desires concerning such parole" (Bryan 1944c, 1). Their "desires" seemed to fall into three categories:

> Group 1: According to Bryan, "Many of them stated that they preferred to remain in the Department of Justice Internment Camps if they could not return to Hawaii" (1944c, 1). A few weeks earlier, on 24 February 1944, nearly two hundred Hawai'i men imprisoned in Santa Fe had submitted their petition to be returned to Hawai'i (discussed in chapter 6). Six of the seven fathers who lost their sons at the battlefront signed this document put forth by Shigeo Shigenaga: Morihara, Mizutari, Murakami, Hotta, Nagami, and Maehara all distinctly signed their names, requesting their return to Hawai'i, one of the reasons being a wish to have the comfort of relatives or friends in times of distress, a foreboding of coming events—at the time, Usaku Morihara alone had lost his son. As stated earlier, that February petition was rejected by the authorities for not being sent through proper channels.
>
> Group 2: Other internees, including Morihara, Hotta, and Tokairin, chose to be paroled to War Relocation Authority camps.
>
> Group 3: A final group chose to be paroled elsewhere on the mainland.

Bryan reports that "the hearing records and pertinent information" of those desiring parole—forty-two cases in all—were submitted to the Alien Enemy Control Unit of the Justice Department "for recommendation regarding parole" (1).

Military Sons and Internee Self-Advocacy

Reflecting their understanding of the power of words and petitions, despite being forbidden citizenship and the citizen's right to petition, some internees exploited the compounded ironies of this situation, arguing for their own or their collective release on the basis of their sons' military service. Gen. Bryan, in his 3 April memo, also makes reference to a petition from Ichiji Adachi of Kona, Hawai'i Island, to the commanding general, dated 14 March 1944: "In this petition a total of forty-five internees, held at Santa Fe, New Mexico, presented their petition to return to the Territory of Hawaii. They are all in the category under discussion" (1944c, 1). Thus, in addition to the collective 24 February petition discussed earlier, the smaller group of forty-five fathers of military sons in Santa Fe collectively petitioned to be returned home to Hawai'i. Unfortunately, no copy of this document is available.

But no sooner had the internees who had been transferred from Fort Missoula, Montana (the cohort originally sent from Camp Livingston to Fort Missoula), arrived in Santa Fe on 6 April, than Adachi drafted another "Petition for Parole to Hawaii" to General Robert C. Richardson Jr., commanding general, U.S. Armed Forces in the Central Pacific Area, on 10 April 1944. It was "signed by 21 internees of this Station, who have just arrived from Missoula, Montana, and respectfully request your favorable consideration thereon" (Adachi 1944, 1). In their argument, they first cited their sons' military service: "[We] are the fathers of the boys who have joined the armed forces of the United States. Some of them are now fighting on the Italian front, some have already paid their supreme sacrifice to their country [Morihara being one], some are about to be sent abroad and some are still undergoing training at different army camps" (2). The fifth and sixth reasons listed by the petitioners return to consideration of their sons' loyalty and the importance of their fathers' release to the sons' morale and sense of service to their country:

That, we know, our sons in the armed forces will do their best to serve their country whatever circumstances they are placed in, but should they be notified of their fathers' parole to Hawaii on the strength of their loyalty, we believe their one big worry will be eliminated.

That some of the brothers of our sons in the army are of draft age. In the absence of their fathers, they have been forced to shoulder the responsibility of maintaining [the] household economy. However, should we be granted parole back to Hawaii, we are confident that they would eagerly join the armed forces, as they would then have no anxiety whatsoever about their homes. (2–3)

This last offering of younger sons would seem to reveal the fathers' desperation. It is signed by Issei from this study: Ryosei Aka, Katsuichi Miho, and Jinshichi Tokairin, among others.

The response to Adachi's 14 March collective petition came from Colonel Kendall J. Fielder, Office of the Assistant Chief of Staff for Military Intelligence, on 15 April 1944. After the standard words of acknowledgment, Fielder points out that "to be considered, such requests or petitions should be initiated individually and forwarded through official channels"—another bureaucratic roadblock, like that experienced by the February 1944 petitioners. The only hopeful information is that "the following seventeen internees have been previously considered and a recommendation for their parole on the mainland has been or is going forward to the Office of the Provost Marshal General" (Fielder 1944a, 1); among them were Issei mentioned before: Usaku Morihara, whose son Arthur Akira was killed in action in October 1943; Reverend Ryuten Kashiwa, with two soldier sons; Teiichiro Maehara, with two soldier sons; Reverend Kakichi Okamoto, with one soldier son; Ryozo Izutsu, whose son Tadami was wounded in action; and Matsujiro Otani, with two, eventually four, soldier sons.

A few weeks later, on 2 May 1944, Col. Fielder wrote another response to Adachi's 10 April petition for parole to Hawai'i, claiming that it had been "very carefully considered by a Board of Officers appointed by the General for that purpose." Reflecting a seemingly sympathetic point of view of an earnest and benevolent authority, the writer continues:

> It has been the policy of the Military authorities in Hawaii to give every consideration to fathers of American soldiers and on several occasions they have been paroled from internment when otherwise such parole would not have been granted. On the other hand it has been the policy to permit no persons who have been evacuated from Hawaii for internment on the mainland or for relocation on the mainland to return to Hawaii.
>
> After careful deliberation the Board has recommended that the adopted policy be adhered to and the commanding General has approved that recommendation. Therefore your petition to be permitted to return to Hawaii has been denied. . . .
>
> In the event the status of the war and the availability of shipping to Hawaii warrants [sic] a change in policy the fathers of American soldiers will certainly be the first to be given permission to return to the Territory of Hawaii. (Fielder 1944b, 1)

In the end, officials claimed enforcement of policy in preference to all manner of argument for the internees returning to Hawai'i. What I find significant is the internees' repeated efforts made to that end.

Although Ryosei Aka participated in collective petitions, such as that filed by Adachi on behalf of the Missoula arrivals in April 1944, his personal petitioning took a somewhat different approach. Recall that Aka was one of the small contingent of Camp Livingston internees sent to Fort Missoula, then held in Montana from June 1943 to April 1944, when they were shipped to Santa Fe, and that he signed Adachi's petition. However, as early as 10 November 1942, he had signed an affidavit at Camp Livingston swearing that he was the father of Private First Class Raymond Aka and attesting to his good citizenship with the goal of returning to his family in the Territory of Hawaii:

RYOSEI AKA, being first sworn, deposes and says; that he is the father of RAYMOND YOSHIHIRO AKA, now serving in the Army of the United States as First Class Private, at Houston, Texas;

That he was engaged in the business of Labor, Waimanalo, Oahu, Hawaii, T.H.;

That he entered the United States in the year of 1907, and that he has resided in the United States continuously during the past 35 years;

That he has always conducted himself as [a] law-abiding resident of the United States of America, that he has not engaged or participated in any activity which was un-American or subversive, during said period or at any other time;

That the United States is his said son's country as well as the affiant's other Children's and that affiant is loyal to the United States;

Wherefore, affiant respectfully requests that upon due consideration of this affidavit and such other facts as are before the Board of Authority concerned, he will be permitted to join his family now residing 347 Buckle Lane, Honolulu, T.H. and if the Board of Authority deems it advisable to place such conditions or restrictions upon him as it may deem necessary. (Aka 1942)

He signed it, using his English signature, and Arnold L. Price notarized it.

The fact that this document was a form requiring blanks to be filled in with appropriate information would suggest that others in a similar situation at Camp Livingston may have also signed their own affidavits, although this is the only one I have come across so far. Not until 2 February 1943, however, did Aka write a brief, pointed letter to the commanding general, Hawaiian Department, enclosing the affidavit:

Sir:

I, Ryosei Aka, hereby respectfully request that upon due consideration of the affidavit herein enclosed and such other facts that may come before the hearing board of authority concerned, I will be permitted to join my family or to return to my home.

This is intended to be [a] petition for rehearing and your prompt consideration in the matter will be greatly appreciated. (1943)

Four months later, on 25 May 1943, Colonel William R. C. Morrison in the Judge Advocate General Department (JAGD), Office of the Military Governor, Iolani Palace, Honolulu, replied with regrets:

> This office regrets to inform you that your petition for a rehearing of your case has been denied and that it will be unable to grant your request for permission to return to your family in the Territory of Hawaii or to return to your home here. However, if you make the necessary arrangements to reserve a place for your family in either a war relocation center or a family internment camp on the Mainland and if you are then willing to have your family evacuated from the Territory of Hawaii, this office will consider the possibility of your reunion with your family under such circumstances.

Offering a prisoner unification with his family only if he is "willing to have [his] family evacuated from the Territory of Hawaii" to become prisoners on the mainland? Yet another cruel and compounded irony confronting the internees.

Possibly in response to Aka's request, FBI director Hoover must have requested information from the DOJ, prompting Assistant Attorney General Wendell Berge to respond on 22 June 1943, with a copy in Aka's file. This judgment has broader implications in that it applies to the subconsular agents as a group, noting their benign function, the War Department's opposition to "proceeding against [them]" because they were already interned, and the insufficient grounds for their prosecution:

> Reference is made to your recent memorandum . . . concerning a possible prosecution of the subject, who was a so-called "consular agent" in Hawaii and engaged in functions commonly performed by a notary public.
>
> The facts in this case are not sufficient to warrant prosecution particularly in view of the fact that the War Department opposed proceeding against so-called "consular agents" and since the subject is now interned by the military authorities for the duration of the war.[2]

Aka persisted, and a year later in Santa Fe, on 21 April 1944, he wrote to Loyd H. Jensen, the officer in charge of the Santa Fe Detention Station:

Dear Mr. Jensen:

REQUEST FOR ASSISTANCE RE EARLY PAROLE TO MINNEAPOLIS

I have two sons serving in the U.S. army, Sgt. Raymond Y. Aka and Corp. Roy Aka, both of whom [are] now stationed at Camp Savage, Minn. Probably on the strength of above fact, while at Missoula I was questioned as to where I would like to go in case of a parole, to which question I named the following address:

Mrs. Shizu Aka, 1941 Aldrich Ave., So., Minneapolis. . . .

Mrs. Shizu Aka being the wife of Raymond Aka, above mentioned.

I now hear that my second son, Roy Aka, may be sent overseas any time. This being the case, it is my earnest desire to be paroled to above named address, so that I may see my son before he leaves and give him a good send off. Also I wish to take up some sort of work in a free zone, as life without work is something I cannot stand.

I, therefore, respectfully request you to take up with the proper authority so that I may be paroled to my daughter-in-law's at an earliest possible date.

Thanking you for your assistance in this matter.

Nearly a year and a half had passed since he filled out his affidavit, and Raymond was now a sergeant. That both sons were stationed at Camp Savage indicates that they were in the MIS.

Jensen must have sent Aka's letter through channels quite expeditiously, as Colonel Francis E. Howard, the director of the Prisoner of War Division, OPMG, wrote to Edward Ennis, the director of the AECU, on 4 May, to which Ennis responded six days later about Aka being "a proper case for parole on the mainland." Apparently, Ennis disregarded an earlier memo from W. F. Kelly containing a questionable interpretation of Aka's letter to family members in Japan while the internee was incarcerated at Fort Missoula. With the subject head "Censorship intercepts indicative of pro-Axis sentiments" and another heading "DETAINEE EXPRESSES CONFIDENCE IN JAPAN'S VICTORY," Aka's message actually reads, "Even for a second, I do not forget the Father land. It is possible that some time the flowers blossoming in the spring will come. And I want you to wait for that time." The censor's note claims that the "reference to spring indicates a possible early victory for Japan" (Kelly 1944b). An equally plausible interpretation, of course, could be an end to the war and the coming of peace.

Within a month, on 13 May 1944, Aka was paroled, as requested, to his daughter-in-law's address in Minneapolis. Assistant Provost Marshal General Bryan wrote the order, which reflects the cooperation between the War and Justice Departments:

The Commanding General . . . has recommended that the internee be released from internment upon the condition that he be excluded from the Territory of Hawaii for the duration of the War; that the Director, Alien Enemy Control Unit, . . . by letter dated 10 May 1944, concurred in the recommendation of the parole of the internee; and that the internee should be paroled; NOW THEREFORE:

IT IS ORDERED that said order of internment be, and the same hereby is vacated and set aside; and it is

FURTHER ORDERED that this enemy alien be paroled under the *general supervision of the Immigration and Naturalization Service;* that such parole be accomplished in the same manner as paroles for those interned by the Department of Justice; that the parole is conditioned upon the execution of and compliance with the sponsor and parolee's agreement provided by the Immigration and Naturalization Service; that it is made a condition of the parole that the internee not return to the Territory of Hawaii prior to the termination of the war; that the parole under any other conditions or the release of this alien enemy will be effected only by order of a competent representative of the War Department; that the War Department may revoke this parole upon its own initiative and will also revoke this parole upon the recommendation of the Department of Justice. (1944d)

By the time Col. Howard replied to Ennis, on 24 May, Aka had been sent to Minneapolis by bus two days earlier and reunited with his family. I find the copious and redundant paperwork surrounding one internee's parole to be a remarkable use of resources.

After nearly a year, with no apparent response to his son Hideo's March 1944 request from the 100th Battalion petitions, Jinshichi Tokairin took it upon himself on 27 January 1945 to write from Santa Fe to General Robert C. Richardson Jr., commanding general in the Pacific, presenting his petition:

That I, Jinshichi Tokairin, Father of Hideo Tokairin, a Pfc. in the U.S. Army, respectfully request to appeal to you for my release or parole from this internment camp to be return to Hawaii.

It is my pleasure and pride to advise you that my son Hideo Tokairin belong to the 100th Battalion and [has] been engaged recently in [the] France and Italy campaign. He just completed three years oversea service and he was transferred to Hawaii in December 1944. Now he is stationed at Schofield Barrack. (Tokairin 1945a)

Although Hideo's father clearly identifies with his son and his military service, he does not mention the Purple Heart or Bronze Star that Hideo earned in the Italian campaign and, if he happened to know about it, perhaps missed a rhetorical opportunity. He does, however, endeavor to characterize his own "long residence in Hawaii" in patriotic and law-abiding terms while declaring allegiance to the United States, in support of his release to Hawai'i:

> I declare that I will be absolutely [sic] loyal to this country under the United States' Constitution.
> As I love Hawaii and this country I have no intention to go back to Japan, but determine to be loyal to this country with my family in the future. (Tokairin 1945a)

A few days later, he writes to his daughter Miyeko regarding the relief he felt knowing that Hideo had returned to Hawai'i safely. At the same time, he expresses some envy in contrasting his own situation in exile. He acknowledges the family's efforts to advocate for his release and return to Hawaii and includes a copy of his own letter to Richardson (Tokairin 1945b).

Members of other families—sons and daughters—were also busy writing on behalf of their interned fathers. Three case studies (see Okawa 2015b) provide examples of efforts from the families of Matsujiro Otani, Rev. Kodo Fujitani, and Ichiji Adachi that illustrate the diligence and persistence—as well as the frustration—of internee family advocates.

The "Point System"

On 4 January 1945, Lieutenant Colonel Eugene V. Slattery, JAGD, authored a memorandum to the Commanding General's Review Board, from the OIS, Iolani Palace Grounds, with the subject heading "Considering Return to the Territory of Hawaii Certain Persons Formerly Interned on the Mainland" (Slattery 1945a). Despite the considered return of internees to the Territory of Hawaii before the war's end, which meant a divergence from reiterated policy, the memo reveals a curious and disturbing point system, rating internees in reference to their military sons and other factors. Even a few examples call this method into question and are cited here in full regarding several internees related to this study:

> [Introduction:] This office submits a synopsis of ten cases of individuals on parole on the Mainland of the United States who have sons or daughters in the armed forces of this nation who desire to return to the Territory of Hawaii. The purpose of this memorandum is to evaluate the facts in each case and establish the proper grouping for each individual.

Ryosei (Yoshinari) Aga (Aka) . . . Age, 57; interned 27 February 1942; transferred to Mainland 27 March 1942; *two sons in the army in 1942;*[3] arrived in the Territory 17 January 1907; made one return trip to Japan in 1936; wife and eight children residing in the Territory; is an Okanawan [*sic*]; although listed as a consular agent in the Hawaiian-Japanese Annual and Directory, denied that he was a consular agent but admitted that he made certain reports to the Japanese consul while employed as a Japanese language school teacher; no organizational ties; made no contributions to Japanese war causes; asserts he owes allegiance to America; wants America to win; expects all of his four sons to be called for service in the United States Army; and has no desire to return to Japan. Internee Hearing Board unanimously recommended parole, Intelligence Reviewing Board recommended internment, and ordered interned by The Commanding General. *Subject is entitled to seven points because of his age, period on the Mainland and the fact that he has two sons in the Army.* Accordingly, it is recommended that he be placed in Group I. (1, emphasis mine).

Kodo Fujitani . . . Age, 59; transferred to the Mainland 23 May 1942; *one son in Army since January 1944;* born in Japan 27 June 1886; arrived in T.H. 7 June 1921; 17 years education in Japan and a university graduate; took physical examination for military service in 1910; wife and seven children in the Territory, while he has one son, one brother and one sister in Japan; engaged as Buddhist priest since 1921, consular agent for ten years, Japanese language school teacher and principal for fourteen years; assisted in collection of comfort kits; registered the births of six of his children with Japanese government; hopes for peace in the present conflict; plans to repatriate to Japan as late as 10 January 1944 but changed his mind on 24 January 1944. Considerations of subject's age, length of time on the Mainland *and the fact that he has a son in the Army entitles him to four points. However, since subject would be considered dangerous but for the fact that he has a son in the Army, two points have been deducted and it is, accordingly, recommended that he be put in Group III.* (1, emphasis mine)[4]

Yet a day later, on 5 January 1945, an order was issued and signed by Slattery that Rev. Fujitani be "placed in Group II" (1945b).

Kiyoji Hotta . . . Age, 62; transferred to Mainland 7 August 1942; *one son in the Army;* arrived in T.H. in 1907; served in Japanese Army during Russo-Japanese war as a corporal for twenty months; four return trips to Japan in 1919, 1934, 1936 and 1938; wife and children in the Territory; children all dual citizens, none having been expatriated; owns a store and real estate on Maui; in 1938 purchased property in Japan worth Y1500; purchased $35,000 in gold bonds of the Tokyo Electric Company which he claims was sold to the American Government; in the event of invasion would be neutral unless the American Government "wants me"; if the Islands were captured by the Japanese and he was ordered to fight he must obey; wanted to return to Japan because he was born there; still wants to return to Japan but since his children do not want to go he cannot go back at this time. *A consideration of the pertinent facts would entitle subject to a maximum of five points.* Accordingly, it is recommended that he be placed in Group II. (1945a, 3–4, emphasis mine)[5]

Ryozo Izutsu . . . Age, 61; transferred to Mainland 16 September 1942; *one son in the Army;* born in Japan 2 April 1884; grammar school education there; wife and seven children but four have been expatriated; a brother and a sister in Japan; arrived in the Territory November 1906; made one return trip in 1907; has Y10,000 on deposit in Japan; contributed $25 to Japanese War Relief; owns $800 in U.S. War Bonds; in 1927 made up his mind to reside here permanently; alleged to be a leader in the Japanese community on Kauai; all of his children are christian [*sic*] and seven of them have attended the University of Hawaii or some other educational school higher than high school; stated he would like to see the United States win this war. *Subject is entitled to five points* under the plan presented to the Board at the last meeting. Accordingly, it is recommended that he be placed in Group II. (4, emphasis mine)[6]

Besides the number of an internee's military sons figuring high in Slattery's criteria and calculation in determining a prisoner's early return to Hawai'i, it would seem that the internee's having Christian ties outweighed his having Buddhist ties and that his son's or sons' being killed or wounded in action, curiously, did not factor in at all. Despite the point system being an attempt to avoid subjectivity, it would seem that much came down to subjective interpretation and judgment.[7] Such attempts at a measurement of "worthiness" might be compared to the short-lived point system devised by Calvert L. Dedrick to measure the loyalty of the Nisei in WRA confinement; this is discussed extensively by Eric Muller, who describes it as "simple-minded" and "perverse" (2007, 48).

The net effect of efforts by internees and their families was not always the desired parole, but individuals in government and military agencies—including Richardson, the military governor; Morrison and Slattery, JAGD, OMG; Bryan, the assistant provost marshal general; Tollefson, OPMG; Ennis, director of the Alien Enemy Control Unit, DOJ; and Williams and Jensen, the officers in charge of the SFIC, INS,

DOJ—becoming increasingly aware of a fundamental contradiction in the Japanese civilian internee situation: sons serving the country that had locked their fathers up. What could call the War and Justice Departments' imprisonment of Japanese immigrants—and the authorities' assumptions about their loyalty—into question more concretely and obviously than that, raising moral and humanitarian questions, ironies compounded when those sons were dying on the battlefield?

Some officials, such as Ennis and Tollefson, responded swiftly. But the machinery of government, coupled with glitches in communication and the martial law governing the islands until October 1944, prevented at worst and slowed at best any efforts to right this wrong, to rectify the contradictions. Internee fathers and their advocates eventually received letters that the internee would be paroled on the mainland or sent to a WRA camp or not sent back to Hawai'i or sent back sooner than later or eventually sent back with the main body of internees months after the war's end. Some Issei, like Rev. Fujitani, were offered parole on the mainland but chose to stay with their communities at SFIC rather than being released to the impersonal and unknown outside world. The diligent efforts of Matsujiro Otani's family led to his incremental release—first to the Granada WRA camp at Amache, Colorado, and, despite his being "scheduled to return to Hawaii" as early as January 1945, finally an early release to the islands in October 1945, well after the war's end and only a few weeks before the general internee population was returned home (Okawa 2015b).

For all 161 fathers in Santa Fe from the Territory of Hawaii who had one or two, or more, sons in the military, waiting for their sons' safe return must have been agony—a universal plight for those with loved ones in harm's way. But these men were in forced exile, separated by thousands of miles from their families, those who might have provided some comfort to the fathers of Akira Morihara or Yukitaka Mizutari or Toshio Murakami or Kihachiro Hotta or Hiroshi Nagami or Iwao Takemoto or Saburo Maehara. The relief felt by Jinshichi Tokairin when he learned about his son Hideo's return to Hawai'i from Europe was undoubtedly shared by many fathers. In the end, it is heartening for those who are descendants to know how ardently some of our fathers, grandfathers, and their families resisted those who would oppress them—if only for the record. While the Issei chose to adapt to their lives in exile in order to survive, many were neither passive nor accepting of their fate; rather, they and their families persistently and repeatedly argued against their imprisonment and for the internees' return to their beloved families and island homes.

CHAPTER 9

Return from Exile and Rebundling

It is our hope that this effort will help to establish a peaceful
world for future generations.
—Keiho Soga, preface to *Kodama*

Thus did my grandfather and the other civilian internees from Hawai'i live their
lives in exile—isolated from the rest of the world and connected to it, then and
now, mainly by words. Their letters, journals, poetry, petitions, newsletters,
scrapbooks, sermons, artwork, librettos, plays, performances, and other activities become for descendants—their own and others'—the evidence of their
hourly and daily realities as prisoners, targets of what the Civil Liberties Act of
1988 termed the nation's "racial prejudice, wartime hysteria and . . . failure of
political leadership."[1] At the same time, these and other artifacts become the evidence of the Isseis' powerful resistance to and survival of the perils of imprisonment—*Yamato damashii* to use Keiho Soga's words, in the face of Naojiro
Hirano's "barbed wire disease." Their individual and collective lives and their
cultural and literacy acts become what Soga describes as "a demonstration to the
world and future generations to come of the true Japanese spirit of *Yamato
damashii*, the strong Japanese character of calm in the face of unbearably harsh
adversity" (1944). John Culley refers to the Issei as shapers of the internment
experience—a claim illustrated in these chapters—rather than passive and inert
victims (2000). One could say that these were dynamic and productive times for
many Hawai'i Issei, despite their unjust imprisonment.

Early Return: Fathers with Military Sons

So was it, too, for the Nisei. Due in part to the persistence of sons and daughters
at home in Hawai'i and abroad—and the internees themselves—in their petitions, some fathers with sons in the military were allowed to return to the islands
before the war's end. The government relaxed the repeatedly stated restrictions
on return of the Issei to Hawai'i before the termination of the war and sent an

initial group of ten internees back to the islands on 11 July 1945 ("10 Alien Japanese" 1945), more than a month before Japan's surrender. The group included several internees related to this study, introduced in previous chapters and paroled in 1944:

> Ryosei Aka, whose sons, Master Sergeant Raymond Aka and Sergeant Roy Aka, served in the MIS; he was paroled on the mainland to Minneapolis, Minnesota, on 13 May 1944, departing from Santa Fe on 22 May;
>
> Ryozo Izutsu, my grandfather's barrack mate, whose son Pfc. Tadami Izutsu's petition may have been received and considered after all, although Tadami had expressed some doubts; the son was wounded in action as a member of the 442nd RCT in Europe and his father paroled on 22 May 1944, probably to a WRA camp;
>
> Teiichiro Maehara, my grandfather's friend and barrack mate, whose son 1st Lt. Saburo Maehara was killed in action one month before the end of the war in Europe, his second son being 2nd Lt. Edward Goro Maehara. Their father was paroled on 22 May 1944, possibly to a WRA camp; and
>
> Kyoichi Miyata, whose son Private Robert Miyata's letter of 26 September 1943 quite possibly was the catalyst for the "reinvestigation" of civilian internees from Hawai'i with sons in the military; the father was paroled on 4 January 1944, probably to a WRA camp.

It is not clear how the particular list of ten was formulated, though it was likely related to Slattery's criteria and point system, outlined in the previous chapter. Several documents in Ryosei Aka's file are particularly noteworthy regarding the timing and wording of the government correspondence on these men. As early as 16 January 1945, Brig. Gen. Morrison, OIS, wrote a memo to the OPMG at the War Department on the familiar subject of "Japanese Civilian Internees from the Territory of Hawaii with Sons in the Armed Forces of the United States." He was informing the OPMG that the commanding general of the U.S. Army Forces, Pacific Ocean Areas, "deems it proper *at this time* to permit Japanese civilian internees from the Territory of Hawaii presently on parole on the Mainland, who have sons or daughters in the armed forces of the United States, to return to the Territory of Hawaii" (1945a, 1; emphasis mine). The Issei from my study whom I listed were included. Morrison requested that the OPMG "make the necessary arrangements to transport these individuals to the Territory of Hawaii" (2).

Two days later, Brig. Gen. Morrison followed up with a memo, "Return to the Territory of Hawaii of Certain Individuals," to the G-2, Counter-Intelligence

Division, in San Francisco, informing it of the commanding general's recommendation and request for travel arrangements to the OPMG (1945b). On the same day, Major Robert B. Griffith, also from the OIS, wrote to the Trans-Pacific Travel Control Bureau, informing it that the commanding general had approved the return of the ten individuals to the territory (1945a). That was in January 1945, certainly before it could be predicted when the Pacific War would end, and thus it was an encouraging development that the military had approved the Issei fathers' return home.

However, it was not until six months later that the promise actually was fulfilled. That it may have happened suddenly, despite the authorities' efficient preliminary planning, is also likely, for Aka's family had not been informed of his return home in advance and were not expecting him. In a family history, his daughter Janice tells the poignant story of his arrival on 11 July 1945, after three and a half years of exile: "He arrived in Honolulu unannounced . . . and sat quietly on the porch waiting for someone to return home. When [I] arrived, [I] was overjoyed at the sight of him but saddened that he received such a disappointing homecoming" (Okudara n.d.). The next day the *Honolulu Star-Bulletin* announced the names of the ten men along with a story about their return:

> Ten Japanese aliens, residents of Hawaii who were relocated on the mainland after the outbreak of the war, arrived in Honolulu Wednesday as the first such group to be returned to the territory.
>
> With the war moving so far west of Hawaii, it is the desire of Lt. Gen. Robert C. Richardson Jr., commanding army forces . . . with powers of exclusion under a presidential executive order, to revert to normal domestic conditions as rapidly as practicable.
>
> Some of those sent to the mainland for security reasons were interned, while others went to relocation centers. None was guilty of overt acts against the United States.
>
> The first group is the vanguard of other groups that will be returned as shipping becomes available.
>
> Their transportation will not, however, take precedence over travel connected with the war effort, and will not interfere with transportation for soldiers returning from furlough or for rotation replacements.
>
> In deciding priority for return to their homes in Hawaii, their health, age, number of dependents and other factors are considered.
>
> Gen. Richardson has given preference to those parolees with sons or daughters in the armed forces.
>
> Each of the 10 who has returned has at least one son in the United States army. ("10 Alien Japanese" 1945)

In the Matsujiro Otani family collection, a document entitled "Invitational Travel Orders," from the Adjutant General's Office, War Department, dated 24 August 1945, provides the names of scores of Issei internees who, like Otani, had sons in the military, as well as some who did not, all who were to return to Hawai'i in a second group along with him. From this study, they included Kiyoji Hotta, Kyujiro Ishida, and Shinjiro Yoshimasu, who were still interned at Santa Fe, and Rev. Ryuten Kashiwa, Usaku Morihara, and Otani, who were at the Grenada WRA camp in Amache, Colorado (Office of the Adjutant General 1945a). Hotta and Morihara, we know, had each lost a son at the Italian front. Also to accompany these men were the family members of Rev. Odachi, who were waiting in a WRA camp to be reunited with him before he unexpectedly became ill and passed away, but who had to remain at the WRA camp at Gila River, Arizona, until the end of the war. Despite the August memo, however, actual travel orders did not materialize until October 1945.

Generally, it was the older fathers who had military-age sons, many of whom had been drafted before the war, such as Yukitaka Mizutari and Hideo Tokairin, or who volunteered for service after the February 1943 formation of the 442nd RCT, such as Tadami Izutsu and Katsugo Miho. These fathers naturally experienced great anxiety over their soldier sons' physical safety in combat, but they also had the chance of early parole, usually to a WRA camp, or an earlier return to their homes in Hawai'i. In contrast, I observed, the internees with younger families were more anxious about their family's basic sustenance and welfare because of their absence as providers, as was true of men such as Kato, Hoshida, and Rev. Matsuura.[2]

The privileging of fathers with military sons by the government is understandable, given the apparent moral contradiction—how could they incarcerate the fathers while their sons were fighting and dying for the United States on the battlefield? Yet it also highlights the fundamental injustice of the internment in the first place, raising the question, Why should the sons' sacrifice influence the treatment of the fathers if the fathers' imprisonment were justified to begin with? And why should the internees without military sons or daughters have less possibility of parole and suffer longer for crimes they had not committed?

Return of the Majority

On 6 August 1945, an atomic bomb destroyed Hiroshima City in the home prefecture of Rev. Watanabe, Kazumi Matsumoto, Katsuichi Miho, Seichi Fujii, Kango Kawasaki, Rev. Kinai Ikuma, and scores of other Hawai'i Issei.[3] If they could have understood its devastation, they would have been themselves devastated, for, as Susan Southard outlines, the atomic bombing caused not only widespread damage and unimaginable deaths at the time but continuing illness and pain even seventy years later (2015). On 9 August, the United States bombed Nagasaki, and on 15 August, Japan surrendered and the war finally ended. Also on 15 August, Ivan Williams, the officer in charge in Santa Fe, addressed the following announcement to "All Internees, Santa Fe Internment Camp":

> As all of you know, Japan has surrendered to the allied Nations. Peace has once again settled over the entire world. The terrible conflict has caused many many hardships and heartaches to people of all Nations. We should all bow our heads in reverence to the Almighty (whatever our religious beliefs may be) for bringing about Peace to the world.
>
> Above all now in this Camp, we do not want demonstrations of any kind. I personally assure each of you, the same fair treatment will prevail as heretofore. Our work must carry on until the Camp is inactivated.
>
> I cannot at this time assure you, just when your internment will terminate. I wish I could.
>
> I believe, however, our Department will, as soon as feasible, plan to return you to your homes or the place you desire to reside. (1945a)

Despite Williams's reasonable approach to the conclusion of the Pacific War, it wasn't until October 1945 that arrangements were initiated to return the majority of Hawai'i Issei to their homes. On 16 October, the Adjutant General's Office of the War Department issued "Invitational Travel Orders" to the commanding general, Seattle Port of Embarkation, and the chief of transportation, Army Service Forces, marked "Restricted," as it had for the second group (1945b). These orders may have been duplicated for each civilian internee—that is, a complete nine-page roster of each returning internee, by name, HJ-CI number, the agency responsible for travel expenses (INS or WRA), gender, and location at the time—as this document could be found in various family collections, including my grandfather's. Together with a gangway pass to a specific ship, there was a baggage-claim pass and an order from the Office of Internal Security, signed on 22 October 1945 by Lt. Gen. Richardson, commanding general, U.S. Army Forces, Pacific Areas. Unlike the order for the second group, it states clearly:

> *All individual internment orders* heretofore issued by the Commanding General, Hawaiian Department . . . pursuant to the authority granted under the provisions of Presidential Proclamation dated 7 and 8 December 1941, *are hereby rescinded.*

All persons heretofore prohibited from entering the Territory of Hawaii under the provisions of Executive Order No. 9066, dated 19 February 1942, and Executive Order No. 9489, dated 18 October 1944, and letters of the Secretary of War, dated 12 October 1942 and 24 October 1944, *are hereby permitted to return.* (emphasis mine)

Their travel orders were accompanied by an information sheet from the INS office in Seattle, titled "Places for Japanese, returning to Hawaii, to apply for help or advice."

Itsuo Hamada—the versatile Maui businessman, journalist, poet, theater director, and performer—writes in "Bearing Pineapple" of the mixed emotions that he and his compatriots felt upon leaving Santa Fe. It was already autumn.

1   In the height of autumn, flowers are fragrant.
     Reluctantly, I leave Santa Fe
     in a fond farewell.
2   Fighting the tears, [I see]
     sunlight fall[ing] on my friends'
     smiling faces.
3   The warmth of the hands held tightly
     is the testimony of our friendship.
     Parting is sad.

Rev. Watanabe records in his pocket notepad that on the evening of 30 September, a "farewell get-together" was held at the SFIC's Christian church. Then, on 22 October, he was again "fingerprinted," with another official "photo taken." On 25 October, his notes state, "return to Hawaii set for Oct. 30" (1944–1945, 20b, 21a).

Kawasaki had been elected the spokesman of the Hawai'i "returnees," so in organizing those being transported to Seattle by train, he appointed captains in charge of the men, who were grouped according to the four main islands, plus Honolulu. On the day of departure, 30 October 1945, Kawasaki notes that he had been in Santa Fe for "2 years, 4 months and 16 days," similar to my grandfather, who had followed him nine days later from Lordsburg. Kawasaki said their good-byes to the officials on behalf of the HJ (Hawai'i Japanese) returnees, paid "for freight shipping of stones for 6 Hawaii Island men," carried out an inspection of the hand baggage, and at noon, "327 HJ board buses for departure for Santa Fe Station" (SB). Their original number of nearly 700 had declined because some of the internees had been paroled on the mainland, repatriated to Japan, transferred to other internment camps, or died.

Hamada's memoir states that he and about 80 percent of the Hawaiʻi group left Santa Fe on that 30 October, and he describes their departure, capturing their intense feelings: "We left Santa Fe with many memories in our hearts and headed north for Seattle, Washington. It was jubilation, like jubilation at dawn, the kind of jubilation that only those who suffered and cried in the darkness know! The rope that bound us mentally and emotionally was untied—the confinement ended. We were freed and no longer prisoners. . . . It was like mountain flowers blossoming after a night of spring rain. After all, we never had committed any crime. The hardship of four years of confinement was something I cannot describe in words" (n.d.).

While still in Santa Fe, the returnees had been informed that each of them could take two suitcases on the train, but the day before departure, that number was reduced to one, and when they arrived in Seattle, Kawasaki tells us, "there was no suitcase of clothes" accessible to them. "And thus, we did not have [a] change of clothes, even underwear, from Oct. 30 to Nov 13. Dirty and grimy we landed at Honolulu!" (SB).

Before their "grimy" return, however, Kawasaki describes boarding the train to Seattle at 2:30 p.m., passing through Las Vegas, New Mexico, to Denver, Colorado. On the train ride, he observes the conditions and the men:

Spokesman [Kawasaki himself] and Dr. [Ben] Tanaka visit the other cars twice daily to see everything is OK.

The coaches are old, probably 40 to 50 years old, unclean; toilets don't flush; there is no drinking water. Utter congestion: 60 men to a car.

And yet, the men are happy in the thought that every minute and every mile, they are approaching their "Sweet Home."

The diner service is excellent. Butter for bread and cream for coffee seem ancient acquaintances. Ice cream for dinner! (SB, 31 October 1945)

He records stopping in Laramie, Wyoming, for cigars and cigarettes, passing the Minidoka WRA camp, small towns in Idaho to Boise, then to Portland, Oregon, jotting down mileage and notable geographical sites along the way. When they finally arrive in Seattle, he notes that they have traveled 2,037 miles from Santa Fe and a total of 8,309 miles since leaving Hilo. In Seattle, their accommodations, communication, and movement were quite restricted and regimented. Then, at noon on Wednesday, 7 November, "all HJ leave [Immigration] Station on buses to Pier 42," and Kawasaki, as the leader, called the roll of returnees: "All present. All board Army Transport Ship Yarmouth," and at 4:00 p.m., they set

sail for Honolulu, accompanied, Kawasaki notes, by "a few J-A veterans returning to Hawaii" (SB, 7 November 1945).

At home in the islands, families were notified by the Swedish vice-consul
Gustaf W. Olson (representing Japan's protecting power in Hawaiʻi), in form letters such as this one about their relatives' return:

> Dear *Mrs. Aoyagi*: Re: Seisaku Aoyagi
> We have been advised by the Commanding General, USAFMIDPAC
> that your relative or relatives are listed in a group scheduled to arrive here
> from the mainland about November 15, 1945.
> A place will be designated at the pier for families to assemble to meet
> them. Further information as to the exact pier, time and designated place
> cannot be given now, but we should have that information a few days
> before their arrival. Please contact us on November 9, 1945 for more
> details. . . .
> Outside islanders will be transported home either by plane or surface
> transportation on or soon after the day of their arrival in Honolulu. If
> they do not wish to accept army transportation and wish to remain here
> for a few days to visit relatives or friends, they may do so, but will have to
> take care of their own transportation back. (1945)

The journey for some is captured in a tanka by poet Sojin Takei:

> Sailing the same sea—
> How smooth this voyage is
> After four long years.
> The present world
> Is a dream within a dream.
>   (1984, 70)

On the troop ship *Yarmouth*, however, there was another reality: Kawasaki
explains that because they were on an army troop ship, they were "forced to do
all the work in connection with our passage, such as KP, LP, clean-up of hall-
ways, etc." On that Tuesday, 13 November, he writes:

> The forward latrine had stuck up and became unusable a few days ago,
> and KK negotiated for the use of the stern latrine. Capt. Kelly, com-
> mander, calls up KK and says: Unless the forward latrine is cleaned up
> and pass[es] inspection, no one will be allowed to land at Honolulu. From
> early morning, practically every one had dressed up, gone on deck to see

the approaching land. KK find[s] it impossible to get men to clean up the latrine, so full of shit. Finally, he succeeded in getting Mr. Adachi Ichiji, Rev. Okawa Gendo, of Waipahu, and Ikawa Morito, Hanapepe, Kauai, WRC, Topaz, Utah, to assist: scrubbing, washing, etc.

    5 p.m. We saw no Diamond Head, no Waikiki. When we finished the job, the ship was already at berth, Pier 26. . . . We debarked. . . . KK tel'd home "I'm back." (SB)

For Kawasaki, my grandfather, and other Big Island men, from their original departure from Hilo years earlier and now from Santa Fe to Seattle to Honolulu to Hilo, Kawasaki records a grand total of 10,918 miles.

Rebundling

SOME UNANSWERED QUESTIONS

Decades later, as a descendant in a more technologically interconnected world sensitive to consequences, something that continues to plague me, though it is beyond the scope of this study, is what happened to the Issei internees upon their reentry in Hawai'i. What happened to them personally after they returned home to their families? As Odo observes, "For most of the Hawai'i internees, the experience [of internment] was devastating. Many were at the peaks of their careers, whether as entrepreneurs or leading figures in Buddhist or Shinto institutions or in the Japanese language media. The road back to cultural and racial rehabilitation would be, for all but a few, simply impossible; others had risen to assume leadership roles in their absence and the very institutions in which they had risen to prominence would never recover their prewar luster" (1994, 7).

The "few" may have gone back to their productive, busy lives, especially if family members were able to maintain their businesses while they were absent or they were not displaced because of the shuttering of religious or educational institutions. Buddhist priests such as Rev. Fujitani, Kashiwa, and Matsuura eventually became bishops of their respective sects. Of the Japanese school principals, however, Noriko Shimada states that "initially they had a hard time adjusting to postwar conditions, because they could not return to their privileged prewar positions, but had to accept any job they could find in order to live" (1998, 135–136). Eventually, some schools were reopened, and Issei such as Futoshi Ohama assumed leadership roles. Many internees may have refused to allow the wartime imprisonment to define them, but injustice and selective incarceration must take their toll on persons more so than on positions.

After all, during nearly four years of incarceration and exile, the internees had encountered trauma and degradation, especially in the early months—with continual and humiliating strip searches, physical abuse and isolation, and the constant loss of freedom and threat of punishment. Tetsuden Kashima, in his examination of internee mistreatment, writes that "to better their conditions, [the Issei] were willing to submit to harsh treatment, endure personal deprivation, and risk physical injury" (2003, 183), punishment by choice for their self-advocacy, as seen, for example, in Lordsburg, in addition to the punishment flagrantly meted out by their captors. Richard Melzer, in his comprehensive discussion of the SFIC, refers to "many suffer[ing] from the psychological effects of captivity not unlike combat prisoners" (1994, 220). Despite the Geneva Convention, no one could be exempt from these conditions.

For Nikkei families in Hawai'i such as mine, the Issei return home reflected a similar theme of silence regarding their experience in internment, as Col. Ando had said of his father during his comments at the SFIC marker dedication in 2002. Although some internees may have felt compelled to write or speak about their imprisonment, as did Soga, Ozaki, Hoshida, and Furuya, I have heard the same words about that silence from others. Like many who have experienced combat, internee survivors had reunions among themselves but may have shared little with outsiders, even and especially family members. It might be called a culture of silence among those who have suffered—and bonded—through extreme hardship.

Furthermore, although the internees were never charged or convicted of crimes and their imprisonment was documented to have been unjust by the Civil Liberties Act of 1988, this exoneration came more than forty years too late for many, for the Japanese concept of *haji* (shame), of being singled out under a veil of suspicion, may have had insidious effects on their lives upon their return. Kashima discusses the "stigma of imprisonment" in terms of "intrafamilial, interpersonal, and intergenerational" relationships (2003, 216), mainly regarding the West Coast mass incarceration, yet as Odo suggests, the civilian internees from Hawai'i were even more isolated (1994, 6)—and, I would add, this was especially true of those exiled to the mainland.

Of Koichi Iida upon his return, his son Robert Iida said, "He was a changed man. I remember seeing him at the pier when he came back—at the Army pier in Kapalama. He had a beard. And I remember he looked sad" (quoted in Borreca 1999). In our family, my grandfather was eventually reassigned to the church on Maui where he had served in the 1920s and 1930s before being sent, in 1936, to 'Ōla'a, where he was replaced after his arrest. He continued his ministry with the

Japanese-speaking congregations in central Maui until his retirement[4]; that was the quiet, austere grandfather I knew. But my grandmother is said to have commented that my grandfather came back "a changed man," the same words used by Robert Iida about his father. Although I had heard the comment as an adolescent when I first heard about Rev. Watanabe's imprisonment, I learned long after she died that it had been my grandmother's observation. Neither my mother nor my aunt could explain what she had meant beyond some reference to his not being as gentle as he had been before; I can only regret never being able to ask her how he had changed—or to ask him, for that matter, about the war years. In any event, his grandchildren born during and after the war were deprived of knowing the person my grandmother remembered. Could I have seen more than a glimpse of the impish man who enjoyed my Spam sandwiches? My grandfather died of cancer in 1968, when I was away from home, teaching in a Virginia women's college. I knew nothing of his suffering then or during his internment decades before that.

Another study might delve into how the returning internees were affected by their unjust imprisonment—how they changed, if they did, and how they coped with their return, though so many witnesses are gone now. Did some of them suffer from depression or what is now labeled post-traumatic stress disorder (PTSD)? Following their return, did levels of alcoholism or other substance abuse rise? Or did the spirit of *Yamato damashii* really prevail?

What other consequences of the Hawai'i Issei exile can be identified? According to the 1 October 1945 roster compiled by the SFIC internees, thirty inmates are listed as having died in internment; of those from Hawai'i, how many died of preexisting illnesses versus illnesses acquired in the camps? How many, like Ishida, lived but continued to suffer from those illnesses? How many, like Oshima, were killed, supposedly trying to escape, when they were, in fact, acting out of despair? For families such as Rev. Odachi's, the separation upon arrest had been final for two of his four children—they lost their father to illness and death before reunification. For other families, such as Craig Hirashima's, the deprivation of their father by his internment was magnified when he died in the tidal wave of 1946, only months after his return.

And what became of the eight Hawai'i Issei women on the list of those interned on the mainland as alien enemies? Six of them were imprisoned in Seagoville, Texas, the other two in New Mexico and California, as of November 1942 (OPMG 1942a). What were their fates? Although I began research on my grandfather's story and hence focused on the experience of the Issei men, I continue to wonder what happened to the women—their journeys, their personal and family circumstances, their treatment, anxieties, and losses.[5]

Despite more temporal distance, descendants' studies such as the current one, integrating English and translated Japanese texts and interviews with government documents, are possible. Although this narrative has foregrounded some of the unpublished writing, both prose and poetry, collected from internee families, with the exception of petition letters (see Okawa 2015b) and brief narrative passages from daughters here, the bulk of documents concern the observations and experience of Issei and Nisei males. A close reading of as yet unpublished journals and published and unpublished poetry in Japanese by both incarcerated Issei women and men might reveal further insights into the complexities of the Hawai'i internees' lives during imprisonment and following their return.

RECASTING

In *Cane Fires,* Gary Okihiro accurately describes the prewar political position of the Hawai'i Issei as disenfranchised and inferior because of their permanent alien status, and he asserts that "the core of Japanese culture—language and religious belief"—was seen by some to threaten Americanism and justified the detention of Buddhist and Shinto priests, language school principals, and others (1991, 188–189). They would be punished for being Japanese. While this characterization is undeniable, in my observation, the strong communities formed by isolating and concentrating large numbers of Issei in the internment camps—a kind of ghettoizing process—ironically had a reverse effect from that intended by the authorities: John Culley points out that in Santa Fe, camp administrators "developed an elaborate program of recreation, entertainment, education, work, and visits, which also served as a means of controlling internee behavior" (1991). However, the communities that formed around such activities as those described previously actually served to perpetuate, perhaps cultivate, elements of Japanese language and religious belief, that "core of Japanese culture," in ways that may not have occurred naturally in ordinary society amid forces of assimilation.

The DOJ/army internment camps, in the end, became an extraordinary collection of highly literate and learned individuals—clergy, teachers, cultural as well as business and community leaders—the "cultural heaven" mentioned earlier. They practiced their arts, and they taught and shared them with one another through classes and cultural societies. Moreover, if the Issei were politically disenfranchised before the war in Hawai'i, they used all of the resources available to them politically to advocate for themselves in internment. Although their linguistic human rights were threatened, especially in the early months of the war, many not only maintained their language but actually expanded their linguistic repertoire.

One example is the February 1944 collective petition first described in chapter 6. What happened to it reflects the perpetuation of power in the hands of the powerful because it was denied consideration based on protocol. However, I believe its execution, in and of itself, reflects the power of the Hawaiʻi Issei internees' resistance to the established authority, in this case U.S. military and government officials, not so much at that time but for Soga's "future generations." At the time, the experience of the Hawaiʻi petitioners illustrated that the petition process itself has a contradictory political function in both democratic and autocratic societies.[6] Although it provides a seemingly positive recourse for redress, petitioning also assumes and sanctions a hierarchy in which the ultimate power resides in the official authority, which invariably functions to maintain its dominance. A paradoxical, perhaps illusionary, power exists among those seeking redress: They have the power to ask, but their request may or may not be bestowed upon them or even considered, as happened in the case of the Hawaiʻi civilian internees.

That said, the drafters of this document were strategic in their choice to write it. Although they were educated, literate, and cultured, as well as more or less socially privileged and respected as leaders of their communities, they knew little, if anything, of the covert investigations by U.S. intelligence agencies and were reduced overnight to the status of prisoners, subjected to the will and whim of others—not for proven wrongdoing but, as in Rev. Watanabe's case, "on suspicion of being an alien enemy,"[7] merely a matter of immigration status. Permanently disenfranchised by their ineligibility for U.S. citizenship because of their race, they were twice oppressed, being imprisoned for being alien Japanese.

Rather than seeing themselves as inferior and dominated masses, as unidentifiably "generic" (JanMohammed and Lloyd 1990, 10), as their captors did, however, the Hawaiʻi internees identified with the collective as a literate "we." They believed in the power of the written word to redefine their identity, and despite the stereotypes and suspicions of the dominant American society, they present a collective narrative in their petition. They use the story of their lives as good citizens in the form and conventions of the official establishment for a political purpose—making a case for the reversal of exile that they request. Basing their argument on good citizenship certainly reflects their appreciation of the irony of their exclusion from it. And their very use of the petition form can be viewed as a means of protest: using a medium technically prohibited to them by laws prohibiting their citizenship.

Although they may have been more successful in advancing other petitions, as we have seen, we must wonder what the Issei accomplished by writing this particular document. Their argument in February 1944 is compelling and heartfelt, but it assumes an audience. For their efforts, they seemed to encounter the worst of fates; rather than their petition being denied, it never reached the officials—for reasons of protocol (supposedly because they wrote a collective petition rather than individual ones)—and it wasn't considered at all. For their descendants, however, it can be seen as a powerful symbolic document from behind barbed wire, notwithstanding its failure. I know I was heartened to see my grandfather's signature among its pages.

Under oppressive conditions, the very act of reconstructing a collective identity devoted to home reveals a creativity, activism, and resistance to the official authority. Mira Shimabukuro calls such discourse "writing-to-redress" in her extensive discussion of writing done primarily in the WRA camps (2015, 26–27). She asserts that "writing-to-redress does more than encode or preserve a response. It also serves as a means to expand a rhetorical, and thus, a political activity: the collective struggle to relocate authority away from one's oppressors and back into the community itself" (30). As events evolved, then, the internees wrote this petition for the record alone, yet having unearthed it from the National Archives, I believe each signature, written primarily in English, ultimately represents the assertion of each man preserved collectively for us: In each case, the signer assumes and asserts membership in a democratic system despite its rejection of him.

For me as a granddaughter, delving into such archival and government documents raised predictably troubling questions and responses—many of them described in the preceding paragraphs and chapters—to official policy and conduct, errors, contradictions, inefficiency, racial biases, hypocrisies, and the humiliation of the Issei prisoners counter to the tenets of the Geneva Convention. Many documents, after all, attempt the same objectification of these men as that accomplished by their expressionless mug shots. At the same time, it was through documents such as this petition and others that I learned of the ways that the Issei from Hawai'i (and the mainland) empowered themselves, advocated for themselves, maintained their dignity in light of and despite their subjugated positions. Priscilla Wegars points out that in both the Kooskia and Lordsburg internment camps, internees used the provisions of the 1929 Geneva Convention "to such great advantage . . . that the U.S. government fought hard to have its provisions denied to current prisoners at our Guantanamo Bay detention facility in Cuba" (2010, 195).

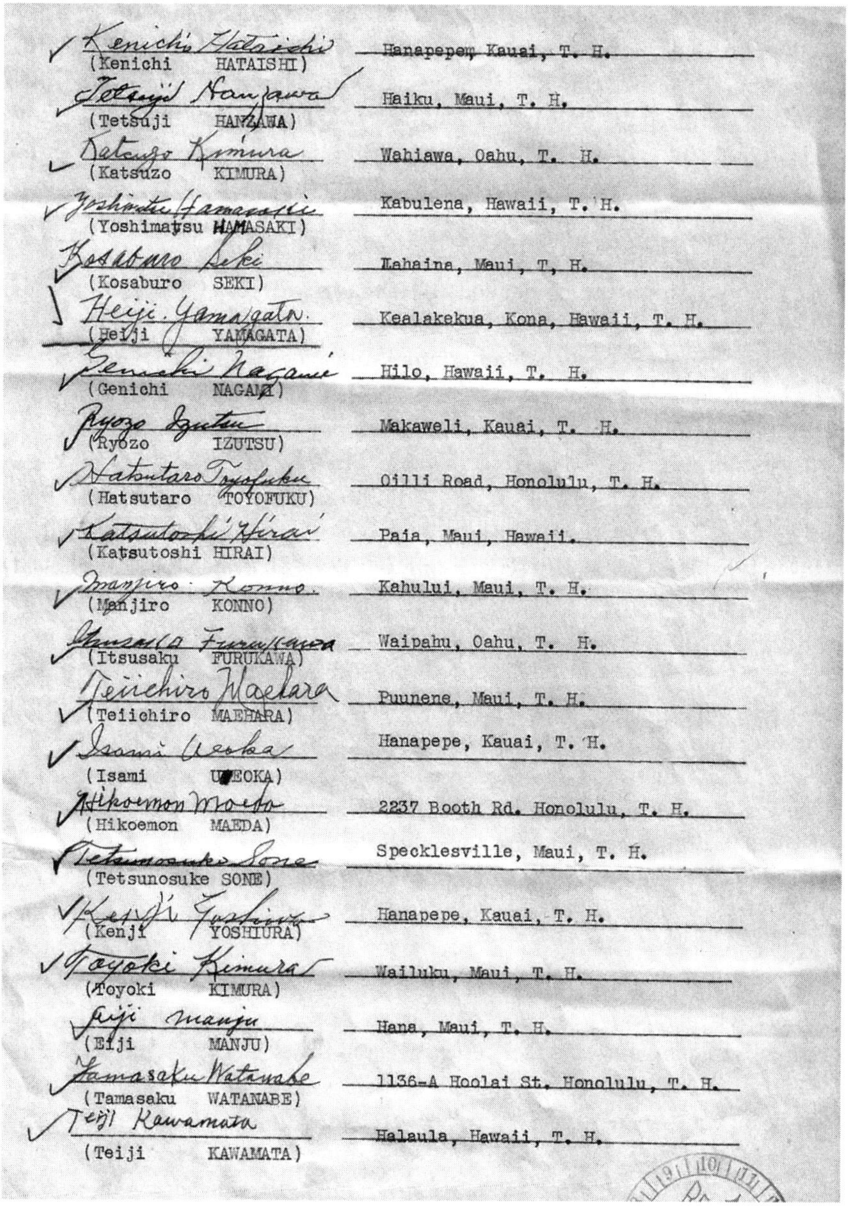

Signature	(Printed Name)	Location
	(Kenichi HATAISHI)	Hanapepe, Kauai, T. H.
	(Tetsuji HANZAWA)	Haiku, Maui, T. H.
	(Katsuzo KIMURA)	Wahiawa, Oahu, T. H.
	(Yoshimatsu HAMASAKI)	Kabulena, Hawaii, T. H.
	(Kosaburo SEKI)	Lahaina, Maui, T. H.
	(Heiji YAMAGATA)	Kealakekua, Kona, Hawaii, T. H.
	(Genichi NAGAMI)	Hilo, Hawaii, T. H.
	(Ryozo IZUTSU)	Makaweli, Kauai, T. H.
	(Hatsutaro TOYOFUKU)	Oilli Road, Honolulu, T. H.
	(Katsutoshi HIRAI)	Paia, Maui, Hawaii.
	(Manjiro KONNO)	Kahului, Maui, T. H.
	(Itsusaku FURUKAWA)	Waipahu, Oahu, T. H.
	(Teiichiro MAEHARA)	Puunene, Maui, T. H.
	(Isami UEOKA)	Hanapepe, Kauai, T. H.
	(Hikoemon MAEDA)	2237 Booth Rd. Honolulu, T. H.
	(Tetsunosuke SONE)	Specklesville, Maui, T. H.
	(Kenji YOSHIURA)	Hanapepe, Kauai, T. H.
	(Toyoki KIMURA)	Wailuku, Maui, T. H.
	(Eiji MANJU)	Hana, Maui, T. H.
	(Tamasaku WATANABE)	1136-A Hoolai St. Honolulu, T. H.
	(Teiji KAWAMATA)	Halaula, Hawaii, T. H.

FIG. 9.1. Internee signatures on a petition requesting return to Hawai'i, SFIC, 24 February 1944 (Hawaiian Aliens; Records Relating to Japanese Civilian Internees during WWII, 1942–46; Records of the Alien Enemy Information Bureau; Records of the Office of the Provost Marshal General, RG 389; NACP).

Government documents also showed how in the prison camps the Issei productivity proved their mettle and how this was received by their official advocates from Spain as well as by U.S. officials. The Hawai'i internees and their mainland counterparts were most formidable in their ability to organize personnel, activities, and goods. Loyd H. Jensen, the SFIC commander for one period, being praised by an International YMCA official for running "the best internment camp I have seen anywhere in the world," said that the prisoners "would make any camp commander look good. . . . They do all the work that has to be done—maintenance, gardening, cooking—and they're very good at it" (quoted in Mangione 1978, 341). After all, these Issei from Hawai'i were among the most productive members of their home communities, despite their political disenfranchisement and imprisonment—as established leaders, based on action and accomplishment and not inheritance, as immigrants in their adopted land.

Also for me as a granddaughter, delving into Issei letters and journals, petitions and poetry, has involved a kind of reliving parts of their lives behind the barbed wire. This experience has been both infuriating and inspiring. Their literacy in Japanese and English served some of them well in surviving this unwarranted captivity. Many seemed extraordinarily busy and productive, given their restricted circumstances, keeping records, asserting a willfulness to combat "barbed wire disease" and official oppression through exposure to different ideas and skills. Their practice reflected such Japanese values as *tennakujozen* (turning a negative thing into something positive), a good and humorous example seen in the Issei searching at Fort Sam Houston for "fossils of shells and pretty stones" in blistering heat (Hoshida n.d., 307). During their imprisonment, they also had a profound desire to communicate not only with their families but also with posterity. Their legacy lies in those attempts, notwithstanding their postwar silence. Although Soga's mention of "this effort" in this chapter's opening quotation may have been a literal reference to the poetry in *Kodama*, such collections in themselves might be seen as metaphors for the observations, emotions, suffering, memories, hopes, and dreams of the writers—a collective voice that might "help to establish a peaceful world for future generations" (Soga 1944, n.p.). Whether we in the "future generations" can or will achieve that "peaceful world" remains to be seen, but that does not diminish the Issei intention or legacy.

Many Issei internees also suffered extraordinarily, some from illness, some from worry and separation, as we can understand in these pages. As the years of exile wore on, they longed more intensely for their families, their lives, their livelihoods, the island climate and culture, and, of course, their freedom, sentiments captured in their collective February 1944 petition, in which they identified themselves as men of Hawai'i. Those who were eventually paroled to WRA camps (such as Rev. Matsuura and Hoshida) or reunited with their families at Crystal City, Texas, were spared at least that deprivation.

If the authorities' intent was to destabilize the Hawai'i Nikkei communities by removing their leaders, they had to have succeeded, at least in part, depriving the communities of their religious, intellectual, and economic base. If the government's purpose was to break the Issei spirit, however, it failed. By their extensive organizing, indulging in activities of the mind and spirit, and maintaining their physical well-being, the Issei prisoners resisted that compliance and subjugation. What was an appearance of cooperation, which so pleased such officials as Jensen, in fact was an assertion of their will to manage their lives and maintain their integrity and dignity.

Vigilance

> When the war is over
> And after we are gone
> Who will visit
> This lonely grave in the wild
> Where my friend lies buried?
> —Keiho Soga (1984, 64)

With this poem and others that echo it, Soga and his fellow poet prisoners charge those of us in subsequent generations to remember this man, to remember them, to not forget what happened in Santa Fe, Lordsburg, Livingston, Missoula, and the other Justice Department and army prison camps, to not erase their existence in this time and these places from our memory.

Some may wonder why we must comply with such a request. Isn't the extensive research on the WRA imprisonment proof enough of the World War II injustice against the ethnic Japanese? Why not allow the Issei internment to fade away as their widespread silence would seem to have it? Many who returned seemed to continue on with their lives, although only those who lived at least until 1988 had the satisfaction of claiming reparations. Can there be too many stories?

Unless we subscribe to the idea that lives lived are "unidentifiably 'generic,'" to borrow a phrase cited earlier, unlimited numbers of stories must be told and preserved for our collective memory. This means maintaining our personal, family, and ethnic histories. In 2006, four years after I started this research project and as my mother's health took a turn, I wrote myself a note: "I am writing this manuscript in the context of the unfolding realization that my mother, in whose person the family memory has been stored, is not infallible, but vulnerable to the challenges of time and remembering at age ninety." Over the years of collecting others' stories and writing about them, I lost her, but she continues to encourage me in this endeavor, for I will forever recall her not-so-gentle admonition, "You finish that book!" a sentiment echoed by many others in her generation. In the absence of our family memories and ethnic histories, isn't it left to us, then, to unearth and reconstruct them one by one?

How much more critical is this endeavor for our national memory and history? Significant scholarship and narratives exist on the WRA concentration camps, perhaps because of the injustice to U.S. citizens and their numerically widespread influence. Much less attention has been paid, however, to those prisons targeting immigrants and overseen by the Justice Department and army, with their existence being excluded from some history books or being trivialized by or unknown to teachers and their students. American Civil Liberties Union attorney Wayne Collins, who fought for Nikkei justice for decades, referred to "the damage done to these innocent people without cause" as "utterly evil" and "a war crime" (quoted in Wegars 2010, 198). Yet this "evil" must be remembered—in its multiple manifestations.

During my first teaching experience at a Virginia women's college in the late 1960s and early 1970s, a history professor colleague rushed up to me one day, asking if I knew about the imprisonment of the American Japanese during World War II; he had a doctorate in history from the University of Virginia but was shocked and incredulous that this had happened. I was shocked by his ignorance, especially given that he was a historian and it had to do with an event that had happened during his lifetime. More recently, in my twenty-first-century midwestern university American literature classes, there were invariably those students who had never heard of this event in World War II U.S. history—and who felt cheated by having not been informed of it.[8]

Clearly, this absence of knowledge leaves the ignorant susceptible to demagoguery and manipulation. Hitler and others capitalized on ignorance and fear in the last century. So, too, is that possible in this century. Madeleine Sugimoto, the daughter of American artist Henry Sugimoto and a child of two Arkansas WRA camps, is reported in the *Guardian* newspaper to believe that "even young Japanese Americans . . . [are] largely ignorant of what had been done to their parents and grandparents by their own government" and that "the collective amnesia that surrounds this blot on American history is not a purely academic matter but a burning priority of today," given the irresponsible references being made to the persecution of other groups (Pilkington 2016). Decidedly, in the preservation of our history, there is the need for vigilance: Cultural memory can be a strong antidote to xenophobia and racism, but events must be broadly and deeply understood.

In November 2000, the National Japanese American Memorial, privately funded, was dedicated in Washington, DC, to memorialize the WRA incarceration and the sacrifices of the Nisei in combat. A letter by President Bill Clinton was quoted in the ceremony: "We are diminished when any American is targeted unfairly because of his or her heritage. This memorial and the internment sites are powerful reminders that stereotyping, discrimination, hatred and racism have no place in this country" (quoted in Daniels 2013, 197). Yet, less than a year later, after 9/11, George W. Bush signed the USA Patriot Act, and in November, as Roger Daniels points out, he "took another soiled leaf from the wartime record of Franklin Roosevelt and issued a military order—'Detention, Treatment, and Trial of Certain Non-Citizens in the War against Terrorism'—which decreed that all such persons, if tried, would be tried by military commissions appointed by him" (199).

In contrast, after 9/11, the Japanese American Citizens League (JACL) did more than merely remember the Nikkei imprisonment; in its postwar incarnation, it defended the civil rights of Muslim Americans in the wake of the jihadist terrorist attacks, fearing that another group might fall victim to race hatred and violence (see Wegars 2010, 226). In 2015, the JACL once again "condemn[ed] the dangerous and irresponsible Islamophobic and anti-immigrant rhetoric being used to vilify and demonize Muslim and Arab communities." Comparing contemporary events to those preceding and during World War II, it asserted emphatically: "Our country's own history has proven that hateful racist rhetoric can lead to destructive and sometimes fatal consequences for the scapegoated communities. The WWII incarceration of Japanese Americans was a culmination of decades of anti-Asian and anti-Japanese sentiment that festered along the west coast" (2015a). In a statement a week later, the JACL again called attention to the threat of bigotry and hate: "As the largest and oldest Asian American civil rights organization in the United States, JACL will continue to oppose the anti-Muslim hate, xenophobia, and bigotry undermining our nation's values and ideas, and call on fellow Americans to do the same" (JACL 2015b).[9]

We also need to appreciate the nuances of historical events to learn from them. For example, we must not allow the Issei/immigrant story of imprisonment in the Justice Department and army internment camps to be confused with that of the later WRA forced removal of civilians, as these imprisonments differed in timing, prisoners, sites, treatment, administration, rules, rights, duration, and official intention and culpability. Kashima outlines the extensiveness and complexity of the U.S. wartime incarceration of Japanese immigrants and their American-born children—its genocidal reach even to orphans, what Daniels refers to as "almost total ethnic cleansing" (2013, 201). So must the accuracy of subsequent portrayals. A much-celebrated *Hawaii Five-0* television episode depicted the internment in Hawaiʻi as having involved children and families (a boy misinterprets events and, as an elderly man, misdirects revenge for his father's death) and was lauded as a great success in its prime-time attention to the subject. But it was historically inaccurate in conflating the mainland incarceration of families with the Justice Department's imprisonment of Issei and Kibei/Nisei adults at camps such as Honouliuli on Oʻahu. Deprivations were different. There was a vast disparity between the "abnormal" conditions in the all-male internment camps, holding resident aliens isolated from their families, and the family prison camps at Crystal City and those run by the WRA, housing several generations.

With discoveries of artifacts and archaeological evidence at sites such as Honouliuli, a recent attention to internment sites in New Mexico—both funded in part by the National Park Service—and a more widespread appreciation for personal stories via the internet and social media, there is a new public interest in such narratives, but they must be accurate to do justice to those who lived them. They must be accurate, too, to give us insights into the circumstances faced by contemporary communities and the actions threatening them. Individual stories provide us with the detail and subtlety for a more complete understanding of complex events. After all, the Hawaiʻi Issei narrative of exile is a part of the history of all Americans, as is the responsibility of vigilance.

In the process of unbundling and rebundling these stories of the Hawaiʻi Issei exile over more than a decade, what originated for me as a text-based study of language and literacy thus expanded into a multidimensional, multigenerational, multigenre project, composed of faces of young men and women, now old, of fathers and grandfathers, now gone, and of multiethnic voices speaking through oral and written histories in the present and material culture of the past. My personal family memory has become communal. My grandfather's individual life has melded into a community of lives, as the biography of one man has become a composite of the stories of many of the hundreds of men who, over the course of a sunny morning in December 1941, became "alien enemies" in their country of residence.

Santa Feans

From the World beyond the Barbed Wire

Several years ago, my long journey in this research process took another serendipitous turn and added another dimension to this story of the Hawai'i Issei in exile: Lucia Ortiz Trujillo made me aware of a Santa Fean's perspective—one that strangely verifies the reality of those within the barbed wire for internee descendants like me.

At a 2007 academic conference in Albuquerque, New Mexico, I spoke casually with a young woman named Lisa Pacheco about my research on the Hawai'i internees at the SFIC. Later, in an email, Lisa recounted what her grandmother remembered from her childhood in Santa Fe during the war:

> My Grandma Lucy was eight years old when [Japan] bombed Pearl Harbor. During the next summer (1942) she was nine years old. She was playing with a group of kids her age in her older sister Melinda's neighborhood on Manhattan Ave., near the train station.... She recalled that there were Japanese men being transported to the internment camp. On more than one occasion the train pulled into the station and the Japanese men would throw candy bars to my grandma and the other kids. At that time, candy bars were hard to come by and she and the other kids really looked forward to the Japanese men's generous gifts. They would get really excited when they heard the train coming and run toward it in hopes of getting candy bars. She remembers walking around with the same kids all the time and when they were in the area that is now called Casa Solana, they'd walk near the camp and see all the guards and fences and people inside. She said if it wasn't for the candy, she might not even remember any of it. (2007)

This made me wonder, could one of those men on the train or one of the people they saw inside the fences have been my grandfather? Lucy Trujillo's story made me realize the value of the memories of those who lived outside the barbed wire, who may have chanced by the camp or peered in—who were there at the same *real time* as my grandfather and the hundreds of other Hawaiʻi men. I discovered that living voices come from unexpected sources, connecting us through space and time.

With the help of several Santa Fe community volunteers, I began to collect stories of Santa Feans with some memories of the SFIC. This was only a pilot project but an important one in terms of timing: Many who were adults during World War II are gone; many who were children are ageing.

During the war, the camp was shrouded in mystery and rumor. Despite an article in the *New Mexican,* dated 14 March 1942, titled "State Takes Japs Calmly" and subtitled "None of Santa Fe Internees 'Dangerous,'" some Santa Feans, then children, verified what became a narrative of anxiety, animosity, and fear, especially following reports of the Pacific conflict in the Philippines. Kermit Hill, now a retired history teacher, took riding lessons at a stable near the camp a few years after the war when he was five or six and knew it as the "Jap Camp" (2011). He recalled the barracks with black tar paper, the high fence, the guard towers. An undated letter from his mother, Zella, to his father, Robert, fighting overseas in Europe, reflected the anxiety of Santa Feans in a fleeting sentence or two: "The old C.C.C. camp is being prepared for a bunch of Japs. The whole town is in an uproar about it."

David Mason, Kermit's classmate, is now a retired navy and commercial airline pilot and has still earlier memories of the SFIC. His father had moved the family from Albuquerque to Santa Fe in March 1945, having become the owner-manager of Santa Fe Hay & Grain. Through his business, he met Santa Feans who had livestock, among them Bundy Avant, an SFIC guard and

> the owner/operator of a horse riding stable . . . [probably a mile west of the internment camp]. My father made arrangements with Mr. Avant to give us . . . transportation to the stables, riding lessons and riding time in exchange for reduced feed bills. . . . It was during the Spring of 1945 that my three older siblings and I started riding at the Avant stables. I was not yet three years of age, but I loved riding. (D. Mason 2011a)
>
> I was riding when I first saw the camp—my first recollection. It appeared to be wide open with wooden barracks. . . . I remember the towers . . . the two towers, which is why I thought it was a prison camp. And the barbed wire on the top. You could see the men walking around in the yard; I think they were raking the yard and constantly keeping the yard clean. . . . The place was immaculately clean—that I do recall. Raking the dirt and the rocks, making it nice and clean. (2011c)
>
> As a child I don't recall the term "internment camp" ever being used to describe the facility . . . it was "*the Jap Camp*" with the emphasis on the

word "Jap." There was no doubt in my mind these men behind the fences were our enemies. (2011a)

Once as we were riding by the camp, in ignorance I got off my horse, picked up a piece of cactus on a stick, chucked it across the fence, and tried to hit one of those "Japs" because they were the enemy. Even as a three year old, I could do my part in the war, I guess. (2011b)

Sharon Mason, who later became David's sister-in-law, moved to Santa Fe in 1942 from Michigan when she was four and lived on the east side of the river across from the SFIC. Like David and others, she has a vivid memory of the guard towers and barbed wire fences, knew it as the "Jap Camp," but also remembers listening a lot to the radio news. The radio and movie theater's *Movietone News* portrayed continuous stories of Japanese fighting in the Pacific, and she became plagued by fears of the Japanese nearby, especially at night—"What if they get out and come after me?" (S. Mason 2011)

However, I found that those who had actual contact with the Japanese men in the SFIC had different responses: Loyd H. Jensen, the camp commander quoted earlier, credited the Issei prisoners for the smooth operation of the camp, praising them for making "any camp commander look good" (quoted in Mangione 1978, 341).

Jerry West, the son of Hal West, a Works Progress Administration (WPA) artist and a border patrol guard at the SFIC, is himself a Santa Fe artist and a retired biology teacher. In "A Local Santa Fe Bystander's View of the Japanese Internment Camp," a pamphlet compiled in 2002 for the SFIC Marker dedication mentioned in chapter 1, West writes about his father:

Our Dad Hal West . . . went to work . . . at the Japanese Internment Camp, in the old CCC buildings on West Alameda. . . . Hal didn't talk much about those years, but I do remember some offhand remarks and comments. [He] was always impressed by the kindness and gentleness of the men, their quiet and peaceful manner, their industriousness. Like many Santa Feans, [he] was impressed by the ability of these men to garden. They grew vegetables that we Northern New Mexicans had never seen. We were all amazed at what they produced in this arid land. (2–3)

"Hal and others didn't necessarily hate the Japanese," Jerry told me in an interview. "They were doing their job" (2011).

Herman Grace, a retired state government official, was also the son of a SFIC guard and public servant, Augustine "Tinnie" Grace, who served in the U.S.

Cavalry National Guard and patrolled the perimeter of the SFIC on horseback. In an email to me, Herman describes his father's experience with the internees:

> When I grew older, my father took me on many hunting trips, and in the evening before a roaring fire, he would tell me the stories of his life. One of these stories related to his patrol of the camp on horseback and of the Japanese people he befriended and who befriended him in turn. He described them as "pious, caring people."
>
> After the Bataan Death March of April, 1942, it was widely publicized that many soldiers from Santa Fe were in that march, and those who survived related gory stories of what happened and the treatment they received as prisoners of war. These stories created animosity in the residents of Santa Fe toward the Japanese [Americans] who had been torn from their homes and transported to the internment camp. My father, "Tinnie," did not share these feelings. He met the men at the camp and saw how industrious they were. He said they had no problem communicating because they spoke English. [He] believed the government established the camp without proper planning and the internees had inadequate food supplies. They started growing gardens when they arrived, but were missing staples.
>
> My father was a kind man who responded to the need he saw exist[ing] at the camp. He told of the barbed wire fence and that he sometimes let some of the men outside its boundaries [to hike in the mountains or to hunt quail] because they had no place to escape to and weren't a danger to anyone. He tried to "de-institutionalize" things. (Grace 2011)

Reverend Charles J. Kinsolving came to Santa Fe from Texas to serve as the rector of the Episcopal Church of the Holy Faith in 1935. Born in Santa Fe in 1936, his son John was about five years old when Pearl Harbor was attacked, and he recalled,

> Everyone here, with the exception of my father, referred to it as the "Jap Trap." . . . Nothing out there in those days, pretty stark. It was a dirt road that followed the river, a dirt road called the Alameda. . . . I recall walking [past] there several times to visit my friend Jimmy Bell. . . . We'd see [the internees] in the summer time wandering around the yard . . . but we didn't pay much attention. (Kinsolving 2011)

Rev. Kinsolving, however, started a program of visits to the SFIC twice a month. "[He] would go down on Sundays—every other Sunday in the afternoon,"

John recalled, "and spend some time there talking with the Japanese who were interned in the camp. . . . He conducted services for those who were already confirmed Episcopalians and he conducted evening prayer for any of the others that wanted to attend." But Rev. Kinsolving's altruism and evangelism had consequences:

I do remember my father being threatened by phone. . . . I remember my dad saying, "another *damned* phone call" and my mother would say, "oh, no." He would just hang up, wouldn't argue with anybody. Feelings were very high in Santa Fe, because many men who died and even those who survived the Bataan Death March were from Santa Fe—so feelings were very high. So people who tried to help the Japanese were not looked on in a very nice way. That lasted throughout the war; my father was very faithful in going out there. (Kinsolving 2011)

Former mayor of Santa Fe Joe Valdes was thirteen years old in 1943 and worked as a clerk doing odd jobs at Cash and Carry Grocery on Palace Avenue, where his father worked as a butcher. He remembers guards from the SFIC bringing three or four, sometimes six, internees at a time to their store to choose the specialty items that they sold there:

The internees were allowed to walk around. We didn't feel that we had to be on guard; we knew they were all Japanese Americans and I had no fear of them. The guards treated them well, a kind of mutual respect, no strong-arming. The men had the freedom of going to the store and picking things that they had in their own diet—letting them buy what they wanted for themselves.

I . . . took things as they came. [The men] were relatively quiet, dressed well, spoke Japanese—didn't bother me.

The store had a delivery service and we'd deliver the groceries to the camp. . . . The first time I saw [it], I was riding in the delivery van up Alameda . . . the minute you turned you could see the fields in front of it, the people gardening—they raised a lot of vegetables. It was a long road to where the gate was, a narrow entrance, nothing stood out except for the towers and fence. (Valdes 2011)

In the process of gathering stories, I met the Jesus Rios family, who have for more than eighty years run the Rios Wood Yard, which I've come to understand is a kind of institution in Santa Fe. Rudolfo, born in 1939, has clear memories of growing up in the presence of the SFIC:

I was about 5–6 years old and . . . my dad would tell us about the prisoners that were on Casa Solana. We'd pass by [to] deliver a lot of wood further down—all of that was empty; we could see the high fences, and when it was warm the men would be out sometimes without shirts. We'd pass by and my dad would drive slow, and try to explain as best he could to a child what was going on.

I thought they had them in there gardening, because they *were* gardening. Some of them were kneeling down and working the dirt and to me they looked like children, because . . . they were smaller people, and I asked my dad, "What are they doing to those kids?" [He said,] "They're not kids, they're *men*."

You're young, you ask, "But what did the men do, what did they *do*?" My dad said, "They didn't do anything; the government picked them up because they're supposedly not 'Americans'; they're afraid that they'll help Japan. Without even knowing, they just brought them here."

When you're very young you don't expect your government to be doing this either. They *hadn't* done wrong, but since they were of another race, they brought them in without charging them with anything, herded them up like cattle and brought them here. My dad would try to explain that they're human beings just like us, but the war is against their nation. It was a sad time.

After the Japanese left, we worked there—the lumberyard was delivering building material, and I was already in my twenties—25—and the picture came back: the dirt was *so rich right there*. You could see why they were planting whatever they were planting, because the ground was black, black, rich, rich, very rich.

It [comes] back, it still does. When I pass through there, I tell my kids now, they had the Japanese Americans right there, they brought them in like cattle and put them in there. I can still see where the encampment was. I can see it mentally. What stayed in my mind most were the men working and you'd see them from far away. (R. Rios 2011)

Rudy's younger sister Frances echoed their parents' concerns and questioning of the government's actions: "They always believed in the rights of human beings, it didn't matter what race you were" (F. Rios 2011).

Endurance and Change

The Rios children inherited values from their parents about the value of human lives, just as the soldier sons inherited the values of their imprisoned fathers. And like the wood yard, the values endure—Rudy echoing his father, telling his children

Notes

Introduction

1. Poem originally published in Okawa 2008, 91. The opening paragraphs and chap. 1 are derived from this essay.

2. See chap. 2 for Roosevelt's memo.

3. What appears to be a government list, dated 10 August 1944, documents the names of eight Issei women who were also exiled to mainland camps ("List of Internees from Hawaii Transferred to the Mainland").

4. See Clark 1980, Burton et al. 2002, and Okihiro 2013 for details about these and other facilities that housed Issei prisoners.

5. Ichioka's essay was originally published in 2000 in *Amerasia Journal* 26 (1): 33–53.

6. Fiset 2001 notes how this limitation led to problems with recruiting Japanese language censors during wartime.

7. See chap. 2 on language issues; see Tamura 1993 for a detailed discussion of the language shift among the Nisei. An exception to this limitation was exemplified by the Nisei linguists in the Military Intelligence Service, mentioned in chap. 7.

8. Terms on exclusion orders signed by Lieutenant General John DeWitt, figs. A and C in CWRIC 1997. Reference is to immigrants ("aliens") and American citizens ("non-aliens").

9. Clark 1980, 7, 12; Fiset 1997, 29. Kashima (2003) discusses the agreement, the division of responsibilities between the Justice and War Departments, and the revised agreement in considerable detail (23–27 and 117).

10. Okihiro 2013, 229–238, 241–249.

11. This group is distinguishable from the Issei and Nisei incarcerated only in the islands at army camps like Honouliuli, researched initially by the Resource Center staff, Japanese Cultural Center of Hawai'i, and discussed in relatively recent research by Falgout and Nishigaya (2014) and the National Park Service (2015).

12. Although they may refer to fellow internees, these writers provide narratives of DOJ/army internment life, principally from their individual viewpoints. Soga's, Ozaki's, and Furuya's memoirs and notes were forthcoming in Japanese in the postwar period but have been available in English translation only since 2008: Soga's accounts, for example, were serialized in the *Hawaii Times*, a Japanese language newspaper, after his return from the mainland and culminated in the publication of *Tessaku seikatsu* in 1948. This detailed reportage of his imprisonment in the Territory of Hawaii and mainland internment camps was translated by Kihei Hirai and published as *Life behind Barbed Wire* (2008). Kumaji Furuya published *Haisho tenten* in 1964, documenting in detail his wartime experiences in facilities such as

Camp McCoy, Camp Livingston, and Fort Missoula. Translated by Tatsumi Hayashi, it was published as *An Internment Odyssey: Haisho tenten*, under Furuya's pen name Suikei, in 2017, giving readers access to the longest journey in miles and number of camps traversed by Hawai'i internees.

13. Nakano and Nakano 1984, intro., vii.

14. Sections of Hoshida's original text, together with family letters, were compiled and edited by Heidi K. Kim in *Taken from the Paradise Isle* (2015).

Chapter 1: Discovering

1. Two causes of the massive wartime incarceration of American citizens and their Japanese immigrant parents, according to the Civil Liberties Act of 1988, cited in the introduction.

2. For information on the 442nd Regimental Combat Team, including the 100th Infantry Battalion (Separate), see chap. 7.

3. I wish to thank Nancy Bartlit, who cochaired the organizing committee with me, and committee members Carrie Vogel, Sue Rundstrom, Janice Baker, Michael Boyle, and former New Mexico History Museum director Frances Levine and her staff.

Chapter 2: The Fate of the "Wingless Birds" I

1. Selected segments of this chapter relating to Tamasaku Watanabe are based on an essay originally published as "Letters to Our Forebears: Reconnecting Generations through Writing" (Okawa 2003b). Copyright 2003 by the National Council of Teachers of English. With permission.

2. The phrase appears in Rev. Watanabe's petition requesting release from the Santa Fe Internment Camp. Unless otherwise noted, all citations annotated with "TWP" are from the Tamasaku Watanabe Papers (TWP), Honolulu.

3. Okihiro (1991) outlines the early Japanese experience in Hawai'i in stark detail—the social and economic roots of white colonial prejudice and fear of the Japanese, how this was related to the larger anti-Japanese movement on the mainland, and what actions government and military officials took in establishing martial law as a result, both before and during World War II. He also documents pre-1920s efforts by the landed oligarchy and military to address "the Japanese problem."

4. See Okihiro 1991 and Kotani 1985 for details on the strike.

5. For "free white person(s)," see Legisworks.org. Chap. 1 of Daniels's book provides an extensive overview of the political and legal conditions confronting the American Japanese prior to and following the outbreak of World War II.

6. See "An Act Relating to Foreign Language Schools and Teachers Thereof" 1920; and "An Act to Amend Section . . . of Act 30 of the Special Session Laws of 1920 . . . a New Section . . . Relating to Foreign Language School" 1923.

7. For descriptions and discussions of linguistic, legal, and educational implications of these events, see Hawkins 1978; Kotani 1985; Tamura 1993; and Asato 2006. In the legislative records of the 1920s, I also encountered other efforts to restrict the Japanese community, specifically targeting the local Japanese press by regulating foreign language newspapers.

8. See Okihiro 1991 for a more extensive discussion.

9. Because the Japanese government considered the American-born children of Japanese parents to be Japanese citizens, legal expatriation documents had to be filed for dual citizens to claim exclusive U.S. citizenship.

10. See Fiset 1997, 28; and Kashima 2003, 22–23, for details on data collected. Greg Robinson (2003) carefully documents the assumptions underlying Roosevelt's decisions to incarcerate the Nikkei population, regardless of citizenship.

11. This language appears in the first draft but is crossed out.

12. See Coffman (2003, chap. 5) and CWRIC (1997, 268–274) for a discussion of factors distinguishing the Hawai'i Japanese experience from that of the mainland Japanese.

13. This FBI language was attached to the file for Sohei Hamano, who was apparently a Nisei (Folder: Hamano, Sohei, n.d.).

14. See Daniels 2013, 7–8; and Fiset 1997, 28–29, for details. Daniels mentions that the Justice and War Departments' joint committee's plan was for arrested aliens to go before a local Alien Enemy Hearing Board, but the "final decision in each case would be made by the attorney general" (7); in practice, the decision for internment seems to have been made by a joint military-FBI/DOJ intelligence board. Fiset cites "members of the Japanese Consulate" as being "listed as Group A suspects" (29), but as this narrative illustrates, the subconsular agents in the Territory of Hawaii were not employed by the consulate.

15. On the "legitimacy of the early arrests," see Kashima 2003, 72–73.

16. Recollections from three of his children differed in the details of their father's arrest; it seemed most prudent to rely on the narrative of Mr. Tokairin himself, published almost twenty years after the interview was conducted (1989, 5).

Chapter 3: The Fate of the "Wingless Birds" II

1. Kango Kawasaki, "Internment Records (Dec. 8, '41–Dec. '45)," compiled as Scrapbook, n.p., Kawasaki Family Collection, Hilo, HI. Unless otherwise cited, all references to "SB" refer to this source.

2. Regarding the discrepancy between the two dates, 21 and 23 February, although Rev. Watanabe may have left Hilo on a later ship, it is also possible that the second date is an error.

3. For more detailed accounts of these events, see Kashima 2003; CWRIC 1997; and Weglyn 1996.

4. The CWRIC cites 21 December as the date of Emmons's address.

5. See Soga 2008, 229ff.; and Saiki 1982, 221ff. Prisoners not sent to mainland internment camps were moved from Sand Island to the Honouliuli Internment Camp, called Jigokudani, or Hell Valley, in central O'ahu. See Falgout and Nishigaya 2014 and National Park Service 2015, for a detailed discussion of recent research on this prison camp.

6. A small group of internees from the Hawaiian Islands volunteered to go to the Kooskia Internment Camp in Idaho from Camp Livingston, but none were Issei from my study (see chap. 4).

Chapter 4: In Exile I

1. "Bearing Pineapple" is the title of the unpublished English language translation of a text originally written by Hamada in Japanese.

2. See the "Lists of Issei Civilian Internees in This Study by Transfer Boat" in chap. 3.

3. Aka wrote drafts of letters in English to various family members, dated 19 June 1942 to 7 August 1943. Unless otherwise noted, all citations annotated with "DL" refer to these letters.

4. Official medical reports from National Archives files, undated, can be found in the Ishida Family Collection, Honolulu.

5. See chap. 7 for further details on Ishida's experience.

6. In her exemplary detailed study, Priscilla Wegars describes this as "a virtually forgotten World War II detention facility that the INS operated for the Justice Department between late May 1943 and early May 1945 in a remote area of north central Idaho. This unique wartime experiment was a road building project employing Japanese alien internee volunteers" (2010, xix).

7. See censorship rules in chap. 6 in relation to Kango Kawasaki's letters.

8. Unless otherwise cited, all Watanabe letters are annotated with a date and refer to documents in TWP.

9. Translated by Rev. Y. Fujitani.

10. This first wave of mainland internees was temporarily moved from Santa Fe to Lordsburg, then returned to Santa Fe.

Chapter 5: In Exile II

1. In *The Art of Gaman: Arts and Crafts from the Japanese American Internment Camps, 1942–1946* (2005), Delphine Hirasuna includes a few pieces made by internees imprisoned at Fort Missoula and the SFIC; although they reflect the ingenuity of the artists, none are attributed to Hawai'i Issei. Also, Allen H. Eaton's classic 1952 study *Beauty behind Barbed Wire: The Arts of the Japanese in Our War Relocation Camps* explores the extensive range of arts and crafts produced in the WRA camps, many of which were also seen in the DOJ/army camps though completely overlooked by the author.

2. This Fujitani collection was donated to the Japanese Cultural Center of Hawai'i in Honolulu.

3. Wording on ribbons trans. Haruko Kawasaki. Because this service was held after the war's end, it is possible that restrictions in place during internment, such as access to florists and funds, had been relaxed.

Chapter 6: In Exile III

1. See Fiset (2001) for a detailed discussion of U.S. wartime censorship of alien enemy mail, including policies and practices of the INS, the FBI, and the Office of Censorship, with origins before the actual outbreak of war and "the INS taking the lead" after the attack on Pearl Harbor. Fiset cites postal censorship as commencing on 12 December 1941.

2. Kango Kawasaki to Sumie Kawasaki, 7 May 1942. Unless otherwise noted, all Kawasaki letters are from the Kawasaki Family Collection, Hilo, HI.

3. Discussion of my grandfather's involvement in my childhood is derived from an essay originally published as "Finding American World War II Internment in Santa Fe," Okawa 2009. Copyright 2009 by the Museum of New Mexico Press. With permission.

4. Poems translated by Yusei Kato; asterisks indicate lines revised by Tatsumi Hayashi and the author.

5. "Publishing," it should be noted, involved cutting stencils in Japanese by hand before mimeographing the entire text.

6. In another of life's ironies, I noted that S. I. Hayakawa, the Japanese Canadian author of Kawasaki's requested book, with whom I had taken a summer linguistics course while in college, became a leading proponent of linguistic imperialism as a cofounder of the U.S. English movement.

7. Although outside the purview of this study, it should be noted that Issei women in the Minidoka WRA camp similarly petitioned authorities, according to Mira Shimabukuro (2015).

8. A third petition, mentioned in chap. 4, was the joint effort of ministers from three religious faiths, Rev. Fukuda, the Konkokyo minister introduced earlier, Rev. Watanabe, a Christian, and Rev. Hosho Kurohira, a Buddhist, and also merits attention (see Okawa 2015a).

9. A version of this discussion and the following section on the Watanabe petition first appeared in "Putting Their Lives on the Line: Personal Narrative as Political Discourse among Japanese Petitioners in American World War II Internment," Okawa 2011. Copyright 2011 by the National Council of Teachers of English. With permission.

10. A brief article on Shigeo Shigenaga by Grant Din may be found at DiscoverNikkei.org, http://www.discovernikkei.org/en/journal/2015/11/10/shigenaga-brothers/ (Din 2015).

11. The original lyric is about a gruesome battle in Manchuria during the Russo-Japanese War. The melody is said to be that of "Senyu Bushi" (Song of Comrades in Arms), a Japanese song originally composed in 1905.

Chapter 7: Compounded Ironies I

1. During World War II, the main units staffed primarily or heavily by American-born Japanese (Nisei or Sansei, the second or third generations of American Japanese) were the 100th Infantry Battalion (Separate), the 442nd RCT, which was a racially segregated unit, and the Military Intelligence Service (MIS). See Crost (1994) for a broad account of Japanese American World War II military service; and more specifically, Murphy (1955) on the 100th Battalion; Tsukano (1985) on the 442nd; and McNaughton (2007) on the MIS.

2. This list provides further vital information: the internee's CI number, the name(s) of his son(s) and his/their rank and ASN (Army Serial Number), and the status of the internee's parole on the mainland at the time.

3. The unit became controversial and orphaned at the outbreak of war because it was heavily composed of Japanese American draftees, who could not be "undrafted" by the military but whom wartime paranoia and racism rendered suspect.

4. Odo (n.d.) refers to 23 March 1943 as the date on which the 442nd RCT was activated.

5. Although the highly decorated World War II military service of the 100th Infantry Battalion (Separate) and the 442nd RCT is relatively well-known, less known is the U.S. Army's MIS, which also involved predominantly Japanese American troops. The MIS trained selected Nisei as Japanese language interpreters and translators, in some cases recruiting those already proficient in the language from other units. MIS activities were shrouded in secrecy for decades because of their highly classified nature, but McNaughton credits the Nisei linguists with shortening the Pacific War and significantly bridging the cultural divide between Japan and the United States during both the war and the occupation (2007, v). Some segments of this discussion of the sons' visits first appeared on the New Mexico Digital History Project website and were published as "Ironies of World War II: Hawai'i Japanese Internee Fathers and American Military Sons in Santa Fe" (Okawa 2012). Copyright Rio Grande Books, 2012. With permission.

6. For a detailed history of the HTG and the Varsity Victory Volunteers, see Odo 2004.

7. This does not diminish the loss of the mothers, which is an equally important story outside the purview of this project.

8. Unless otherwise cited, information on the seven sons was obtained from Lee 1949; and Russell K. Shoho's (2007) excerpts from and elaborations on the Lee entries in AJA 2007.

9. Masako Yoshioka, short essay on her brother Yukitaka Mizutari, 17 April 2000, included in "KIA Profiles," in AJA 2007.

10. At the time, his father would have been absent from the family, interned for several years.

11. Verified by Colonel Bert Nishimura, Andrew Ono, and Samuel Sasai.

12. This information is also found in "KIA Profiles," in AJA 2007, and was presented in an exhibit at the Smithsonian Institution's Museum of American History in 2002, according to family records.

13. By this time the 100th/442nd had established its reputation as a formidable, efficient, and aggressive fighting unit, and army divisions fighting in southern France now were competing for them.

14. The following note has been extracted from Ono's unpublished "Rescue of the Lost Battalion" (n.d., 59): "Although accurate statistics on men wounded or killed in action during the specific battle in the Rescue of the Lost Battalion are impossible [to determine] due to the army's practice of assessing a monthly count, Masayo Duus relates an interaction directly after the battle that reflects the devastation felt by the unit:

On November 12 at 2:00 P.M., the troops of the 442nd stood lined up at attention for an assembly called by General Dahlquist to honor them for their achievements. The sound of the bugle echoed through the forest. A military band played the "Star Spangled Banner" dispiritedly. The general walking along in front of the troops, turned to Lieutenant Colonel Miller with a dissatisfied look on his face.

"I ordered that all the men be assembled," he said.

"Yes sir," answered Miller firmly. "All the men are what you see."

When the 442nd had entered the Vosges a month or so before, its strength was 2,943 men. Of those 161 had died in battle, 43 were missing, and about 2,000 were wounded (882 of them with serious wounds). Of the dead 13 were medics. The regiment had dwindled to less than a third of its authorized strength. (Duus 2007, 217)"

15. Shoho (2007) writes that Lt. Maehara was killed near Ripa, Italy, as does correspondence from Lt. Col. Virgil Miller to Colonel Sherwood Dixon, which attributes Maehara's death to a German mortar shell (22 June 1945; further source information is unavailable).

16. Written by unidentified internees for Katsuichi Miho (trans. Kihei Hirai), in Jinshichi Tokairin's folder of miscellaneous writings (Tokairin n.d.).

17. It is not clear to what Aka is referring when he writes about his son's "register[ing] for the draft," as the drafting of Japanese Americans had been suspended as of 7 December 1941, and Nisei volunteers were not accepted until 1 February 1943.

18. Another version of this adage reads as follows: "*Chu ni aran to hosseba, kou ni arazu / Kou ni aran to hosseba, chu ni arazu.*"

19. Wegars cites a letter to a soldier son from his Issei father, an internee from New York at the Kooskia Internment Camp, which sheds more light on the question of divided loyalties: "Once you put on the uniform of the U.S. Army, your body your mind have nothing more to do with Japan. You belong completely to America. Don't do anything that's ridiculous or cowardish. Bloody war awaits you. Go with strong resolve that you are to give all, to fight well, for the defen[s]e of your country. . . . I send you off as true soldier's father should, telling you to go bravely and to fight wholeheartedly" (2010, 114).

Chapter 8: Compounded Ironies II

1. Previously, in an 8 January 1944 letter to W. F. Kelly of the INS, DOJ, Bryan had provided a list of four options, with the addition of a fifth, "continued internment," requesting that Kelly "call upon the officer in charge of the internment camps where these internees are held to ask each of them his desires in this matter"; however, on the option of "outright release," Bryan comments, "It is not believed wise by this office despite the recommendation of the Commanding General to accord this category of internee an outright release on the mainland" (1944a, 1–2).

2. Wendell Berge, memorandum to FBI Director, 22 June 1943, Aka Family Collection, Honolulu. This source was possibly retrieved from RG 60; further information is unavailable.

3. According to listings in *Echoes of Silence: The Saga of the Nisei Soldiers of WWII*, both of Aka's sons were in the MIS at Camp Savage, Minnesota (AJA 2007).

4. It should be noted that Rev. Fujitani was not "on parole on the Mainland," as stated in the introduction to the list, but rather had remained in the SFIC after being denied acceptance into a WRA camp.

5. No mention is made of his son Kihachiro's having been KIA in Europe the previous year (see chap. 7).

6. No mention is made of his son Tadami's having been wounded in Europe (see chap. 7).

7. A contrast with internee fathers who did not have sons in the U.S. military can be seen in Slattery's judgment regarding my grandfather, apparently based on a different point system. On 22 June 1945, Lt. Col. Slattery wrote a memo stating that the Commanding General's Review Board "reached the decision that the aforementioned person [Tamasaku Watanabe] be paroled on Mainland; Group V (6 pts.)," but his rationale reveals a subjective value system: "Although Subject was a Consular Agent and admits being loyal to Japan, his immediate family resides in the Territory and his three children are exclusively United States citizens; furthermore, his children have been well educated in American universities and hold responsible positions in the Territory. It is the opinion of this office that Subject would not activate his expressed loyalty in a manner inimical to the peace, safety, and security of the United States. Accordingly, it is recommended that Subject be paroled on the Mainland and placed in the afore-mentioned group on the Return to Hawaii List" (Slattery 1945c).

Chapter 9: Return from Exile and Rebundling

1. The Civil Liberties Act of 1988, quoted in the introduction.

2. This led some internees such as Hoshida and Rev. Matsuura to seek reunification with their families, although they were imprisoned in WRA camps.

3. Ironically, it was secretly developed thirty-five miles away from the SFIC, at Los Alamos.

4. Rev. Watanabe had been the church's first permanent minister during his initial twelve-year tenure. Following the outbreak of war, the church changed its name and expanded its congregation.

5. It would be interesting, for instance, to compare the experiences of some or all of these Issei women with those of the two Nisei women imprisoned at Honouliuli, discussed by Amy Nishimura (2014, 199–216).

6. A version of this discussion first appeared in "Putting Their Lives on the Line: Personal Narrative as Political Discourse among Japanese Petitioners in American World War II

Internment" (Okawa 2011). Copyright 2011 by the National Council of Teachers of English. With permission.

7. The language on his arrest warrant (see chap. 2).

8. In a journal response to a film depicting an Issei father's arrest, a student wrote, "Having to leave your life behind at the drop of a hat for something you had no part in—that's unbelievable. These are things our schools didn't teach. Not mine anyway. I knew there had been internment camps, but that was it. It's crazy. That's the only way I can think to describe it." Another wrote, "I can't believe I never knew about this stuff before this class."

9. The JACL website documents the organization's continuing efforts to condemn acts of racism and xenophobia, such as anti-immigrant executive orders and hate crimes against Jewish communities. More recently, it has denounced the immigration ban, border concentration camps, and the inhumane treatment of children. Daniels (2013) outlines post-redress efforts to memorialize and interpret the incarceration, both legal and physical, as well as the abrogation of civil liberties post 9/11.

References

Frequently Used Abbreviations (see also Note on Abbreviations)

NARA I: National Archives and Records Administration, Washington, DC
NARA II: National Archives and Records Administration, College Park, MD
RG: record group
TWP: Tamasaku Watanabe Papers, Honolulu, HI

Primary Sources: Archival (Family, Government, Newspaper), Contemporary

"10 Alien Japanese Are Returned from Coast." 1945. *Honolulu Star-Bulletin*, 12 July.
"An Act Relating to Foreign Language Schools and Teachers Thereof." 1920. Act 30 (Senate Bill No. 32). In *Laws of the Territory of Hawaii Passed by the Eleventh Legislature, Special Session 1920*, 10–24 November.
"An Act to Amend Section . . . of Act 30 of the Special Session Laws of 1920 . . . a New Section . . . Relating to Foreign Language Schools." 1923. Act 171 (House Bill No. 139). In *Laws of the Territory of Hawaii Passed by the Twelfth Legislature, Regular Session 1923*, 21 February–2 May.
Adachi, Ichiji. 1944. Petition for Parole to Hawaii to Gen. Robert C. Richardson, Jr., 10 April. Folder: Adachi, Ichiji; Box 176; RG 494/338; NARA II.
Aka, Ryosei. 1942. Affidavit, 10 November. Folder: Aka, Ryosei; Box 176; RG 494/338; NARA II.
———. 1942–1943. Draft letters (DL). Aka Family Collection, Honolulu.
———. 1943. Letter to Commanding General, 2 February. Folder: Aka, Ryosei; Box 176; RG 494/338; NARA II.
———. 1944. Letter to Loyd H. Jensen, 21 April. Aka Family Collection, Honolulu.
Akahoshi, Shingetsu. 2002. Interview with the author, 20 September, translated by Reiko Odate Matsumoto. Fairfax, VA.
Alien Enemies Act. 1798. *Laws of the United States*. Philadelphia: Richard Folwell. https://www.varsitytutors.com/earlyamerica/milestone-events/alien-enemies-act.
Allen, George N. 1942. Report on Tamasaku Watanabe (referencing Reverend Takie Okumura), 9 April. Folder 146-13-2-21-209, Box 242, RG 60, NARA II.
Ando, Joe. 2002. Comments at Santa Fe Internment Camp Historical Marker Dedication, 20 April. Santa Fe, NM.

Aoyagi, Seisaku. N.d. Notes, translated anonymously. Aoyagi Family Collection, Hilo, HI.

Bicknell, George W. 1941a. "Memorandum: Seizure and Detention Plan (Japanese)," 21 November. FBI file 100-2-1777.

———. 1941b. Warrant for Tamasaku Watanabe, 7 December. Folder: Watanabe, Tamasaku (Gyokusaku); Box 2643; RG 389; NARA II.

Borreca, Richard. 1999. "Relatives Interned, They Went to War: Japanese-Americans from Hawaii Fought to Disprove Doubts about Their Loyalty." *Honolulu Star-Bulletin*, 13 September.

Bryan, B. M. 1944a. Memorandum to W. F. Kelly, 8 January. Folder: Reports Gen. Bryan to Gen. Gullion, Box 6, RG 389, NARA II.

———. 1944b. Memorandum to Commanding General, Thirty-Fourth Division: "Reinvestigation of Detention of Civilian Internees Related to Members of the 100th Infantry Battalion," 14 March. Folder: Reports Gen. Bryan to Gen. Gullion, Box 6, RG 389, NARA II.

———. 1944c. Memorandum to Commanding General, U.S. Army Forces in the Central Pacific Area: "Japanese Civilian Internees from the Territory with Sons in the Armed Forces of the United States," 3 April. Folder: Reports Gen. Bryan to Gen. Gullion, Box 6, RG 389, NARA II.

———. 1944d. Order to Department of Justice, 13 May. Aka Family Collection, Honolulu.

Cardinaux, Alfred. 1942. Report, 21 November. Folder: Lordsburg II, Box 30, RG 59, NARA II.

———. 1943. Report, 2 June. Folder: Lordsburg I, Box 30, RG 59, NARA II.

Chávez, Thomas. 2002. Comments at Santa Fe Internment Camp Historical Marker Dedication, 20 April. Santa Fe, NM.

Civil Liberties Act of 1988. 1988. "Restitution for World War II Internment of Japanese-Americans and Aleuts," 10 August. Pub. L. No. 100-383, 102 Stat. 904.

Commission on Wartime Relocation and Internment of Civilians (CWRIC). 1997. *Personal Justice Denied*. Seattle: University of Washington Press.

de Garay, José M. 1942. Letter/Report to the Spanish Ambassador re: "Visit to Camps of Interned Japanese in This District," 14 August. Folder: Lordsburg II, Box 30, RG 59, NARA II.

Eberhardt, Charles C. 1944. Report, 10–11 July. Folder: Santa Fe, Box 20, RG 59, NARA II.

Egan, Charles. N.d. "Voices in the Wooden House: Angel Island Inscriptions and Immigrant Poetry, 1910–1945." MS.

"English Lesson." 1942. *Lordsburg Times*, 30 December. Tamasaku Watanabe Papers (TWP), Honolulu.

Ennis, Edward J. 1944. Memorandum to Francis M. Howard, 10 May. Aka Family Collection, Honolulu.

Farrington, Territorial Governor, et al. v. T. Tokushige et al. 1926. Cir. No. 4667, 22 March. In *The Federal Reporter, Cases Argued and Determined in the Circuit Court of Appeals and District Courts of the U.S. and the Court of Appeals of the District of Columbia*, 2nd ed., 11:710–715. St. Paul, MN: West Publishing Co.

Fielder, Kendall J. 1944a. Letter to Ichiji Adachi, 15 April. Folder: Adachi, Ichiji; Box 176; RG 494/338; NARA II.
———. 1944b. Letter to Ichiji Adachi, 2 May. Folder: Adachi, Ichiji; Box 176; RG 494/338; NARA II.
Folder: Hamano, Sohei. N.d. Box 194; RG 494/338; NARA II.
Fujii, Seichi. N.d. Notebook. Fujii Family Collection, Honolulu.
Fujimura, Kiyoshi. 1988. "He Died in My Arms: The Story of T/Sgt. Terry Mizutari." In *John Aiso and the M.I.S.,* edited by Tad Ichinokuchi, 96–97. Los Angeles: Military Intelligence Service of Southern California.
Fujitani, Kodo. N.d. Inscribed poem on S. Akahoshi painting, translated by Y. Fujitani. Fujitani Family Collection, Honolulu.
Fujitani, Yoshiaki. 1980. Note on photo of two men. Fujitani Family Collection, Honolulu.
———. 1998. "*Kuni no On*—Gratitude to My Country." In *Japanese Eyes . . . American Heart: Personal Reflections of Hawaii's World War II Nisei Soldiers,* edited by Hawaii Nikkei History Editorial Board, 94–102. Honolulu: Tendai Educational Foundation.
———. 2003. Email to the author, 4 October. Honolulu.
———. 2004. Conversations with the author, May–August. Honolulu.
———. N.d. Interview with Warren Nishimoto. In *The Hawai'i Nisei Story: Americans of Japanese Ancestry during World War II.* Hawaii Nisei Project, http://nisei.hawaii.edu.
Fukuda, Yoshiaki. 1990. *My Six Years of Internment,* translated by Konko Church of San Francisco. San Francisco: Konko Church of San Francisco.
Fukuhara, Harry. 2008. Interview with the author, 2 January. Honolulu.
Furuya, Kumaji (Suikei). 1964. *Haisho tenten.* Honolulu: Hawaii Times.
Furuya, Suikei. 2017. *An Internment Odyssey: Haisho tenten,* translated by Tatsumi Hayashi. Honolulu: Japanese Cultural Center of Hawai'i.
Grace, Herman. 2011. Email to the author, 25 January. Santa Fe, NM.
Griffith, Robert B. 1945a. Memo to Trans-Pacific Travel Control Bureau, 18 January. Folder: Aka, Ryosei; Box 176; RG 494/338; NARA II.
———. 1945b. Letter to Tamasaku Watanabe, 23 June. Folder: Watanabe, Tamasaku (Gyokusaku); Box 312; RG 494/338; NARA II.
Gufler, Bernard. 1942. Confidential report on visit of F. de Amat, Spanish Consul in San Francisco, to Alien Enemy Internment Camp, Lordsburg, NM, 8–9 December. Folder: Lordsburg I, Box 30, RG 59, NARA II.
Hamada, Itsuo (Toseki). N.d. "Bearing Pineapple," translated by Izumi Kuroiwa. Hamada Family Collection, Hilo, HI.
Hamasaki, Kazuichi. N.d. Conversation with David Fukuda, 3 February. Nisei Veterans Memorial Center, Wailuku, Maui, HI.
Hill, Kermit. 2011. Interview with the author, 23 April. Santa Fe, NM.
Hill, Zella. N.d. Note to Robert K. Hill. Santa Fe, NM.
Hirano, Naojiro. 1944. Notebook. Hirano Family Collection, Hilo, HI.
Hirano, Wataru. 2004. Interview with the author, 9 June. Honolulu.

Hoover, J. Edgar. 1941. Memorandum to L. M. C. Smith, Chief, Special Defense Unit, Washington, DC, 31 May. FBI file 146-13-2-21-209 (for Tamasaku Watanabe), Box 242, RG 60, NARA II.

———. N.d. Memorandum. Folder: Lordsburg II, Box 30, RG 59, NARA II.

Hoshida, George Yoshio. N.d. "Life of a Japanese Immigrant Boy in Hawaii and America." MS. University of Hawai'i at Mānoa Archives, Hamilton Library, Honolulu.

Hoshida, George Yoshio, and Tamae Hoshida. 2015. *Taken from the Paradise Isle: The Hoshida Family Story*, edited by Heidi Kim. Boulder: University Press of Colorado.

Hotta, Shoma. 2017. Conversation with David Fukuda, 3 February. Nisei Veterans Memorial Center, Wailuku, Maui.

Ikuma, Edward. 2002. Interview with the author, 13 October. Honolulu.

———. 2015. Interview with the author, 20 May. Honolulu.

Ishida, Hisao. 1945a. Letter to Officer-in-Charge Ivan Williams, January. Ishida Family Collection, Honolulu.

———. 1945b. Letter to Officer-in-Charge Ivan Williams, 17 August. Ishida Family Collection, Honolulu.

Ishida, Kyujiro. 1944a. Letter to Hisao Ishida, November. Ishida Family Collection, Honolulu.

———. 1944b. Letter to Mrs. Henrietta Schoen, Santa Fe Internment Camp Hospital, 6 November. Ishida Family Collection, Honolulu.

Izutsu, Tadami. 1997. Interview with Ted Tsukiyama, 22 May. Japanese Cultural Center of Hawaii, Honolulu.

———. N.d. Izutsu Family Memoir. Izutsu Family Collection, Honolulu.

Japanese American Citizens League (JACL). 2015a. "JACL Condemns Dangerous Anti-Muslim Rhetoric." 2015. Press release, 9 December. Accessed 8 July 2016. https://jacl.org/jacl-condemns-dangerous-anti-muslim-rhetoric/.

———. 2015b. "JACL Stands with Asian American Leaders to Rally against Anti-Muslim Hate." Press release, 16 December. Accessed 8 July 2016. https://jacl.org/jacl-stands-with-asian-american-leaders-to-rally-against-anti-muslim-hate/.

Kato, Isoo. N.d. "Memoirs of World War II Internment" (includes journal and letters), translated by Haruko Kato Tagawa. MS. Kato Family Collection, Honolulu.

Kawasaki, Kango. 1941–1945. Scrapbook (SB): "Internment Records (Dec. 8, '41–Dec. '45)," Kawasaki Family Collection, Hilo, HI.

———. 1942–1943. Letters to Sumie Kawasaki. Kawasaki Family Collection, Hilo, HI.

Kelly, W. F. 1944a. Memorandum to Col. Howard F. Bresee, 17 March. Folder: Hawaiian Aliens, Box 5, RG 389, NARA II.

———. 1944b. Memorandum to Edward J. Ennis, 23 March. Aka Family Collection, Honolulu.

Kinoshita, Ichiji. N.d. Kinoshita Family History. MS. Kinoshita Family Collection, Honolulu.

Kinsolving, John. 2011. Interview with Janice Baker, 15 August. Santa Fe, NM.

Koyama, Kafu. 1943. "Circumstances of Publishing This Directory," *Santa Fe Japanese Internment Camp Directory*, 1 November, translated by Joh Sekiguchi. Santa Fe Review Office, Santa Fe Internment Camp, Santa Fe, NM.

"List of Internees from Hawaii Transferred to the Mainland." 1944. Santa Fe Detention Station, Santa Fe, 10 August. Kuniyuki Family Collection, Honolulu.

Lloyd. N.d. Letter to Governor John E. Miles. Folder 342, Box SN 13226, Governor John E. Miles Papers, State Archives of New Mexico.

Maehara, Ichiro. 1997. Interview with Nisei Veterans Memorial Center, October. Wailuku, Maui, HI.

Mason, David. 2011a. Email to the author, 20 January. Santa Fe, NM.

———. 2011b. Email to the author, 23 January. Santa Fe, NM.

———. 2011c. Email to the author, 23 April. Santa Fe, NM.

Mason, Sharon. 2011. Interview with the author, 18 November. Albuquerque, NM.

Matsumoto, Kazumi. 2003. Interview with the author, 2–3 July. Kalāheo, Kauaʻi, HI.

Matsumoto, Reiko Odate. 2002. Interview with the author, 25 August. Annandale, VA.

Matsuura, Gyokuei. 1942. Letters to Masue Matsuura. Matsuura Family Collection, Aiea, HI.

———. 2003. Interview with the author, 20 June. Aiea, HI.

———. 2004. Oral history interview with T. Tsukiyama, 13 February. Japanese Cultural Center of Hawaiʻi, Honolulu.

Miho, Katsugo. 1944. Letter to Katsuichi Miho, 28 August. V-mail correspondence. Miho Family Collection, Honolulu.

———. 2003. Interview with the author, 14 April. Honolulu.

Miho, Laura Iida. N.d. "Torn Loyalties." Essay. Miho Family Collection, Honolulu.

Military Intelligence Board. 1942. Internment order, 12 April. Honolulu. Folder: Watanabe, Tamasaku (Gyokusaku); Box 2643; RG 389; NARA II.

Miyasaki, Sumie Kawasaki. 2008. Interview with the author, 17 July. Hilo, HI.

Morrison, Wm. R. C. 1943. Letter to Ryosei Aka, 25 May. Folder: Aka, Ryosei; Box 176; RG 494/338; NARA II.

———. 1945a. Memorandum to Headquarters, OPMG, Honolulu, TH, 16 January. Folder: Aka, Ryosei; Box 176; RG 494/338; NARA II.

———. 1945b. Memorandum to Counter-Intelligence Division, "Return to the Territory of Hawaii of Certain Individuals," 18 January. Folder: Aka, Ryosei; Box 176; RG 494/338; NARA II.

———. 1945c. "Alien Control in Hawaii." Report draft, August. Box 892, RG 494/338, NARA II.

Nagami, Teruo. 2009. Interview with the author, 14 July. Hilo, HI.

Nagasako, Kengo. N.d. Notes. Mizutari Family Collection, Hilo, HI.

Nakamura, William. 1957. "Rev. Watanabe to Be Honored Sunday Morning." *Maui Times,* February. TWP, Honolulu.

Nakano, Jiro, and Kay Nakano. 1984. *Poets behind Barbed Wire.* Honolulu: Bamboo Ridge Press.

Nishikawa, Fusako M. 2002. "My Brother, My Hero." College paper, 3 October. Mizutari Family Collection, Hilo, HI.

Nitta, Hazel Murakami. 2017. Comments to David Fukuda, 17 January. Nisei Veterans Memorial Center, Wailuku, Maui, HI.

Odate, Chikou. 2000. "Friends in Prayer," February, translated by Yusei Kato. Odate Family Collection, Annandale, VA.

Office of the Adjutant General. War Department. 1945a. "Invitational Travel Orders," 24 August. Otani Family Collection, Honolulu.

———. 1945b. "Invitational Travel Orders," 16 October. TWP, Honolulu.

Office of the Provost Marshal General (OPMG). 1942a. "Location of Enemy Aliens from Territory of Hawaii Interned in U.S.A., November 27, 1942." Folder: Hawaiian Aliens, Box 5, RG 389, NARA II.

———. 1942b. Record of the Hearings of a Board of Officers and Civilians Convened Pursuant to Paragraph 33, Special Orders No. 320, Headquarters, Hawaiian Department, dated at Fort Shafter, TH, 19 December 1941. In the case of *Kodo Fujitani*, 30 April. Folder: Fujitani, Kodo; Box 2609; RG 389; NARA II.

———. 1942c. Record of the Hearings of a Board of Officers and Civilians Convened Pursuant to Special Orders No. 33, Headquarters, Hawaiian Department, dated at Fort Shafter, TH, 2 February 1942. In the case of *Tamasaku (Gyokusaku) Watanabe*, 13 February. Folder: Watanabe, Tamasaku (Gyokusaku); Box 2643; RG 389; NARA II.

———. 1942d. Record of the Hearings of a Board of Officers and Civilians Convened Pursuant to Special Orders No. 33, Headquarters, Hawaiian Department, dated at Fort Shafter, TH, 2 February 1942, as Amended by Special Orders No. 65, Headquarters, Hawaiian Department, dated at Fort Shafter, TH, 7 March 1942, as Amended by Special Orders No. 80, Headquarters, Hawaiian Department, dated at Fort Shafter, TH, 24 March 1942. In the case of *Isoo Kato*, 15 April. Folder: Kato, Isoo; Box 2618; RG 389; NARA II.

———. 1942e. Record of the Hearing of a Board of Officers and Civilians Convened Pursuant to Special Orders No. 320, Headquarters, Hawaiian Department, dated at Fort Shafter, TH, 19 December 1941. In the case of *Kazumi Matsumoto*, 17 January. Folder: Matsumoto, Kazumi; Box 240; RG 494/338; NARA II.

OPMG / U.S. Department of Justice. 1945. "Japanese Civilian Internees from Hawaii with Sons in the Armed Forces of the United States—Consolidated and Revised List," 20 June. Folder: Hawaii 1945, Box 5, RG 389, NARA II.

Ogawa, Howard I. 1944. "The Death of a Hero: This Is How Sgt. Mizutari Fought—and How He Died." Mizutari Family Collection, Hilo, HI.

Ohama, Katsumi. 2001. Email to Jane Kubota, 7 September. Honolulu.

———. 2006. Email to the author, 4 July. Honolulu.

Ohara, Kenjyo. 1993. Interview with Reverend Y. Fujitani. Japanese Cultural Center of Hawai'i, Honolulu.

———. 2003. Interview with the author, 21 May. Mililani, HI.

Okudara, Janice Aka. 2007. Interview with the author, 1 July. Honolulu.

———. N.d. Aka Family History. MS. Aka Family Collection, Honolulu.

Olson, Gustaf. 1945. Letter to Mrs. Seisaku Aoyagi, November. Honolulu, TH. Aoyagi Family Collection, Hilo, HI.

Otani, Akira. 1943. Letter to Florence Otani Toyoshiba, 14 November. Otani Family Collection, Honolulu.

———. 2003. Interview with the author, 19 April. Honolulu.

———. 2007. Phone conversation with the author, January. Honolulu.

Otani, Matsujiro. N.d. "Reflecting on My Eighty Years," translated anonymously. MS. Otani Family Collection, Honolulu.

Otsuka, Hikoju. N.d. "Song of Internment." In "Memoirs of World War II Internment," by Isoo Kato, translated by Haruko Kato Tagawa. MS. Kato Family Collection, Honolulu.

Ozaki, Otokichi (Muin). 1984. Untitled tanka. In *Poets behind Barbed Wire*, translated and edited by Jiro Nakano and Kay Nakano. Honolulu: Bamboo Ridge Press.

———. 2012. *Family Torn Apart: The Internment Story of the Otokichi Muin Ozaki Family*, edited by Gail Honda. Honolulu: Japanese Cultural Center of Hawai'i.

Pacheco, Lisa. 2007. Email to the author, spring. Albuquerque, NM.

Petition (Affirmative) to Governor John E. Miles. N.d. Folder 341, Box SN 13226, Governor John E. Miles Papers, State Archives of New Mexico, Santa Fe, NM.

Petition (Negative) to Governor John E. Miles. N.d. Folder 341, Box SN 13226, Governor John E. Miles Papers, State Archives of New Mexico, Santa Fe, NM.

Provost Marshal's Office (PMO), Headquarters Hawaiian Department. 1941. Memorandum to the Family of Seichi Fujii, 26 December. Fujii Family Collection, Honolulu.

———. 1942. Memorandum to the Family of Seichi Fujii, 15 February. Fujii Family Collection, Honolulu.

Richardson, Robert C., Jr. 1945. Order signed on 22 October. Office of Internal Security, Honolulu, TH. TWP, Honolulu.

Rios, Frances. 2011. Interview with the author, 26 April. Santa Fe, NM.

Rios, Rudolfo. 2011. Interview with the author, 20 November. Santa Fe, NM.

Roosevelt, Franklin D. 1936. Memorandum to Chief of Naval Operations, 10 August. Box 216, Folder A 8-5, General Records of the Navy, RG 80, NARA II.

Santa Fe Internment Camp Historical Marker. 2002. Plaque. Santa Fe, NM.

Santa Fe Kirisuto Kyokai. 1943. "Kaiin Kyoyu Meibo" (Roster of the Members and Friends of the Santa Fe Christian Church). Box 332, University of California Los Angeles Research Library Special Collections.

Sasai, Samuel. 2008. Interview with the author, 7 January. Honolulu.

———. 2016. Interview with the author, 29 February. Honolulu.

Schofield, Lemuel B. 1942. "Instruction No. 58, Instructions Concerning the Treatment of Alien Enemy Detainees." 28 April. Folder: 1300 Detainees, Box 3, RG 85, NARA I.

Shigemasa, June Odachi. 2007. Interview with the author, 9 June. Hilo, HI.

Shigenaga, Shigeo, et al. 1944. Petition by Enemy Alien Civilian Internees of Japanese Nationals Now at Santa Fe Detention Camp, 24 February. Folder: Hawaiian Aliens, Box 5, RG 389, NARA II.

Slattery, Eugene V. 1945a. Memorandum to Commanding General's Review Board, OIS, 4 January. Folder: Fujitani, Kodo, Box 189, RG 494/338, NARA II.

———. 1945b. Order, 5 January. Folder: Fujitani, Kodo, Box 189, RG 494/338, NARA II.

———. 1945c. Memorandum, 22 June. Folder: Watanabe, Tamasaku (Gyokusaku); Box 312; RG 494/338; NARA II.

Soga, Yasutaro (Keiho). 1944. Preface to *Kodama*, January, translated by Reiko Odate Matsumoto. Santa Fe Internment Camp, Santa Fe, NM. Santa Fe Bungei Kyokai (Literary Society of Santa Fe). Odate Family Collection, Annandale, VA.

———. 1984. Untitled tanka. In *Poets behind Barbed Wire*, translated and edited by Jiro Nakano and Kay Nakano. Honolulu: Bamboo Ridge Press.

———. 2008. *Life behind Barbed Wire*, translated by Kihei Hirai. Honolulu: University of Hawai'i Press.

"State Takes Japs Calmly: None of Santa Fe Internees 'Dangerous.'" 1942. *New Mexican*, 14 March.

Takei, Sojin. 1984. Untitled tanka. In *Poets behind Barbed Wire*, translated and edited by Jiro Nakano and Kay Nakano. Honolulu: Bamboo Ridge Press.

Tokairin, Hideo. 2004. Interview with the author, 1 July. Wahiawa, HI.

Tokairin, Jinshichi. 1943. Letters, translated by Hanayo Sasaki. Tokairin Family Collection, Honolulu.

———. 1945a. Letter to Robert C. Richardson, 27 January. Tokairin Family Collection, Honolulu.

———. 1945b. Letter to Miyeko Tokairin, 1 February. Tokairin Family Collection, Honolulu.

———. 1989. "The Life History of a Nikkei of Hawaii." Interview with Kisaburo Ueda. *Journal of the Pacific Society* (January). Tokairin Family Collection, Honolulu.

———. N.d. Miscellaneous writings. Tokairin Family Collection, Honolulu.

Tollefson, A. M. 1943a. Letter to Private Robert S. Miyata, 16 October. Folder: Alien—Sons in Army—Japanese, Box 6, RG 389, NARA II.

———. 1943b. Letter to Director, Alien Enemy Control Unit, 18 October. Re: Edward J. Ennis letter to OPMG (1 October 1943). Folder: Alien—Sons in Army—Japanese, Box 6, RG 389, NARA II.

———. 1943c. Memorandum to Commanding General, U.S. Army Forces in the Central Pacific Area: "Japanese Civilian Internees with Sons in Armed Forces of the United States," 18 October. Folder: Alien—Sons in Army—Japanese, Box 6, RG 389, NARA II.

Trujillo, Lucia Ortiz. 2018. Conversation with the author, 16 July. Santa Fe, NM.

U.S. Army. N.d. "Military Intelligence Service Language School." Fort Snelling, MN. Mizutari Family Collection, Hilo, HI.

U.S. Department of Justice. 1941. Notecard, 9 April. FBI file 146-13-2-21-209 (on Tamasaku Watanabe), Box 242, RG 60, NARA II.

U.S. Statutes at Large. 1798. "An Act Respecting Alien Enemies," 6 July. Avalon Project. Lillian Goldman Law Library, Yale University. Accessed 19 March 2017. http://avalon.law.yale.edu/18th_century/alien.asp.

Valdes, Joseph. 2011. Interview with the author, 26 April. Santa Fe, NM.

Watanabe, Tamasaku. 1922. Diary. Sacramento, CA; Honolulu; and Wailuku, Maui. TWP, Honolulu.

———. 1941a. Affidavit, 9 August. TWP, Honolulu.

———. 1941b. Diary, 7 December. 'Ōla'a, TH. TWP, Honolulu.

———. 1942–1945. Letters to Sumi Watanabe Okawa, Lordsburg and Santa Fe, NM. TWP, Honolulu.

———. 1944a. "Anger Creates Illness." Essay, 26 March, translated by Haruko Kawasaki. *Fuku-in* (Santa Fe Christian Church newsletter). TWP, Honolulu.

———. 1944b. "Thoughts on Daniel." Sermon, 24 October, translated by Haruko Kawasaki. *Fuku-in* (Santa Fe Christian Church newsletter). TWP, Honolulu.

———. 1944–1945. Small notebook from Santa Fe Internment Camp, translated by Rev. Y. Fujitani. TWP, Honolulu.

———. 1945. Petition to Maj. Stephen M. Farrand, OPMG, 9 May. Santa Fe, NM. TWP, Honolulu.

———. N.d. "A Claim of Tamasaku Watanabe." TWP, Honolulu.

———. N.d. "The Practical Difficulties in Working a Larger Parish Plan." MS. TWP, Honolulu.

West, Jerry. 2002. "A Local Santa Fe Bystander's View of the Japanese Internment Camp." MS. Santa Fe, NM.

———. 2011. Interview with the author, 23 April. Santa Fe, NM.

Williams, Ivan. 1944. Telephone message to Midwestern Area Red Cross, 22 November. Ishida Family Collection, Honolulu.

———. 1945a. Announcement, 15 August. Santa Fe Internment Camp, Santa Fe, NM. Folder: 1300 Gen Files, 1300/n, Box 4, RG 85, NARA I.

———. 1945b. Letter and memorandum to W. F. Kelly, 23 August. Ishida Family Collection, Honolulu.

Yoshida, Teruko Fujitani. 2003. Interview with the author, 25 May. Honolulu.

Yost, Israel A. S. 2006. *Combat Chaplain: The Personal Story of the WWII Chaplain of the Japanese American 100th Battalion.* Honolulu: University of Hawai'i Press.

Secondary Sources

Americans of Japanese Ancestry (AJA) World War II Memorial Alliance. 2007. *Echoes of Silence: The Saga of the Nisei Soldiers of WWII.* Montebello, CA: AJA World War II Memorial Alliance. Compact disc.

Anders, Mary Ann. 1996. "Cross of the Martyrs." *Bulletin of the Historic Santa Fe Foundation* 23, no. 1 (March): 1–2.

Asato, Noriko. 2006. *Teaching Mikadoism: The Attack on Japanese Language Schools in Hawaii, California, and Washington, 1919–1927.* Honolulu: University of Hawai'i Press.

Barbour, John. 2008. "Exile as Cultural Translation and Religious Orientation." Paper presented at the International Auto/Biography Association Biennial Conference, Honolulu.

Brazier, Philip, and Bob Thompson. 2002. "A Brief History of Puna Congregational Christian Church." *Building God's Family One Heart at a Time,* 5 May. Kea'au, HI.

Burton, Jeffrey F., Mary M. Farrell, Florence Lord, and Richard Lord. 2002. *Confinement and Ethnicity: An Overview of World War II Japanese American Relocation Sites.* Seattle: University of Washington Press.

Choy, Peggy. 1991. "Racial Order and Contestation: Asian American Internees and Soldiers at Camp McCoy, Wisconsin, 1942–43." In *Asian Americans: Comparative and Global Perspectives,* edited by Shirley Hune, Hyung-chan Kim, Stephen S. Fugita, and Amy Ling, 87–102. Pullman: Washington State University Press.

Clark, Paul F. 1980. "Those Other Camps: An Oral History Analysis of Japanese Alien Enemy Internment during World War II." Master's thesis, California State University–Fullerton.

Coffman, Tom. 2003. *The Island Edge of America: A Political History of Hawai'i.* Honolulu: University of Hawai'i Press.

Crost, Lyn. 1994. *Honor by Fire: Japanese Americans at War in Europe and the Pacific.* Novato, CA: Presidio Press.

Culley, John J. 1985. "Trouble at the Lordsburg Internment Camp." *New Mexico Historical Review* (July): 225–248.

———. 1991. "The Santa Fe Internment Camp and the Justice Department Program for Enemy Aliens." In *Japanese Americans from Relocation to Redress,* edited by Roger Daniels, Sandra C. Taylor, and Harry H. L. Kitano, 57–71. Seattle: University of Washington Press.

———. 2000. "Enemy Alien Control in the U.S. during World War II." In *Alien Justice: Wartime Internment in Australia and North America,* edited by Kay Saunders and Roger Daniels, 138–151. St. Lucia: University of Queensland Press.

Daniels, Roger. 1997. Foreword to *Imprisoned Apart: The World War II Correspondence of an Issei Couple,* by Louis Fiset. Seattle: University of Washington Press.

———. 2013. *The Japanese American Cases: The Rule of Law in Time of War.* Lawrence: University Press of Kansas.

Din, Grant. 2015. "The Shigenaga Brothers' Detention on Angel Island and the Continent during World War II." *Discover Nikkei,* 10 November. Accessed 26 September 2016. http://www.discovernikkei.org/en/journal/2015/11/10/shigenaga-brothers/.

Duus, Masayo Umezawa. 2007. *Unlikely Liberators: The Men of the 100th and 442nd,* translated by Peter Duus. Honolulu: University of Hawai'i Press.

Eaton, Allen H. 1952. *Beauty behind Barbed Wire: The Arts of the Japanese in Our War Relocation Camps.* New York: Harper & Brothers.

Falgout, Suzanne, and Linda Nishigaya, eds. 2014. *Breaking the Silence: Lessons of Democracy and Social Justice from the World War II Honouliuli Internment and POW Camp in Hawai'i.* Social Process in Hawai'i, vol. 45. Honolulu: University of Hawai'i Press.

Fiset, Louis. 1997. *Imprisoned Apart: The World War II Correspondence of an Issei Couple.* Seattle: University of Washington Press.

———. 2001. "Return to Sender: U.S. Censorship of Enemy Alien Mail in World War II, Parts I and II." *Prologue* 33, no. 1: 21–35.

Gondo, Chie. 2004. "Viewing Post-War Japanese Movie Showings in Honolulu through the Activities of Hawaii Nichibei Kinema." *Ritsumeikan University Art Research Center Bulletin* 4 (March): 139–148.

Hawkins, John N. 1978. "Politics, Education, and Language Policy: The Case of Japanese Language Schools in Hawaii." *Amerasia Journal* 5, no. 1: 39–56.

Higa, Karin M. 1992. *The View from Within: Japanese American Art from the Internment Camps, 1942–1945.* Seattle: University of Washington Press.

Hirasuna, Delphine. 2005. *The Art of Gaman: Arts and Crafts from the Japanese American Internment Camps, 1942–1946.* Berkeley, CA: Ten Speed Press.

Howes, Craig. 1993. *Voices of the Vietnam POWs.* New York: Oxford University Press.

Ichioka, Yuji. 2006. "A Historian by Happenstance." In *Before Internment: Essays in Prewar Japanese American History,* edited by Gordon H. Chang and Eiichiro Azuma, 280–300. Stanford, CA: Stanford University Press.

JanMohammed, Abdul R., and David Lloyd. 1990. "Toward a Theory of Minority Discourse: What Is to Be Done?" In *The Nature and Context of Minority Discourse,* edited by Abdul R. JanMohammed and David Lloyd, 1–16. New York: Oxford University Press.

Kashima, Tetsuden. 1991. "American Mistreatment of Internees during World War II: Enemy Alien Japanese." In *Japanese Americans from Relocation to Redress,* edited by Roger Daniels, Sandra C. Taylor, and Harry H. L. Kitano, 52–56. Seattle: University of Washington Press.

———. 1997. Foreword to *Personal Justice Denied,* by CWRIC. Seattle: University of Washington Press.

———. 2003. *Judgment without Trial: Japanese American Imprisonment during World War II.* Seattle: University of Washington Press.

———. 2008. Introduction to *Life behind Barbed Wire,* by Yasutaro Soga, translated by Kihei Hirai, 1–16. Honolulu: University of Hawai'i Press.

Kim, Heidi. 2015. Introduction to *Taken from the Paradise Isle,* by George Yoshio and Tamae Hoshida, edited by Heidi Kim, xxi–xxxii. Boulder: University Press of Colorado.

Kimura, Yukiko. 1988. *Issei: Japanese Immigrants in Hawaii.* Honolulu: University of Hawai'i Press.

Kotani, Roland. 1985. *The Japanese in Hawaii: A Century of Struggle.* Honolulu: Hawaii Hochi.

Lee, Lloyd L. 1949. *In Freedom's Cause: A Record of the Men of Hawaii Who Died in the Second World War,* 47–140. Honolulu: University of Hawai'i Press.

Mangione, Jerre. 1978. *An Ethnic at Large: A Memoir of America in the Thirties and Forties.* New York: G. P. Putnam's Sons.

McAvoy, Audrey. 2014. "Internments Can Happen Again, Scalia Warns." *Honolulu Star-Advertiser,* 4 February.

McNaughton, James C. 2007. *Nisei Linguists: Japanese Americans in the Military Intelligence Service during World War II.* Washington, DC: Department of the Army.

Melzer, Richard A. 1994. "Casualties of Caution and Fear: Life in Santa Fe's Japanese Internment Camp, 1942–46." In *Essays in Twentieth Century New Mexico History,* edited by Judith Boyce De Mar, 213–240. Albuquerque: University of New Mexico Press.

Muller, Eric. 2007. *American Inquisition: The Hunt for Japanese American Disloyalty in World War II.* Chapel Hill: University of North Carolina Press.

Murphy, Thomas D. 1955. *Ambassadors in Arms: The Story of Hawaii's 100th Battalion.* Honolulu: University of Hawai'i Press.

Nakamura, Kelli Y. N.d. "'Into the Dark Cold I Go, the Rain Gently Falling': Hawai'i Island Incarceration." MS.

National Park Service. 2015. "Honouliuli Gulch and Associated Sites." Final Special Resource Study and Environmental Assessment. Japanese Cultural Center of Hawai'i, August. http://www.npshistory.com/publications/hono/srs.pdf.

Nishimura, Amy. 2014. "From Priestesses and Disciples to Witches and Traitors: Internment of Japanese Women at Honouliuli and Narratives of 'Madwomen.'" In *Breaking the Silence: Lessons of Democracy and Social Justice from the World War II Honouliuli Internment and POW Camp in Hawai'i,* edited by Suzanne Falgout and Linda Nishigaya, 199–216. Social Process in Hawai'i, vol. 45. Honolulu: University of Hawai'i Press.

Nora, Pierre. 1996. "General Introduction: Between Memory and History." In *Conflicts and Divisions.* Vol. 1 of *Realms of Memory: Rethinking the French Past,* edited by Lawrence D. Kritzman, translated by Arthur Goldhammer. New York: Columbia University Press.

Nye, Naomi Shihab. 2002. *19 Varieties of Gazelle: Poems of the Middle East.* New York: HarperCollins.

Odo, Franklin. 1994. "The Japanese in Hawai'i during World War II: The Challenge of Internment." In *Reflections of Internment: The Art of Hawaii's Hiroshi Honda,* 3–9. Honolulu: Honolulu Academy of Arts.

———. 2004. *No Sword to Bury: Japanese Americans in Hawai'i during World War II.* Philadelphia: Temple University Press.

———. N.d. "442nd Regimental Combat Team." In *Densho Encyclopedia.* Accessed 8 October 2015. http://encyclopedia.densho.org/442nd%20Regimental%20Combat%20Team/.

Okada, Koichiro. 1995. "Forced Acculturation: A Study of Issei in the Santa Fe Internment Camp during World War II." Master's thesis, New Mexico Highlands University.

Okawa, Gail Y. 2003a. Introductory exhibit panel, *Honoring Our Grandfathers: Japanese Immigrants in U.S. Department of Justice Internment Camps, 1941–45,* April. Hamilton Library Bridge Gallery, University of Hawai'i at Mānoa, Honolulu.

———. 2003b. "Letters to Our Forebears: Reconnecting Generations through Writing." *English Journal* 92, no. 6 (July): 47–51.

———. 2008. "Unbundling: Archival Research and Japanese American Communal Memory of U.S. Justice Department Internment, 1941–45." In *Beyond the Archives: Research as a Lived Process,* edited by Gesa E. Kirsch and Liz Rohan, 93–106. Carbondale: Southern Illinois University Press.

———. 2009. "Finding American World War II Internment in Santa Fe: Voices through Time." In *Telling New Mexico: A New History,* edited by Martha Weigle with Frances Levine and Louise Stiver, 360–373. Santa Fe: Museum of New Mexico Press.

———. 2011. "Putting Their Lives on the Line: Personal Narrative as Political Discourse among Japanese Petitioners in American World War II Internment." *College English* 74:50–68.

———. 2012. "Ironies of World War II: Hawai'i Japanese Internee Fathers and American Military Sons in Santa Fe." In *Sunshine and Shadows in New Mexico's Past: The Statehood Period,* edited by Richard Melzer, 161–171. An Official New Mexico Centennial Project. Los Ranchos, NM: Rio Grande Books.

———. 2015a. "A Collaborative Petition: Three Ministers." MS.

———. 2015b. " 'Dear Mrs. Roosevelt': Family Advocacy on Behalf of Hawai'i Internees in Mainland Exile." MS.

Okihiro, Gary Y. 1991. *Cane Fires: The Anti-Japanese Movement in Hawaii, 1865–1945.* Philadelphia: Temple University Press.

———. 2013. "Department of Justice Camps, U.S. Army Internment Camps." In *Encyclopedia of Japanese American Internment,* edited by Gary Y. Okihiro, 229–238, 241–249. Santa Barbara, CA: Greenwood.

Ono, A. N.d. "Rescue of the Lost Battalion." MS.

Palama Gakuen. 1960. *Palama gakuen soritsu 50 shunen kinenshi 1910–1960* (Palama Gakuen 50th-Year Anniversary Book, 1910–1960). Honolulu: Palama Gakuen.

Pilkington, Ed. 2016. "Japanese American Internment Survivor Hears Troubling Echoes in Trump Rhetoric." *Guardian* (UK), 28 May. Accessed 5 June 2016. www.theguardian .com/us-news/2016/may/28/japanese-american-internment-survivor-donald -trump-rhetoric?CMP=fb_us.

Robinson, Greg. 2003. *By Order of the President: FDR and the Internment of Japanese Americans.* Cambridge, MA: Harvard University Press.

Saiki, Patsy Sumie. 1982. *Gambare! An Example of Japanese Spirit.* Honolulu: Kisaku.

Shimabukuro, Mira. 2015. *Relocating Authority: Japanese Americans Writing to Redress Mass Incarceration.* Boulder: University Press of Colorado.

Shimada, Noriko. 1998. "Wartime Dissolution and Revival of the Japanese Language Schools in Hawai'i: Persistence of Ethnic Culture." *Journal of Asian American Studies* 1, no. 2 (June): 121–144.

Shoho, Russell K. 2007. "KIA Profiles." In *Echoes of Silence: The Saga of the Nisei Soldiers of WWII.* Montebello, CA: AJA World War II Memorial Alliance. Compact disc.

Slackman, Michael. 1984. "The Orange Race: George S. Patton, Jr.'s Japanese-American Hostage Plan." *Biography* 7, no. 1: 1–22.

Southard, Susan. 2015. "What U.S. Citizens Weren't Told about the Atomic Bombing of Japan." *Los Angeles Times,* 7 August.

Tamura, Eileen H. 1993. "The English-Only Effort, the Anti-Japanese Campaign, and Language Acquisition in the Education of Japanese Americans in Hawaii, 1915–40." *History of Education Quarterly* 33, no. 1 (Spring): 37–58.

Tsukano, John. 1985. *Bridge of Love.* Honolulu: Hawaii Hosts.

Tsukiyama, Ted T. 2013. "Chu Naran to Hosseba." *MIS Veterans Newsletter* 20 (February).

Van Valkenburg, Carol Bulger. 1995. *An Alien Place: The Fort Missoula, Montana Detention Camp, 1941–1944.* Missoula: Pictorial Histories Publishing Co.

Van Voss, Lex Heerma. 2001. Introduction to *International Review of Social History, Supplement 9: Petitions in Social History,* 1–10. New York: Cambridge University Press.

Wegars, Priscilla. 2010. *Imprisoned in Paradise: Japanese Internee Road Workers at the World War II Kooskia Internment Camp.* Asian American Comparative Collection. Moscow: University of Idaho.

Weglyn, Michi Nishiura. 1996. *Years of Infamy: The Untold Story of America's Concentration Camps.* Seattle: University of Washington Press.

Index

Page references to illustrations are in boldface type.

About the Author

Gail Y. Okawa is professor emerita of English at Youngstown State University, Ohio, and a visiting scholar at the Center for Biographical Research, University of Hawai'i at Mānoa. She is interested in the links between language/literacy, culture, and race in relation to history, social justice, and education. Having earned bachelor's, master's, and doctoral degrees in English, she has published numerous essays in national journals and collections and has presented papers and lectures nationally and internationally. Since 2002 when she was a visiting scholar at the Smithsonian Institution, she has been exploring the experiences of Japanese immigrants from Hawai'i, including her maternal grandfather, who were imprisoned during World War II in internment camps on the U.S. mainland. Her project expanded to include the visits of sons in Nisei military units to their interned fathers, and stories of internees' sons who were killed in action, as well as to record memories of the Santa Fe Internment Camp among the city's present-day residents.